Contents

I write for the man who's in love. For the man who walks by with
his pain in his eyes. The man who listened to him. The
man who looked away as he walked by. The man who
finally collapsed when he asked his question and no one
listened. (Aleixandre, 1979, pp.193–194).

(And the women too.)

Since what we do affects other people, and what we do with the increased
powers of technology has a still more powerful effect on people and on
more people than ever before — the ethical significance of our actions
reaches now unprecedented heights. But the moral tools we possess to
absorb and control it remain the same as they were at the 'cottage industry'
stage. Moral responsibility prompts us to care that our children are fed,
clad, and shod; it cannot offer us much practical advice, however, when
faced with numbing images of a depleted, dessicated and overheated planet
which our children and the children of our children will inherit and will
have to inhabit in the direct or oblique result of our present collective
unconcern. Morality which always guided us and still guides us today has
powerful, but short hands. It now needs very, very long hands indeed.
What chance of growing them? (Bauman, 1993, p. 218)

Our relationship to the social is, like our relationship to the world, deeper
than any expressed perception or any judgement. It is as false to place
ourselves in society as an object among other objects, as it is to place society
within ourselves as an object of thought. In both cases the mistake lies in
treating the social as an object. We must return to the social with which we
are in contact by the mere fact of existing, and which we carry about insep-
arably with us before any objectification. (Merleau-Ponty, 1962, p. 362)

If only it were all so simple! If only there were evil people somewhere insidiously committing evil deeds, and it were necessary only to separate them
from the rest of us and destroy them. But the line dividing good and evil

cuts through the heart of every human being. And who is willing to destroy a piece of his own heart? (Solzhenitsyn, 1974, p. 168)

Because we have freed ourselves of the older overt forms of authority, we do not see that we have become the prey of a new kind of authority. We have become automatons who live under the illusion of being self-willing individuals. This illusion helps the individual to remain unaware of his insecurity, but this is all the help such an illusion can give. Basically the self of the individual is weakened, so that he feels powerless and extremely insecure. He lives in a world to which he has lost genuine relatedness and in which everybody and everything has become instrumentalized, where he has become a part of the machine that his hands have built. He thinks, feels, and wills what he believes he is supposed to think, feel, and will; in this very process he loses his self upon which all genuine security of a free individual must be built... This loss of identity then makes it still more imperative to conform; it means that one can be sure of oneself only if one lives up to the expectations of others. If we do not live up to this picture we not only risk disapproval and increased isolation, but we risk losing the identity of our personality, which means jeopardizing sanity. (Fromm, 1991, pp. 218–219)

What the wise man prefers is the concrete world, *for it is this which manifests physis*. And we do not find physis if we do not engage the wakeful world, if we do not see, hear, or know the concrete. Wisdom is not flight from but an engagement in the concrete world (as becomes especially clear with respect to the polis). The wise man prefers this. (Guerrière, 1980, p. 115)

Preface

I'm not trying to prove anything, by the way. I'm a scientist and I know what constitutes proof. But the reason I call myself by my childhood name is to remind myself that a scientist must also be absolutely like a child. If he sees a thing, he must say that he sees it, whether it was what he thought he was going to see or not. See first, think later, then test. But always see first ... Most scientists forget that ... So, the other reason I call myself Wonko the Sane is so that people will think I am a fool ... Anyway, I also thought you might like to see this. (Adams, 1985, p. 157)

I am not trying to prove anything in this book. If, in the end, there are a few more question marks, a little more awareness and a few more *un*certainties about what we say and think and do, I will have achieved the aim of this work. It is not meant to be a textbook on morality. It does not mean to contain prescriptions for the conduct of psychotherapy or psychoanalysis. The problem is at the same time too simple and too complicated to resolve by writing about it — ever. This book is but a kind of post-modernist meditation on the problem of 'right action'. As Elie Wiesel asked, 'How are we to speak of it? How are we not to speak of it?' It is not a new endeavour, but I hope it is never entirely in vain.

I grew up to be a psychologist and psychotherapist in a country where scientific research money was allocated to help young black men channel their angry and aggressive feelings into 'more constructive channels' than resisting the repressive regime of the time. These young men had been deprived of votes, schooling in their own language, the most basic human rights of free speech and free movement at the risk of terror, torture and death. I heard many black people complain, when they were counselled after detention experiences, that white, liberal middle-class psychologists could just never understand them — never — because they lack the generations of experience of the current economic and existential conditions, and particularly because they simply could not speak to them in their language.

As an adolescent Black South African said to me:

> How can they expect me to trust the person who is counselling me in the very language that the torturer used in extracting my confessions from me in prison? Again they ask me to say what I really think and feel — it is the same thing — just the good cop this time, but they are still white, living in rich houses, wearing rich shoes and no matter how kind they look, they are part of the system which although changed has caused too much suffering, too many deaths, too many broken dreams for too long. Of course I go along with it, as I always have, but my heart I keep away and it is my heart which is shattered.

Black people in Great Britain have also complained to me that they sometimes feel that counsellors and psychoanalysts see them for their own education: *'They always say they want to learn about my culture. But I don't want to teach them about my culture, I want them to help me!'* In many cultures, of course, the existence of spirits in the form of visitation from the gods (as in South America), or in the presence of ancestors and spirits around us at all times (such as in Africa), is an ordinary way of experiencing reality. I recently witnessed a conversation in which a white European person was attempting to build a bridge between Eurocentric and Afrocentric psychologies. The analyst used the phrase, *'Of course, the spirits of our ancestors are within us'*. Being a Kleinian and therefore familiar with the imagery of the introjection of part- and whole objects, this was a sincere attempt to build a bridge. The black psychologist of African origin protested the values inherent in this imagery vehemently. He said that there is a *world of difference* between the idea that our ancestors are *in* us by some form of theoretical objective psychodynamic construct, and the experiential reality of the fact that the honoured ancestors are fully and fulsomely here with us now, that is, next to us, around us, interacting with us at all times as real forces, influences and recipients of the effects of our actions — *real* presences. I still wonder if it was coincidence that this white person disappeared from the room when a ritual libation was held to honour these unseen — but very present — others.

The well-meant *'I also want to learn from you about your culture'* is sometimes experienced as another imposition from an insensitive, uncaring 'liberal' who wants to use the pain of the patient as another vehicle for feeling righteous or 'good'. And yet — is this to mean that such efforts should not happen or are in vain? I think not. But I believe they should be seen in all their infinite complexity with the myriad motivations and desires, fears and fantasies which are shot through the apparently good intentions as well as the darker, more shady contours of envy, glee, identification with suffering or victimhood of completely different magnitudes and scales.

I have seen scapegoating of the different since my earliest days in school, when teachers explained that *everybody must be treated the same* — even when everybody was demonstrably utterly different, needing different things, needing to articulate the unusual, the exceptions, the unpopular aspects, the beauty and challenge of individual difference — deviations from the statistical mean of average, normal, conforming, acceptable, appropriate. Sometimes equality of opportunity exactly must mean that everybody is *not* treated the same. Morality is often born from precisely those who do not accept the *status quo* and who question the values, morals and truths which the democratic majority hold to be self-evident.

Years later I encountered this again and again and again: 'Everybody will be treated exactly the same'. Of course, it is always a lie. It also happens to be bad psychology. And stupid management. Everybody is not the same. If everybody *was* exactly the same it would make some kind of sense, but it is the idiom of autocratic control. It is the clarion call to mediocrity, blandness, uniformity — it is the schooling of the fascist army and the oppression of the dehumanised factory, the bland lines of people stripped of their individuality which find its ultimate expression in the shaven heads and naked bodies with numbers who are disposed of in neat and tidy rows in neat and tidy gas ovens where exceptions are ruled out. Only when we are stripped of whatever made us human, can we all be treated exactly the same. William Blake said, 'the same law for the lion and the ox is oppression.' (Ostriker, 1977).

If I sound outraged or strong at moments in this book, this is what I feel now as I write it. I have learned painfully and chasteningly, that ethics, as well as morality, continues to change and grow. This appears to be true for me and for others. It is quite possible that in time, I may feel completely different or even opposite to many of the things, ideals and principles I hold as valuable and true and worthwhile striving for at this moment. I trust I will be able to bear changing my mind, my priorities and be able to review my actions as I shift with the movement of my own progress towards death and the march of my world's time. Only rarely is there complete correspondence at the physical, emotional, nominative, normative, rational, theoretical and transpersonal levels of human experience. The only inescapability is our relationship.

As a child of the so-called post-modern era, I have been busy with the material in this book for as long as I have had consciousness. The history of my country of origin and also my personal history predisposed me to be particularly sensitive to issues of responsibility, which are explored in the following pages. These are: our responsibility for ourselves *and* for others; our ineradicable existential interconnectedness with others and the devastating effects of bystanding. I grew up surrounded by multiple definitions of reality, each one utterly convinced of the truth of their version and willing to spill blood until 'the bitter end'. At the same time equally large numbers of people, both in South Africa and in the rest of the world, were equally vehement that there was *nothing* they could do about it. Many people fled the existential guilt of contributing by their mere existence in that country to the legalised oppression of so many people to pursue their work elsewhere. I was one of those.

At the time of writing this preface, South Africans have just adopted a new constitution which, for the first time in living memory, provides the possibility of the beginnings of a just society; with the average, random distribution of racism, torture, injustice and unequal distribution of resources. Around 1994, many people were leaving for a variety of stated reasons. Many were white and financially, socially and in terms of moral self-righteousness benefited from apartheid, but left as soon as legal justice was possible. That could be coincidence or it could indicate that their previous claims to supporting the just cause were perhaps essentially cosmetic — useful for their self-esteem as long as no professional sacrifice and no risk to their pocket was required. Some white South Africans are now returning to that hurt and hindered land to help reconstruct a society from such an incredible legacy of cruelty and injustice. Whether or not we can draw a causal relationship between international efforts to boycott South African goods and events — and this is always arguable — most people in Europe and the Americas now have the opportunity of looking back over this period of world history on their awareness, involvement and responsibilities towards the threatened people of that country.

I have long ago given up on the idea that there is one truth — in fact, I remember John Vorster, a South African Prime Minister, saying in a radio interview, *'Never in the darkest night did I have a shadow of a doubt that I was right'*. I have always had the opposite experience, and learnt early to distrust anybody who is that sure about issues of such complexity, whilst also deeply respecting people who make a commitment and are willing to stand up and be counted for their beliefs even when these have been different from mine. I noticed if everybody only looked after themselves we could never complete the work that needed to be done. I noticed even as a little girl that everybody had to look after themselves *and* after others. I understood that we were all fettered, not only the imprisoned helpless ones, but also the keepers, the torturers and the people who made or broke laws out of fear.

I have had the privilege of witnessing another Prime Minister of South Africa, F. W. De Klerk, doing a volte-face, changing his most deeply held articles of faith by doing what amounts to a 180° turn. I also went to Berlin on the night of the 11th November 1989. In a minuscule way, I participated in the joyous festivities and exuberant delight of taking down that particular concretisation of dogmatic conviction. Of course, every solution brings other problems. The effect of having to change from shooting people who were traversing that no-man's-land to helping them across, apparently cost some East German officers so much agony (or 'cognitive dissonance') that they committed suicide. A different kind of suffering emerges even as one kind of suffering ends. And, as I wrote in a poem, *The Opening of the Wall*, at the time:

> Will people from now on not have to pay for their choices? Did you dream of one truth? And did you really expect one act to solve the world? If the world was solved, how would we need each other? After the change is made, the turning point turned, did you really think the problems would be over? No, no the problems are only just beginning, maybe the worst ones. (Clarkson, 1993a, p. 235)

There have, of course, been many other large and smaller incidents in which I have been confronted with the moral insolubilities of life whether near or far away. Yet, at the same time, life continues to demand of me to choose and to make a commitment even though I will probably never know for sure the ultimate moral rightness or wrongness of many of the decisions for which I am responsible by my actions or non-actions. 'The question of the good is posed and is decided in the midst of each definite, yet unclouded unique and transient situation of our lives, in the midst of our living relationships with men, things, institutions and powers, in other words in the midst of our historical existence' (Bonhoeffer, 1955, p. 185).

Regarding the uses of *this* work, I would like to quote Bataille (1986), 'I OWE IT TO MYSELF TO PUT YOU ON GUARD AGAINST AN UNFORTUNATE USE OF WHAT I HAVE SAID' (p. 261). If I take my courage in my hands to offer this book to others, it comes from neither a position of certainty nor of tentativeness but, as far as is possible, from both. And even then, these will fluctuate and change over time. I hope it is an invitation to deeper search and questioning, an evocation of exploration, a call to self-questioning and an engagement with a quest which never ends. What is the good? Of course there will be many contradictions in this exercise. Engagement on this field is paradoxical and at the same time imperative. You may hear tones of judgement or forgiveness which I may have intended or not. As you read this book you may hear a voice with which you do not agree or shades of meaning which evoke other condemnations or pardons which are as foreign to me as they may be an intrinsic part of your own experience. This is your part of the dialogue — share it with me, share it with others.

Please forgive me for my oversights and shortcomings, my fumblings and incomplete attempts to tell a whole story, and listen to the questions of your own conscience instead. I have described writing before as an exercise in humility and I write from a particular cultural and temporal world. This book is not finished and can probably never be finished. A friend characterised it as *a signal* and I felt that she had understood what I meant.

I have but very few answers and, as I grow older, my questions merely seem to multiply. The more I understand, the more I see complexity, and the more I learn, the more I understand the importance of not-knowing. This is my individual experience. But it seems also the experience of my world — the post-modern Zeitgeist which we currently inhabit. The value of the bystander concept, if it has any, lies in its capacity to deconstruct accepted ways of thinking, to create by destroying — to deconstruct — and to act as a celebrant of proliferation, diversity and complexity. The spirit of this book is ultimately about questions, not about answers. It is an attempt to clarify recognition and right action. Please use it in your own way as a sounding-board for your soul. It is about 'the working, not the work; the upset, not the new doctrine; the romantic agony of Job and Jung, not the solidified trophy that crowns the struggle' (Hillman, 1988, p. 16).

The book is divided into three parts: I – What and Who is a Bystander?; II – Bystander Patterns, and III – The Retrieval of Relationship.

Part I — What and Who is a Bystander?

This part focuses on exploring the notion of bystanding and its immediate field. Chapter 1 looks at what bystanding is. Chapter 2 explores bystanding in its cultural and historical context and Chapter 3 investigates the dramatic and narrative elements of bystanding by looking, amongst other perspectives, at the Karpman Drama Triangle and the archetypal concept of Physis (Clarkson, 1995d).

Part II — Bystander Patterns

Here are discussed specifically a selection of the most popular bystander slogans, roughly divided into three chapter sections. Survival is probably the most overriding biological imperative of living organisms. However, human beings have, over the centuries, on occasion chosen to sacrifice their lives for other values, such as religion, love, nationalism, family or friendship. (There are also, of course, many tales and some documented instances of animals sacrificing their lives voluntarily for their young, their mates or even their human companions.) English (1992) suggested that there are three primary responses to survival, freeze, flight and fight, which influence bystanding patterns. Examples of the bystander patterns and scenarios are here organised, arguably, in three clusters which may or may not have significance in terms of such survival responses to danger or emergency. Equally, these clusters can be conceptualised in terms of whether power is denied, feared or abused. I am here thinking of May's notion of power as violent, aggressive, competitive, cooperative or creative. May places creative power at the top of the hierarchy and suggests that as people fail to have creative power, they progressively descend down the hierarchy. Naturally enough these things are never that simple in life. But then, perhaps they are:

- Chapter 4
  It's none of my business (Pontius Pilate)
  I want to remain neutral (I don't want to take sides)
  The truth lies somewhere in the middle (Six one and half-a-
     dozen of the other)
  I don't want to rock the boat (I don't want to raise a difficult issue)
- Chapter 5
  It's more complex than it seems (Who knows anyway?)
  I don't have all the information (Ignorance is bliss)
  I don't want to get burned again (Let them fry!)
  My contribution won't make much difference (Who? Me?)
- Chapter 6
  I'm only telling the truth as I see it (Gossip is juicier than
     responsibility)

I'm only following orders (The Nuremburg Defence)
I'm just keeping my own counsel (I'm all right Jack)
Victim blaming (They brought it on themselves really)

Part III — The Retrieval of Relationship

This section offers some information, guidelines and further regions of exploration for individuals, parents, counsellors, psychotherapists and others. Chapter 7 describes critical choice points in bystanding in ourselves and Chapter 8 discusses bystanding in counselling, psychoanalysis and psychotherapy. Chapter 9 offers my seven level model of epistemology, experience and processing of meaning which can be used to explore and create some manageability in the extremely complex and multiply determined world of ethics and morality in which we live today. People who are familiar with it will be able to read the book, noticing the different levels as they proceed, and using the model or not as they wish as a conceptual framework which has both the scope and the width to contain all the ramifications of our discussion in this realm. Other people may wish to read the last chapter first or to ignore it altogether. 'This too is only one model, one image among many' (Hersh, 1982, p. 162). My hope is that it can act as a summary, both of what has gone before in this book and as a tool for future benefit.

Appendix I summarises how this material relates to the five therapeutic relationships dissected in Clarkson (1995a). Appendix II contains an abbreviated version of this material for use in organisations concerned with culture change or value clarification or empowerment programmes.

Following the recommendations of Muhlhausler & Harré (1991), I will usually use the vernacular gender-neutral device of *they, their,* and *them* to refer to a person in general, unless specified as either male or female. The terms Counselling, Psychotherapy, Psychoanalysis, Analytical or Counselling Psychology, Clinical Psychology and psychological counselling are all used interchangeably. Please read the appellations as they apply to you. There is no intention to enter into debate or even discussion within this volume about the nature of disciplinary disputes or demarcations. I have made such a contribution elsewhere (Clarkson & Pokorny, 1994). The application of this volume to the individual fields needs to be done as theoreticians and practitioners move from the general to the particular and from the generic to the unique. Similarly, the appellations *client* and *patient* are both used depending on context, since I think that either of these may be appropriate ways to describe people who come to psychotherapists or counselling psychologists for help. All client examples are fictional.

I first showed how bystanding was manifested in ordinary life situations as well as in psychotherapeutic practice in 1987. The role of the bystanders ('audience or lookers-on' (Macdonald, 1972, p. 178)) was explored giving a further context to the Karpman Drama Triangle (1968) in terms of both the moving stage backdrop of history and the responsibility for individual and collective change. Some of the motivations and rationalisations for bystanding and the psychological costs thereof were surveyed in *Bystander Games* (Clarkson, 1993b).

From these papers the book grew, both handicapped and helped by its origins. I want to emphasise that bystander apathy is a term that originated in social psychology (Latané & Darley, 1970) and is a human phenomenon which can be spoken about in any number of psychotherapeutic dialects. Perhaps more suitable languages are those of Ethics, Moral Philosophy or even Cultural Studies. I believe the case for non-intervention, neutrality and abstinence from 'rescuing' has been made, and well made. This is the case for intervention made because it *also* needs to be made.

In this book I have developed some of the motivations, nature and dynamics of the bystander role in life, different bystander patterns and their possibilities for transformation, extending the uses of pattern theory into a moral dimension. The thrust of my work has been that it is not only the responsibility of the main players of bystander, victim, rescuer and persecutor roles (or abstractions such as management or governments) that can turn the tides of history, but that perhaps the most important and potent possibilities for change lie with those who would most disclaim such power — the bystanders. I have tried to keep this conversation not too technical and not too aligned with any one psychotherapeutic or psychoanalytical approach, but with a variety of entry points for many people. Hopefully, its seed idea can be developed further in many different universes of discourse. I am aware that there are a great many other grammars, idioms and vocabularies in which I could have conducted this work. Many threads are left unexplored. Its many deficiencies, I hope, will not alienate people from this project — whatever meaning they give it in their own lives — but will inspire them to do better.

If you can use this book, please do and write to me about your findings. I have been, for some years, collecting information from all over the world in a qualitative research project called *Bystander Witness*. It involves researching, arranging workshops and conferences, collecting data, anecdotes, stories, understandings, insights, strategies, and information which illuminate *the bystander phenomenon* in order to make a contribution to a better and more relational world.

THE KILLING OF KINDNESS

We murdered kindness when we turned away
as the filthy beggar lay asleep — drunkenly we hoped —
and died roughly in the doorway her swollen feet wrapped in rags
with the bright blue of the plastic bags like pieces of sky for a pillow.

There once was a man who called for a bowl of water
while the multitude howled and bayed and gathered together
and for votes, for safety, for posterity, for God knows what reason
he washed his hands in front of them knowing that innocence is no excuse.

There was a strange smell in the air and smoke hung above the village
acrid and disturbing day after cloudless day and the months passed and
even the years and we went about our life as if nothing unusual was
    happening
we needed to believe very hard that the very construction of our world was
    not mad.

There were Poles and Gypsies and those who choose to love others like them
and human vegetables and those who were unlucky and in the wrong place
at the wrong time with the wrong people and died and died and died and
    died
sometimes fast and naked sometimes as slowly as it took anyone an eternity
    to notice.

Now they rape girls in schoolrooms, mutilate the little black ones in the
    church
with blazing machetes and they say that hundreds sit and wait for death as
    their bellies balloon
and the trucks don't arrive and the pride of grey suits and the shoal of
    green uniforms
say that we don't understand enough about it and if we interfered it may
    just make it worse.

Of course we are different — or are we? A friend was in trouble, but
   suddenly they were
just somebody with whom you had talked or, maybe someone so close to
   you that you could
not speak up for them at all. Someone fired the letter, supported the
   slander and you turned
away and he or she uncomprehending heard the cock crow in the lonely
   execution at dawn.

Men in white coats in hygienic environments (so therefore it has to be true)
   claim that
plants recognise those who have hurt or killed their fellows and cringe away
   from them feeling
each other's hurt as dogs can, or elephants or even babies until they are
   trained to the new kind
of human (dead to its own body) who can murder a whole planet without
   feeling or faith.

So many suicides from high South African Police station windows when
   suspects killed
themselves by jumping to their deaths voluntarily except that when the
   families buried them
their genitals scorched, their nails pulled out, their nipples amputated -
   Europeans (the name
of the whites in the distant land) drank the wine, ate the oranges and felt sad
   about the situation.

There was a child, bruised like a plum, terrified like a wounded thrush, sick
   from fear and lack
of concentration, stretched like a deerskin in the sun between a father's
   secret attentions and a
mother's whimpering cry for help and nobody knew or they said they didn't
   know and the
teachers couldn't have known, but she never undressed for swimming and
   nobody ever asked her the reason.

There is an old man near you or a young woman, a child or a baby, a dog,
   a friend or a place,
absorbing the violence, the viciousness, the vileness and the vice and someone is standing by
passively looking, merely observing, inwardly cringing, finding good
   reasons for not engaging,
estrangingly ever from feeling the kind-ness, our human kindness, the
   sameness of being and pain.

Once upon a time the fathers and brothers, the mothers and sisters of God
  (many gods)
preached our care for the weak ones, the sick, the crazy, the fallen, the
  different and the
ungrateful even — but the recent soul doctors warn against over-involve-
  ment, caring too
much, hiding in a web of self-watching and suspicion of the *wahanin** the
  *harafish***, the hurt,
the hearts of ordinary people in trouble.

But even this **we and them** again assumes that we are divisible, a you, a
  me and a them
as if we do not share the very ground of our being like the oceanfloor, the
  canopy of sapphire,
the shared tides of living and dying, the hungers for beauty, the yearning for
  awe, the utter
complete neediness for each other even as we pretend that one can be sated
  or free if all are not.

London, July 1994

*(Fox, 1983)
**(Mahfouz, 1994)

PS. At the time of going to press, (thanks to Anne Pickering's introduction) I have just made contact with Di Margetts of Protective
Behaviours Inc. (see Appendix III). I have put in boxes at the end of
each chapter the real-life stories from West's book, *Risking on Purpose*,
(West, 1991) as aids to the imagination — little bridges from theory
to everyday teaching and the ordinary practice of non-bystanding-
responsible involvement.

Also at this time an inspirational example of responsible behaviour presents itself in the story of Bob Bellear, who is the first Aborig-
ine in Australia's 200-year history of white settlement to be sworn in
as a judge. He began his legal career after witnessing a police 'round-
up' of Aborigines in Sydney following a disturbance (*The Times*, 7
May 1996, p. 10).

Acknowledgements

The author gratefully wishes to acknowledge Tessa Adams, Marie Angelo, Rita Cremona, Fanita English, Harriett Goldenberg, Mary Goulding, Gottfried Heuer, Vincent Keyter, Katherine Pierpoint, Denton Roberts, Andrew Samuels, Patricia Shaw, Camilla Sim, Margaret Turpin and all my clients, colleagues and many other friends, for their encouragement, examples and editorial input.

I am grateful to the editors/authors and publishers of the following books and journals for publication of material which forms portions of this book:

- 'Who I Write For' (translated by Lewis Hyde) and 'Human Matter' (translated by Stephen Kessler) from *A Longing for the Light* by Vicente Aleixandre (Lewis Hyde, ed.). Reprinted by permission of Copper Canyon Press, PO Box 271, Port Townsend, WA 98368, USA.
- Selected excerpts from *Reality Isn't What It Used To Be* by Walter Truett Anderson. Copyright © 1990 by Walter Truett Anderson. Reprinted by permission of Harper Collins Publishers, Inc.
- Excerpts from *Postmodern Ethics* by Zygmunt Bauman. Reprinted by permission of Blackwell Publishers.
- The Karpman Drama Triangle (page 47) was originally published in the *Transactional Analysis Bulletin*, Vol. 7, Number 26, April 1968. Reprinted with permission from Stephen B. Karpman and the International Transactional Analysis Association.
- The Seven Level Model (Figure 3, p. 145). Reproduced with permission from the Open University Press.
- 'Nice Day for a Lynching' by Kenneth Patchen (p. 38) from *The Collected Poems of Kenneth Patchen.* Copyright © 1971 by New

Directions Publishing Corp. Reprinted by permission of New Directions Publishing Corp.

- 'About Protective Behaviours' (Appendix III). Reprinted with permission from Di Margetts.
- Excerpts from *Risking on Purpose* by Peg Flandreau West. Reprinted by permission of Protective Behaviours Inc. (USA) and Essence Prevention Network, MISSION SA, Australia.
- Poem by Rumi (p. 250 from *Delicious Laughter: Rambunctious Teaching Stories from the Mathnawi* edited by Coleman Barks. Reprinted by permission from Maypop Books, 196 Westview Drive, Athens, GA 30606, USA.

Every effort has been made to obtain permission to reproduce copyright material throughout this book. If any proper acknowledgement has not yet been made, the copyright holder should contact the publisher.

Dedication

This book is dedicated to Grainger Weston and Denton Roberts, who don't.

Part I
What and Who is a Bystander?

Chapter 1
Bystanding —
What Is It?

As Breytenbach (1988), the celebrated South African poet, wrote from prison:

> see he is versed in harmfulness
> would you not rather show him mercy?
> the feast of words has been consumed,
> no-one is guilty of innocence

Introduction

In the Queens area of New York a young woman by the name of Kitty Genovese was bludgeoned to death over a period of half-an-hour. During this time several dozen neighbours watched from their windows or heard her screaming and did nothing. The only person who eventually called the police only did so after calling a friend in another part of the city to ask for advice.

How is this possible? Did the 'audience' stop their eyes and ears? How could the human witnesses see and hear and not help another person in her agony? Study of this event led to the development of the concept of bystanding, or bystanding apathy, in Social Psychology by Latané and Darley (1970) to describe the behaviour of people in emergencies who are aware of a violent assault or an injustice but do not attempt any effective intervention.

Supposing you are in a bus queue and you overhear someone in the queue give a stranger wrong information — Would you correct him? Or, would you keep silent and mind your own business? Researchers from University College Swansea found that in only four queues out of any 10 did a person intervene to help the stranger. The others simply watched him board the bus to, for example, Birmingham, knowing that he wanted to get to Bradford.

Recently I saw a middle-aged woman whose fundamentalist Christian mother had washed her 3-year-old child's genitals in carbolic acid with a scrubbing brush. Her father had raped her and the mother blamed the little girl for 'leading him on'. She has never retrieved her life. I also sat on an Ethics Board where we discussed how, when a complaint (whether valid or not) is laid against a psychotherapist colleague, other colleagues tend to avoid the individual in the same way as people draw away from relationship with a worker in a factory who is made 'redundant' (Clarkson & Murdin, 1996). This psychological reaction is commonplace in groups, organisations, societies. It is perhaps even herd-based in terms of drawing away from the pack-animal who looks maimed, or bloodied or vulnerable. But then again many animals appear to pity the sick, protect the weak and even attempt to help the injured (Massar, 1996).

In 1945 some nations vowed never to forget the Nazi atrocities committed in the name of racial purity. By 1993 they know the why, when, who and where of ethnic cleansing in Bosnia and Ruanda. The newspapers are full of avoidances and explanations whilst large numbers of people are dying again. This time we really cannot claim ignorance. There may be good reasons. Or mixed ones. But, too often, to bystand is to deny relationship. To deny kindness.

In 1994 in the UK three young girls were sexually assaulted in a tube train while dozens of people looked away without any attempt to intervene. Whether it really happened like that or not is less important than the fact that similar events happen on national, local and individual scales every day. It is likely that the newspaper in your part of the world carries a story like this in any given week. On a more ordinary level, many people have experienced friends and colleagues turning away from them, often at the times of their most dire need. Many people have also refrained from getting involved in other people's troubles even when they could have helped.

It is very difficult to think, feel and act in this most complex field of morality and ethics — yet we cannot escape these issues for as long as we live (see Clarkson, 1995c). Confident in being right, so many wrongs have been committed; lacking confidence perhaps even more. Someone, somewhere — not too far from you at this moment — may be unjustly or cruelly treated and there may well be something you could do to help, but you don't. Sometimes, of course, the person in need is you and others are claiming to be the 'innocent bystanders'.

Even Christ, in the dark painful night of Gethsemane, pleaded in vain for his disciples to stay awake with him. And later, Peter denied him three times, seeking the warmth of the communal fire rather than braving the cold and the fear of being seen to be a disciple:

> Then saith the damsel that kept the door unto Peter,
> Art not thou also one of this man's disciples?
> He saith, I am not.
> And the servants and officers stood there,
> who had made a fire of coals; for it was cold; and they warmed themselves;
> and Peter stood with them, and warmed himself. (St. John 18,17–18)

Of course Peter was afraid. Human beings are frightened of death whether it is by execution, or the symbolic 'dead-making' as in ancient tribal rituals or modern-day professional societies. People are also frightened of losing love or those they love, and 'higher' values are often abrogated in the service of protecting those in our charge:

> A client in a group with a psychotherapist recoiled in horror when someone else confessed that they had 'operated' on cats when they were little. The individual had cut them open and taken out their organs, even though the cats were screaming. The man could not understand or have compassion with the person who told this story. His horrified recoil was expressed in his body, his moral condemnation and his inability to conceive of having empathy with anybody 'who could do that'. The therapist, knowing how much he adored his newborn daughter, then asked: *'And what would you do if someone said they were going to kill your child unless you tortured a cat in the same way — and there was no other option?'* His whole demeanour changed and, rubbing his hands, he said: *'Of course, I would torture the cat — I would torture as many cats as they liked to save my daughter's life.'*

This story is told here for the purposes of illustration and provocation.

Our animal selves fear pain and deprivation. People fear authority, people fear being different, people fear the chaos of ever-proliferating complexity, people fear being 'labelled', people even fear relationships — certainly many people fear intimacy, seeing that it is in intimate relationships that some of the most violent acts have been perpetrated on human beings. Some even say that human beings fear thinking for themselves, that they fear freedom. Some also say that no-one can be free without the freedom of all the others:

> Passers-by ignored the screams of teenage girl being mugged in a city centre. (*Daily Mail* May 15, 1987)

> A gang of youths who attacked a multiple sclerosis sufferer in a busy street were condemned as 'sick and disgusting' yesterday ... As he lay bleeding and crying for help, crowds of shoppers walked straight past. (*Daily Telegraph* May 5, 1987)

> Three people stepped over a woman being raped on a staircase ... (*Daily Telegraph* June 3, 1987)

The tragedy is these reports are commonplace. In the not too distant future it is easy to see how they might be so commonplace as to fail to warrant the attention of newspapers:

> That is the truth about the society we have created, a society where fear of being harmed overrides everything. (*The Mail on Sunday* June 14, 1987, p. 32)

The Bystander

A bystander is the descriptive name given to a person who does not become actively involved in a situation where someone else requires help. Where one or more people are in danger, bystanders could therefore, by taking some form of action, affect the outcome of the situation even if they were not able to avert it. Thus, by this definition, anyone who becomes actively involved in a critical situation, is not a bystander. Of course, people may get involved for good or bad reasons — a human motivation is but mixed at best. It was said of Schindler that:

> generosity was a disease in Oskar, a frantic thing, one of his passions. He would tip taxi drivers twice the fare on the meter. This has to be said too — that he thought the Reich housing authorities were unjust and told Stern so, not when the regime got in trouble, but even before that, in it sweetest autumn. (Keneally, 1994, p. 57)

As in this example, there are many attempts to blemish in some way those qualities of bravery, excitement and resourcefulness on behalf of others that many of us aspire to, but few can emulate in the demanding crucible of real life?

It is bystanding to be witness to, but not to confront, a racist, misogynist or homophobic joke. Letting a friend drive whilst drunk is bystanding. It is also bystanding (and an ethics violation) not to confront or to get help to deal with a colleague whom you personally believe to be disabled or impaired, for example, due to stress, burnout or addiction. According to most professional codes of ethics it would be bystanding, for example, to condone (by knowledge without intervention) a situation whereby one knew a colleague to be in conscious or unconscious conflict with the professional ethical code.

Involvement, engagement or acknowledging one's relationship to another person in trouble does not always mean heroic confrontation. It can take many forms. The transformation of bystanders into silent witnesses or companions of honour is an important outcome of life-transforming counselling and psychotherapy. This occurs, in particular, when the counselling or psychoanalytic approach concerns itself with 'the form-giving, meaning-making part, the narrator who at every waking moment of our lives spins out its account of who we are and what we are doing and why we are doing it'. (Anderson, 1990, p. 137).

Potentially, all psychotherapists, psychoanalysts and counsellors have an important contribution to make to the wellbeing of all of humankind, in addition to the 'cure', analysis or growth of individual clients. Indeed, thinking about most of the moral dilemmas of psychotherapy and psychoanalysis, it seems comparatively rare that those people who come into this profession will deliberately and intentionally set out to hurt. From experience of working with and on ethical issues and procedures, it is my conviction that many ethical errors occur through ignorance, confusion, stress, lack of support, or overwork. However, the issue on which psychoanalysts, psychologists and psychotherapists are most likely to be morally culpable is that of bystanding, that is, knowing that something is wrong but not getting involved, for reasons of ideology, dogma, reputation, cowardice or an excessively *laissez-faire* position.

The Power of the Bystanders

There are so many definitions of power that it would require another book to begin to do justice to the concept. For our purposes, power is seen as the capacity to bring about change — May's (1972) notion of creative power. When humans do not or cannot exercise their power, or when complexity overwhelms them, they often attempt to create the illusion that life is under control, and in this way we enter into power relationships which we hope will be the means for reducing our existential anxiety. Lipman-Blumen (1994) identified five strategies for reducing our existential anxiety:

1. Submission to a sacred force or being.
2. Allegiance to a secular, usually political, ideology.
3. Subordination to a secular institution.
4. Subjugation to a human ruler, benign or otherwise.
5. Assumption of control over other individuals, institutions, situations, and/or resources. (p. 118)

As the largest component in most systems, bystanders often have the most power to change the system. Some years ago, a group of soldiers in Haiti, by their refusal to obey orders, succeeded in securing protection and justice for hundreds of genuine victims of the regime there. As Ury (1991) wrote to negotiators:

> You may not have enough leverage by yourself. Fortunately, almost every negotiation takes place within a larger community that constitutes a potential 'third force' in your negotiation. Involving other people is often the most effective way to deter your opponent's attacks and bring him to agreement without provoking a counter-reaction. (p. 124)

Roberts (1984) reminded us that there are no innocent bystanders because to choose not to be part of a solution is, in fact, to choose to be part of the problem. In Clarkson (1987) it was shown how the audience (the onlookers or bystanders) of any drama usually have the power to allow a production on the stage of life (or Broadway) to continue, change or cease: 'The privilege of innocence held by those who do not enact the central roles of the drama carries with it the existential responsibility for applauding, editing, influencing or aborting the show' (Clarkson, 1987, p. 86). When the bystanders get involved, the situation changes. The central (obvious) roles are those of Persecutor, Victim and Rescuer, or Villain, Scapegoat and Hero. However, any of these three archetypes can rarely stop the performance. They usually lack the power to have the theatre closed. This most potent capacity is almost always within the purview of the actions of the bystanders.

Frequently it is *only* the complicity of those who are watching or who are closing their eyes to the situation which allows a tragedy to unfold. Bystanders or neutral observers are pivotal in the dramas of history as well as in individual stories of cruelty, oppression and injustice. Although bystanding seems less overtly wicked, to the extent to which bystanders refuse to use their action to prevent or intervene in wickedness, at a covert psychological level it can permit or sanction much worse. The great psychologist, Shakespeare, had a sense of this less-appreciated psychological dynamic when he made

Paulina cry out in *The Winter's Tale*: 'poor trespasses, more monstrous standing by' (III. ii. 186–187) (Shakespeare, 1951).

Many people participate passively in violent or oppressive situations. These may be personal, social, organisational or political. By not challenging or intervening they give tacit permission to the abuse of power occurring in their environment. We all do this to some extent. Tacit permission is perhaps the most powerful force for good or evil in the field. 'According to folk wisdom, each of us must decide to be either a part of the problem or the solution and not to decide is to decide' (Roberts, 1984, p. 229). In his article on autocratic power, Jacobs (1987) correctly suggests 'the largest group in the system is the Bystanders' (p. 68). He cites public protest against the euthanasia programme in Germany in 1939 as an example of how bystanders can have great power in situations where they choose to exert this power:

> Prior to the process of becoming aware, the social exists obscurely and as a summons ... This is because the nation and class are neither versions of fate which hold the individual in subjection from the outside nor values which he posits from within. They are modes of co-existence which are a call upon him. (Merleau-Ponty, 1962, pp. 362–363)

Every major social change in favour of justice for homosexual people, against child labour or slavery, against cruelty to animals, for special facilities for those who need them, has come about because of the involvement of bystanders. Until the bystanders become involved, the perpetrator's work goes unchallenged. Frequently, the oppressed minority could not have succeeded in changing the law or the system without the help of people who refused to remain passive and started 'interfering' with the established system. Systems theory shows that changing any one part of a system will affect the remainder (Watzlawick, Weakland & Fisch, 1974). Therefore, if the bystanders in any given system change their behaviour, the rest of the system will be affected and change is more likely to follow.

Moral Complexities

This is not surprising. Modern physics asserts that all observers are part of the field. Indeed, some experiments show that observers determine the field, even the outcome of experiments with rats! (McGuire, 1969). Therefore, if people are aware of a problem they are likely to be perpetuating or aggravating it if they are not working actively to solve it. The presence of a third party may deter an opponent from threatening or attacking you. And, bystanders even slow down the spread of innovations within a population of pigeons! (Lefebvre & Giraldeau, 1994). When children are quarrelling, the watchful eye of a parent will often prevent fisticuffs. As Ury (1991) pointed out, when the general public is watching, even a dictatorial government may hesitate before using violence on protesters.

All social ills, such as torture (Moore, 1985), are the direct consequence of bystanding and all social ills which have been resolved or at least ameliorated (slavery, child labour, cruelty to animals, lack of votes for women) are the result of bystanders (or so-called third parties) becoming involved. Of course, there are situations where it may be better not to get involved. And, there may be difficulties in deciding how to exert the power of *standing by* instead of bystanding. What may the consequences be — fatal, futile or foolish? Yet, we can hardly avoid the questions. 'We have to make choices ... about who the good guys and the bad guys are ... and we also have to make choices about how to make choices' (Anderson, 1990, p. 8).

Individual moral choices are exceedingly complex. We are deeply (but not irrevocably) influenced by our early childhood surroundings. So, much of an individual's ethics are based on family messages, prescriptions and the way parents and other significant others valued or showed examples of heroism, altruism and sharing with others (Oliner & Oliner, 1988). Families and schools which emphasise responsible involvement help children from an early age to learn the skills and consequences of taking responsibility for themselves and others. Unfortunately, most of these so-called authorities are often as confused as we are as to what is the right action. And when they are not, it may be worse! Different cultures are also different — villagers tend to get over-involved because the people know each other's business, whereas a young mother could die with her baby in a flat in London and not be discovered for three weeks.

> In Judaism, the bystander's duty to come to the rescue of his fellow-man who is in peril is religious, ethical and legal. A citizen is expected to engage in the act of rescue both personally and with his financial resources. He is required, however, neither to give his life nor to place his life in substantial jeopardy to save his fellow ... Although failure to come to one's neighbour's rescue incurs no criminal sanction, the legal nature of the duty is evidenced by (1) the right of the rescuer to sue for all financial losses incurred as a result of the rescue operation, (2) the rescuer's immunity to liability, and (3) the exemption he enjoys from all positive legal, civil, and ritual duties while he is actively engaged in the rescue operation. (Kirschenbau, 1980, p. 204)

Information Overload

When discussing bystanding the most frequently mentioned objection is the sheer impossibility of being involved with everything which is going wrong in the world. So often people say *'I can't possibly become involved with everyone who needs help — it's simply too much!'* Newspapers, television and the fact that it is normal for us to be informed about painful detention, terrible torture and undignified death on a daily if not hourly basis, bring with them an almost debilitating paralysis.

In the meantime we must live with the immediate problem, 'what to *do* when some are hurting and others, who have power, don't care?' (Goodman, 1991, p. 130). So much to do — so little time; so overwhelming the need — so small the resources; so impossible to attend to it all — so easy to deal only with problems close by. The world has become chaotic and unpredictable in unprecedented ways. However, what we learn from chaos theory is that there is sometimes a pattern in the chaos. There is even an enhanced possibility of being creative — perhaps even evolving new ways of thinking and living with ethical and moral problems. As evidence of our inextricable inter-relationship with all other living organisms grows, it becomes harder and harder to claim and maintain individual isolation.

Passing judgement on moral or existential solutions any individual arrives at under extreme stress (be it peer group pressure or financial threat, such as job loss) requires caution and empathy. It is monumentally difficult to judge the actions of another person not knowing all the relevant facts and feelings. At the same time, however, it is questionable whether even understandable pressures can really exonerate an individual from his or her share of collective responsibility. The pressures on the Nazi or Bosnian soldiers may be understandable, but does this mean that they are not to be held responsible for their actions? The pressures on an overworked bond dealer or housebound single mother may be overwhelming, but does this obviate them from responsibility?

> To the extent that whatever we hold to be 'the good' in our culture is achieved through the enhancement of relationships, then it is the process of relating that deserves our closest attention. In this sense, we may confront the pervasive pluralism of contemporary life, not with dismay, but with a sense of reassurance: the very richness of patterns of relationship furnishes a resource, a set of potentials that might be absorbed with advantage into neighboring traditions. (K. Gergen, 1994, p. 108)

Responsibility

Responsibility is a keyword in the nexus of themes which cluster around the bystander concept. It is, of course, a topic of great complexity and here I can merely highlight some aspects relevant to this field and this discourse. Response-ability (see Perls, 1969) refers to the ability to respond — to react in some way to the events, invitations and provocations of our world. Not to respond is, of course, also a response. In the words of Sartre, we are condemned to a freedom from which there is no exit — an inextricable accountability for our existence and the actions or non-actions of our existence in our inevitable relationships with others. Another version of this states that the only thing required for evil to triumph is for good men to do nothing. This indicates the unavoidable complicity of all who do not engage in resisting or fighting or transforming evil.

Marcel (1952), who differed radically from Sartre's more fashionable conception of human relationship as infinite nausea, proffered the notion of *fidelity* as the choiceful assumption of responsibility.

> The concrete historical permanence which I give myself in fidelity cannot be derived from a universal law, however valid. The law is abstract and formal and governs particular cases, whereas in fidelity I continuously inform myself from within. Nor does the universal law represent or reveal more fully the objective order to which I must conform, the nature of Being, for in fidelity I am not merely cultivating an ideal, I am making a response: I am not merely being consistent with myself, but I am bearing witness to an other-than-me which has hold of me. Fidelity is not a mere act of will, it is faith in the presence of an other-than-me to which I respond and to which I shall continue to respond. It is this continuous response in the bond of fidelity which is my life and my permanence, and more fully represents and reveals the structure of Being than does conformity to a law. Fidelity is response to a person and can never be rightly practised towards an idea or an ideal, which is idolatry, for a principle can make no demands upon me, because it owes the whole of its reality to the act whereby I sanction it. (Blackham, 1961, p. 76)

Abuses of Responsibility

The concept of responsibility which has been taken most seriously in the traditions of existential and humanistic philosophy is not meant to impose on others the edict 'you are responsible', nor to persecute ourselves and others in this way. There have been some unfortunate side-effects when misinformed or over-zealous people have abused this concept. For example, when the holistic health movement, this concept. For example, when the holistic health movement, including pioneers such as Simonton, Matthews-Simonton and Creighton (1978), brought to people's attention the major ways in which they could be responsible for their own health, some also took it to mean that their illness was their own 'fault'. What was meant to be liberating can become a new oppression.

So, whereas some people took permission to visualise their fight against cancer cells in ways which supported their drive for self-healing and healthy self-esteem, others used it to demoralise themselves and blamed themselves (or worse, were blamed by others) for 'having made themselves sick'. This is indeed victim-blaming (of which we shall hear more later), a version of *'Well, they really brought it upon themselves'*. Anything of potency, pleasure and value (sex, food, religious faith) can, of course, be abused. The original intention behind the notion of taking responsibility for one's own life was not to make people feel bad because they were ill or in trouble; it was to discover the empowerment of more freedom in choices and individual responses to the creation and development of their lives. To accept responsibility for oneself and to invite others to do the same can form an authentic and potent foundation for personal and social change (Smail, 1978).

> Burnet suggests that we are partly responsible for our states of character as being responsible for them at the start [1114 b32; cf. 1114 a4–7]. But responsibility for character at the beginning qualified by inability to alter it when formed is not naturally described as co-responsibility. If we are co-responsible who or what are our partners in responsibility? (Hardie, 1968, p. 179)

Avoidance of Responsibility

Personal responsibility is often avoided by complying with an internalised parent or authority figure that prohibits questioning or effectively challenging authority. An example of this are those people who obediently 'follow orders' to torture others, even though these acts do violence, at least initially, to their own values and/or visceral empathy. This is the fellow feeling which is carried in our very musculature as we hurt or gag in disgust, or even yawn when others do the same.

Visceral empathy is more likely to operate when the other living beings in our vicinity actually *are* in our vicinity and are not remote by virtue of the television screen, thousands of miles away or, by time, into the centuries which will be inhabited by our children's children. According to Bauman (1993):

> Knowingly or unknowingly, our actions affect territories and times much too distant for the 'natural' moral impulses which struggle in vain to assimilate them, or abandon the struggle altogether. Morality which we inherited from pre-modern times — the only morality we have — is a morality of proximity, and as such woefully inadequate in a society in which all important action is an action on distance ... Unassisted, individual imagination cannot embrace actions of such scale, and see through them up to their furthest repercussions. Neither is it called or pushed to stretch itself that far; our moral conscience rests satisfied once responsibility for the near and dear has been taken and fulfilled. The far-away effects of what we do or desist from doing either remain invisible and thus unworrying, or are presented and believed to be taken care of by agencies which neither demand, nor would take gladly our too keen an interest, let alone interference. We do not 'naturally' feel responsibility for such far-away events, however closely they may intertwine with what we do or abstain from doing. (p. 218)

Responsibility and Liability

There are another two emphases pertinent to the discussion of responsibility: the poles of responsibility as liability and responsibility as awareness to relationship. Table 1 highlights these.

Table 1: Two emphases in the discussion of responsibility

Responsibility as liability	Responsibility as awareness to relationship
Own interests	Empathy
Fixed	In flux
Finite	Complex
Limited to self and immediate family, sometimes not even friends	Not limited to any particular grouping, indeed, reaching out to the 'different'
Unauthentic guilt and neurotic guilt	Authentic and existential guilt

'Responsibility as liability' allows people to defer action on the basis that they are not 'liable' for what is happening. A different interpretation of responsibility would be 'to be aware–responsive, able to respond', which is a more relational understanding.

Responsibility and Mental Health

It is to be hoped that, during the course of becoming conscious (for example, exposure to minorities, counselling, psychoanalysis, supervision or training, spiritual awakening, and sincere work and reparation) we, as counsellors, psychotherapists and people will develop greater congruity, authenticity, and courage to act on behalf of ourselves and others in unjust or violent situations. Indeed, several investigators have suggested that self-actualising individuals have strong value systems which they enact in their daily lives, sometimes at the expense of their own comfort or wellbeing (Cornell, 1984). As Boadella (1986) says, psychological health *includes* the 'courage to act in defence of what one believes to be right, even when there is danger' (p. 5).

> Obviously, freedom as a definition of a man does not depend upon others, but as soon as there is a commitment, I am obliged to will the liberty of others at the same time as mine. I cannot make liberty my aim unless I make that of others equal in my aim. (Sartre, 1969, p. 52)

Bystanding is predicated upon the denial of obligation and responsibility for others. Giving away power in this way leads to disempowerment and experiences of helplessness. It also prevents learning. It is propped up by the futile claim that *'I am not my brother's keeper'*, or the illusion that individuals can be islands in the sea of humanity, not connected with or awash with the tidal waves which draw all of us together. Metaphorically, bystanders wash their hands, as did Pontius Pilate, knowingly condemning an innocent to harm while publicly claiming guiltlessness. Sometimes they choose to accept responsibility for making choices that safeguard their own lives and liberty. As Aristotle (1934) pointed out 'When you have thrown a stone, you cannot afterwards bring it back again, but nevertheless you are responsible for having taken up the stone and flung it, for the origin of the act was within you' (III. v.14).

The problems of evil, injustice, unfair persecution, prejudice, and the abuse of power are existential realities. They have probably also been always with us. Our responses to these realities (as people, as counsellors, psychologists and psychotherapists) are mediated by complex processes.

Blackham (1961) quotes Weber:

> There are two fundamentally different ethical conceptions: the ethics of sentiment and the ethics of responsibility ... the believer in an absolute ethic cannot stand up to the ethical irrationality of the world. He who enters politics concludes a pact with devilish powers, since it is a realm where *alone* power and violence are valid means; yet from good may come evil and from evil good. Who does not see this is politically a child. (p. 40)

Responsibility and Guilt

'In attempting to facilitate a patient's awareness of responsibility, the therapist soon discovers an uninvited presence in the therapeutic arena. That presence is guilt, the dark shadow of responsibility' (Yalom, 1980, p. 276). It is possible to distinguish between three types of guilt: neurotic guilt, genuine guilt, and existential guilt. In psychotherapeutic practice (and ordinary life) both therapist and client are often confused about the distinctions between them.

The most distinguishing characteristics of neurotic guilt are exploitative design, repetitiveness, and the fact that the guilt-ridden individuals do nothing effective about solving the problem for which they feel guilty. Neither do they make reparation. This is guilt for guilt's sake. This kind of guilt carries the psychological message that someone else should do something about it (such as forgive you for doing nothing, understand that it is not your fault, etc.).

Authentic (genuine) guilt results from actual aggression against another or a lack of action on behalf of another. The original social function of guilt can be understood as a means of helping children to distinguish between right and wrong and to take action to correct wrongful acts committed impulsively, before autonomous adult functioning is well established. Therapeutically, genuine guilt is dealt with by actual or symbolically appropriate reparative acts. The ability to experience genuine guilt is apparently not only a requisite for the survival of society, but an intrinsic aspect of being human.

Existential guilt is also part of our human inheritance. Existential guilt can be described as deep, personal awareness of the suffering of others (for example, victims of famine or torture) at the same time as one chooses to use one's life and resources differently. It could mean celebrating opportunities with joy and gratitude without demeaning others or ourselves with false, hypocritical protestations of guilt which are recycled for their social 'popularity value' whilst having no effect on future behaviour. Existential guilt involves genuinely taking responsibility for choices and not blaming others, the government, or God! 'Therefore existential guilt ... is compatible with, even necessary for, mental health' (Yalom, 1980, p. 279). Existential guilt leaves the individual feeling humble, responsible, and often deeply and profoundly in touch with our collective identities. Thus, it can be an antidote for and a spur to move us away from bystanding toward responsible involvement.

Responsibility and Relationship

Relationship (or the interconnectedness between people) has been significant in all healing since the time of Hippocrates and Galen. It is one of the major significant features in people's lives, whether this happens as a result of falling in love, being in crisis, educational development, religious conversion or effective psychotherapy. 'We are born of relationship, nurtured in relationship, and educated in relationship. We represent every biological and social relationship of our forebears, as we interact and exist in a consensual domain called "society"' (Cottone, 1988, p. 363). It is for this reason that the client (or patient) is thought of as always in relationship whether this be conceived of in object relations terms or in subject relations terms (as in existential approaches to psychotherapy) (Clarkson, 1991; 1995a).

One thing seems to stand out from most research into the outcome of psychotherapy (see Clarkson, 1995a for review). *The relationship* is the most important factor in all effective psychotherapies — indeed, in all constructive change in small or large systems it is this relationship that, again, underlies the existential impossibility of the individual on an island capable of being understood outside the web of human networks. Our responsible relationship with others is perhaps the fullest expression of being human:

> I find myself engaged along with others in a world which makes demands on me: I respond to others and undertake responsibilities to and for them. So far from my being myself the ground of my certainty in knowing and the motive of my constancy in willing, it is the existence of another that gives me my primary notion of existence and it is in so far as I believe in the existence of others and act on that belief that I affirm my own existence. (Blackman, 1961, p. 74)

It is our 'first nature' to be connected, to be in organismic empathy, to have fellow-feeling. 'Un-connectedness', unawareness, being 'out of empathy' is 'second nature' — learned behaviour. It is not *first nature*. It was probably developed as a defence against our biological and social truth. Second nature usually means that which is automatic or 'a deeply ingrained habit' (Macdonald, 1972, p. 1223). First nature is that which is our truest, most real and most biologically rooted temperamental authentic self. We may have become inured to the plight of our fellow inhabitants of the planet, desensitised to the assaults on the planet, conditioned by philosophies and economies which glamorise individualism against social responsibility. But this is not truly organismic. This is not the situation of living organisms in a healthy field. It is not truly human. Perls, Hefferline and Goodman (1951) affirm this in the following words:

> We have been at pains to show that in the organism before it can be called a personality at all, and in the formation of personality, the social factors are essential ... The underlying social nature of the organism and the forming personality — fostering and dependency, communication, imitation and learning, love-choices and companionship, passions of sympathy and antipathy, mutual aid and certain rivalries — all this is extremely conservative, repressible but ineradicable. And it is meaningless to think of an organism possessing drives which are 'anti-social' in this sense, opposed to his social nature, for this would be a conserved inner contradiction; it would not be conserved. But there are, rather, difficulties of individual development, of growing-up, of realizing all of one's nature. (p. 333)

Even today in this post-modernist swirl:

> we come to accept morality, and moral discourse, as a living and central element in human existence. We see our interpersonal relationships as collaborative efforts in constructing values. We see education as, among other things, a training in the skills of moral reasoning — morality not merely handed down but learned and reacted to and re-created out of experience. And when there is conflict about that, as there inevitably will be, we accept the conflict also as an arena for expressing and creating values. (Anderson, 1990, p. 258)

And the value we are discussing here is that of engagement.

Encouraging or Discouraging Engagement

We are also conditioned by our social groups and the values and examples in our environment. The vivid examples of rock stars, such as Sir Bob Geldof and Sting, amongst others (however we may judge their individual merit) have certainly made it fashionable and interesting for many young people to take some share of the responsibility for the state of our world. Role models, such as Jane Fonda or Robert de Niro, have had an enormous effect in legitimising involvement as a value in our modern society. It is not that their choice of cause is necessarily more right or attractive than others — several young people have told me that it is because some famous people involve themselves in uncomfortable morally ambiguous situations, it makes it more exciting and valuable. Of courses they may also be criticised or suspected of 'only seeking publicity'. Whether people follow, fall out or lead and how they do this, is another story.

For many years, most forms of psychotherapy and psychoanalysis have held it important to maintain a neutral or value-free attitude towards much of society's distress. You often hear counsellors say *'I don't want to impose my values on my clients'*. This attitude is at least partly due to psychology and the ambitions of psychoanalysis to model the discipline on 'science'. But, even scientists have occasion to reflect, as exemplified in the following comment by Franck about scientists' reactions during the years 1932–1933:

> In general we are cautious and therefore tolerant and therefore disinclined to accept total solutions. Our very objectivity prevents us from taking a strong stand in political differences, in which the right is never on one side. So we took the easiest way out and hid in our ivory tower. We felt that neither the good nor the evil applications (of the atomic bomb) were our responsibility. (Kipphardt, 1971, p. 2)

This dilemma crystallised around the case of Robert Oppenheimer who had done more than any other man to create the atomic bomb, but who then refused to continue to work for the North American Government and help to build the even more dreadful hydrogen bomb. He was taken to court for defending his right to make moral judgements about the 'use' of his science. And psychotherapists who work with the infinitely more potent stuff of the human soul imagine that they can be neutral?

Thinking more deeply about this, however, raises more and more very interesting and disquieting aspects. To choose not to communicate your values is the enunciation of a value — perhaps that it is possible to protect anybody with whom we interact in any setting from the impact of our values; perhaps that it is possible to hide our values successfully in the consulting room? More and more counsellors and psychotherapists are beginning to question these positions. Some are vehemently speaking out against such hypocrisy on scientific experimental grounds as well as on moral and social grounds:

> When the patient talks about being angry about something — *'The goddamn developers, they're putting up this building that's going to cut the sun off for the afternoon just down my block, no more afternoon sun'* — does that come into the hour, and if it comes into the hour, how is it talked about? Is it talked about as a personal problem? Is it talked about symbolically, about being 'cut off from the sun' as though the guy were dreaming it? Is it talked about in terms of aggression and hostility and why you have an authority problem and that you always somehow are rebelling and coming in and bitching about what's wrong with the world? *Or is it taken up as a vital part of the citizen's life?* (Hillman & Ventura, 1992, p. 217)

The themes of more national and international counselling and psychology conferences have recently shown concern with the so-called impact of countertransferences (the therapist's own feelings and prejudices) on patients about race, sexuality, gender, ability and so on. There is little literature and no clear position from which trainee counsellors or psychotherapists may take their bearings. One of the most eloquent accusations comes from Hillman and Ventura (1992). It may be argued that psychotherapy is hardly responsible for the state of the world, but the central accusation does hold water. It is no longer possible for counsellors or psychotherapists of all persuasions to avoid the responsibility of considering the implications of their work for individuals or groups by affecting a value-free stance. This theme will be pursued further in Chapter 8.

Ethical Solipsism in Counselling, Psychoanalysis and Psychotherapy

Ignorance of ethical issues in counselling and psychotherapy, from Freud and Fliess's nasal operations on a female patient to cure her of masturbation, to the casual disregard for ethical sexuality in the still-occurring sexual relations with patients has been noticed and studied. However, the concomitant and quite recent phenomenon referred to as 'the vengeance of the victim' (Clarkson, 1995b), and the backlash of psychologists and psychotherapists becoming overly preoccupied in fear with the niceties and particularities of the law, to the exclusion of the spirit, have also been seen.

The question then becomes 'What is the best way to be involved?'. This does not always mean doing something directly or immediately. Is it our business, or must psychotherapy, along with clinical psychology (with justice) be charged with 'ethical irrelevance'? (Boyd, 1992, p. 42).

Carl Jung, as even some of his staunchest allies have now admitted, was prepared to cooperate with Nazi psychiatry in Germany, making anti-Semitic comments about 'Jewish psychotherapy' in the hope, he unbelievably claimed, of keeping it alive. When the Argentine government began locking up and torturing some politically active psychoanalysts, their local psychoanalytic institute would not defend them. Perhaps this was merely from fear. But then, how does one explain the fact that the parent organization, the International Psycho-Analytic Association, though asked by a small number of politically aware colleagues, would not take a public stand, or write a letter of protest to the Argentine Psychoanalytic Society or to the Argentine government? (Masson, 1989, p. 45)

There are those who vociferously defend Jung against such charges of course, believing them to be untrue. Since the beginning of consciousness human beings must have grappled with the problem of evil and, in most cultures and religions, elaborate constructions have been created to help human beings to cope with and to understand what is perceived of as evil. For most of this century psychology attempted to get away from the idea of inherent evil and tried to find excuses and explanations for inexplicable horror in causal factors, such as early childhood development. Towards the end of this century there seems to be more acknowledgement of human evil. Understanding childhood causes has not helped either the victims, the perpetrators, the do-gooders or the observers to metabolise events, such as large-scale rape in Bosnia, mass genocide in Rwanda and the vivid depiction of two 10-year-old boys torturing baby James Bulger to death. Passivity in the face of evil from any vantage point is complicity with it. For psychology to disclaim responsibility even more so. So, honour to organisations and societies, such as the British Psychological Society, which take responsibility (Thompson, 1985).

> According to the primarily theoretical framework adopted in order to comprehend the atttempt to transform unruly inimicality into docile obedience (Foucault, 1979), the secretly vicious disciplinary order is a *cultural–historical process* into which we are born. Psychology's methods of dealing with persons are structurally no different from those in the areas of medicine, criminal justice, education and industry ... and yet I do argue that we as individual persons and as psychologists are responsible for our participation in this order and are free to abandon the project of domination and control, to practice a psychology that recognizes, embraces, liberates and empowers the Other through a practice of open dialogue. This entails not an eradication but a respectful acknowledgement of the presence of inimicality in others and in ourselves. (Wertz, 1995, pp. 452–453)

From Bystanding to Standing By

Unfortunately, psychotherapy has in many forms developed the self-absorption of an unhealthy narcissism which both reflects and effects the spirit of our times (Hillman & Ventura, 1992). It has accepted as a yardstick the individual self and its wellbeing-as if it can be accomplished separate from others. The profession often holds self-actualisation as its primary end-goal of psychotherapy (Maslow, 1968) and/or resignation to the depressive position (Hinshelwood, 1989) or adjustment (Dryden & Trower, 1989) as the highest good. This has resulted in little engagement with social problems and a preoccupation with subjective fantasy and intrapsychic projection, at the expense of involvement with the real-life tissue-issues, such as torture, poverty and social injustice, which are the true daily concerns of every human being. A phobia of rescuing (unhelpful interference), born of overcompensation and misunderstood clinical errors, has led to an absence of genuine help, in particular as far as third parties are concerned. Inauthentic rescuers, of course, can be transformed into helpers. Perhaps all psychotherapy training attempts to do that. Psychotherapy has an enormous debt to pay to society in this respect and potentially an important contribution to make to the wellbeing of all of humankind in addition to the cure and growth of the individual client. Denial of this capacity has far-reaching implications for us all. Cornell (1984) writes:

> [if therapists] are to be significant agents of change, if we are to offer significant medicine to our communities and to the world community, we need to move beyond issues of individual survival and well-being. We need to engage ourselves and others in a broader sense of purpose. (p. 242)

Bystander behaviour in situations where others are at risk or being harmed may be understandable. Recent legal decisions in South Africa even acknowledge the group pressure contribution to bystanding (Colman, 1991a; 1991b). But, is it then also excusable in individuals or groups adhering to a tradition of the so-called helping professions? If all our engagements are only for the individual, how could this possibly equip a person to live in a world which we inextricably share with others?

> Despite some of Berne's prejudices and blind spots, TA [transactional analysis] has a tradition rich in social awareness, a commitment to changing the world in which we live, and continuing emphasis by some clinicians and trainers throughout the world on broadening our individualistic concerns with the compromises and conventions of everyday life towards an action-orientated commitment to the planet which is ours, and the plight of all its peoples. (Clarkson, 1986, p. 4)

However, the transformation of bystanders into witnesses or companions of honour in just combat or righteous resistance is still a much neglected area. Naturally the 'liberators' or the 'terrorists' may make exactly the same claims. And as we know, roles frequently become interchangeable, with removable labels. Traitor or patriot? Rebel or freedom fighter? Opposite sides of a similar coin. Of course, bystanders can also become (in addition to being genuine helpers and genuine witnesses) genuine victims (injured and punished for their involvement) and genuine guardians (structuring, limiting or controlling violence, for example). Some people may repeatedly interfere in the business of others, this may be a way of life to them — perhaps even to the detriment of their friends and the people they are trying to help. Other people may habitually avoid getting involved from a 'fear of interfering' or fear people saying that they are 'busybodies' or incurring some other negative criticism from others or from themselves. However, these attitudes may be the 'pathology' of the person.

Standing by someone, in a positive as opposed to a passive sense, does not always mean frantic activity. It may mean making your gaze felt by standing still and looking silently as a parent terrorises a child in public. A friend recently reported that this action alone appeared to influence a mother, in his view, to change the tone and content of her voice towards her frightened child suffering public humiliation in a suburban shopping mall. It may mean action as subtle as protecting a dying person from interference by state or medicine. As Ilich (1975) describes it:

> Remedies against a painful agony multiplied, but most of them were still to be performed under the conscious direction of the dying who played a new role and played it consciously. Children could help a mother or father to die, but only if they did not hold them back by crying. A person was supposed to indicate when he wanted to be lowered from his bed on to the earth which would soon engulf him, and when the prayers were to start. But bystanders knew that they were to keep the doors open to make it easy for death to come, to avoid noise so as not to frighten death away, and finally to turn their eyes respectfully away from the dying man in order to leave him alone during this most personal event. (pp. 131–132)

A native American woman gathers visible network support

In one Protective Behaviours Training in a northern Wisconsin community, a majority of the participants were Winnebago Native Americans. At one point in the session, while we were discussing networking and the use of resources, a North American woman stood up. She spoke of difficulties with equitable law enforcement and issues of trust. She cited several instances of white police officers either not responding to domestic violence calls, or showing up and over-reacting using verbal abuse and undue force while arresting Native American men. This caused a dilemma for Native American battered women who attempted to obtain police protection from violence. The women themselves were concerned about the racial basis of the abuse the Native American men often received at the hands of the police, and often felt even more vulnerable when the men returned, bruised and humiliated — and even more angry at the woman who had involved the police. Often, the speaker commented, the tribal elders and other members of the tribe felt that such matters should be handled through the Tribal Councils, and frequently were perceived as being prejudiced against the women who attempted to gain white police protection.

While she was talking, several other Native Americans, men as well as women, quietly stood and remained standing. I too, remained standing and quiet, thinking over what she had said. Then, realizing that the five others were still also on their feet, I asked slowly, somewhat puzzled as they did not take a turn to speak,

'What is happening now?'

'We're standing with her', one of the women answered.

The first speaker looked around, and apparently satisfied, sat down. At which point the others sat down also.

Later I wondered, a one-step removed 'what if'. What if we all started doing this. What would our world be like if we did? What if we all, literally, started standing in support when we agree or are interested, sitting only when we disagree or are bored? It could be somewhat disconcerting for speakers to have such immediate and honest feedback, and it might make all speeches, especially political ones, shorter. (West, 1991, p. 61)

Chapter 2
Bystanding —
Cultural and
Historical Context

A dragon was pulling a bear into its terrible mouth.
A courageous man went and rescued the bear.
There are such helpers in the world, who rush to save
anyone who cries out. Like Mercy itself,
they run toward the screaming.
And they can't be bought off.
If you were to ask one of those, 'Why did you come
so quickly?' He or she would say, 'Because I heard
your helplessness'.

(Rumi, 1990, p. 108)

Our Zeitgeist

The fragment of poetry above is some eight centuries old, in a very particular context. It is a fragment of some 60 000 of the most sublime verses the world has known. It was written in moments of mystical ecstasy by a man in love with another man in whom he saw and felt and worshipped God. One could also say that he was in love with God whom he saw and worshipped in another man. Whether their relationship was physically sexual is not known. However, it was love at first sight. Rumi was a great spiritual teacher, a leader of a school, who on this one spectacularly ordinary day became completely entranced by a filthy old beggar 'who did not fit in at all into the Konya society' (Schimmel, 1993, p. 20). Rumi neglected his religious and social duties to spend all his days and nights with the beggar, Shams, in ecstatic conversation and blissful union. Eventually Shams went away, but Rumi pined and pined until Shams was brought back to Mowlana's house, where they continued their relationship. In the end jealousy of their intimacy, and outrage at Rumi's privileging of the old dervish with his company and his gifts, became unbearable. By an account which now appears to be proved, Rumi's heirs and students murdered Shams. They hid their complicity and Shams' body from Rumi who poured out his grief in their midst for years and years afterwards. Is this a bystanding story?

The moral problems of then and there are always more ambiguous. Are we better off here today? I do not believe the situation, frame and concept of bystanding is morally soluble in the way that modernist moral enquiry favours. It was the hope of the Enlightenment project that answers would be found. For many this hope has been bitterly and confusedly disappointed. Perhaps today some people have such clear and unambiguous answers, but this book is not for them. This deliberation here is done in the face of the fact that most of our hard-won answers seem to proliferate further and more complex questions. Increased medical capacity raises issues about embryological research. Fertility cures bring into focus first-time mothers of pensionable age. Choice for childbirth highlights prejudice against the right of people with Down's syndrome to life. The notion of bystanding is contemporary with current social conditions of complexity, ambiguity and uncertainty. Whereas modernism provided solutions to classical problems, post-modernism is providing un-solutions to modernist solutions. The notion of the bystander might be doing the same to psychology as quantum physics and chaos theory is doing to the Cartesian world paradigm.

This spirit of our time (or zeitgeist) has been given many names, several pejorative, all inadequate as they must be when we are attempting to describe and categorise the stream of history in which we are caught. O'Hara (1991) is only one of a number of theoreticians of the cultural climate of our time who have used the term 'post-modernism' to describe collectively a number of different strands of development in the current, most prevalent phenomena in literature, art and architecture — lately even psychology. It is viewed by some as the emerging cultural tradition that reflects upon, interprets and experiences the manifestations of our Western culture at this time, although others, by definition, would disagree.

Although there is much debate about whether the term is useful, adequately defined, or even meaningful, it does encapsulate the attempts of a generation to name the condition of fragmented conceptual realities that characterise our time (Connor, 1989). And, naming (a nominative level operation) is a basic but important step towards understanding or perhaps liberation, as we see in our clients, who may move from reporting *'Daddy messing about'* to *'Daddy raping me'*.

The Moral Demand

> The early postmodern years are bringing, instead of a collapse of morality, a renaissance of searching for principles of life that we variously call morals, ethics, values. And this is not merely a single shift of values, but a continual dynamic process of moral discourse and discovery. Morals are not being handed down from the mountain top on graven tablets; they are being created by people out of the challenges of the times. The morals of today are not the morals of yesterday, and they will not be the morals of tomorrow. (Anderson, 1990, p.259)

But this still cannot provide us with escape from the moral imperative which being alive now posits. Indeed, as three authors (Douzinas, Warrington & McVeigh, 1991) in post-modern jurisprudence will have it:

> Postmodernism must neither replace one set of certainties with another, nor create a new series of bipolarities ... The political imperative of postmodern deconstructive readings is to remain critical and oppositionist, and to challenge any orthodoxy that a complacent and affirmative postmodernism may wish to reimpose. (p. xiii)

Some commentators have emphasised a particular amorality as one of the many voices in post-modernism. However, a description of a time is not a prescription. By that very token I often find that the level of personal, critical and political grappling with moral questions within a post-modernist frame is unsurpassed in urgency, honesty and sheer vertiginous courage. Pre-digested values no longer have either the unquestioned authority or the utopian conviction they once had. We have to work it out for ourselves over and over again in more and more difficult and incommensurate circumstances. Often the more complex the moral situations in which we find ourselves, the less the previous solutions apply and the less we can trust the popular or democratic majority vote to do *justice* to the chaotically multiplying possibilities of fairness and compassion:

> Values, sense and meanings are not to be justified by the same ultimate finality but in the movement of our lives, in their infinite combinations and possibilities [that is, in our finite, our moral, our unique possibility]. We are not directed along the rational tracks of truth towards a future terminus: the end of history and the realisation of a non-alienated totality in the reign of absolute knowledge, where in the dialectical unity of nature and history the sense of existence and being become one. We are not necessarily directed anywhere. We are thus finally free to realise the terrible responsibility of our own her- and his- stories. (Chambers, 1990, p. 95)

Ethics

Staub (1990) differentiates between altruistic behaviour, which is meant to help others with the sole purpose of promoting their welfare, and pro-social behaviour, which is also about benefiting others (but without excluding the possibility of self-gain). A definition of ethics may be useful at this point. Fletcher (1966) offers the following:

> Ethics deals with human relations. Situation ethics puts people at the centre of concern, not things. Obligation is to persons, not to things; to subjects, not objects. The legalist is a *what* asker (What does the law say?); the situationist is a *who* asker (Who is to be helped?). That is, situationists are *personalistic*. In the Christian version, for example, a basic maxim is that the disciple is commanded to love people, not principles or laws or objects or any other *thing*. There are no 'values' in the sense of inherent goods — value is what happens to something when it *happens* to be useful to love working for the sake of persons. Brunner (1947) declared that the notion of value apart from persons is a 'phantasmagoria'. There are no intrinsic values, he says, being a blunt situationist. (p. 50)

An egoistic ethic [erotic] says in effect, *'My first and last consideration is myself'*. This is the essence of an exploitative stance; it is 'what makes Sammy run'. A mutualistic ethic [philic] says, *'I will give as long as I receive'*. We all know this one because it is the common dynamic of friendships. But an altruistic ethic [agapeic] says, *'I will give, requiring nothing in return'*. It explains a Father Damien on Molokai, a kamikaze pilot, a patriot hiding in a Boston attic in 1775, or a Vietcong terrorist walking into a Saigon officers' mess as he pulls out the pin in a bomb hidden under his coat. All these actions, whether correctly (perhaps fanatically) decided or not, are examples of selfless, calculating concern for others. These three ethical postures spell out what is meant by the old saying, 'There are, after all only three kinds of ethics' (Fletcher, 1966, pp. 109–110).

Desensitization and the Normalization of the Obscene

One of the most worrying consequences of the information and problem overload in the moral domain is that of desensitization. 'When people are subjected to too much fear-provoking material, they tend toward numbing, forgetting or feeling so violated that they are hostile to the overall message' (Rogers Macy, 1983, p. 177).

Compassion fatigue is another term which has been used to describe similar phenomena. Put simply, it refers to the fact that human beings, like other animals, have a remarkable capacity for habituation to intolerable circumstances. I read of three children who lived for many years chained to an iron bedstead, were constantly sexually abused, who ate dog food — and survived. We also have the capacity to habituate to the distress of others of our kind. And herein lies our infinite capacity for justifying passivity as we tolerate cruelty in ourselves and others. A *Daily Mail* reader writes in the letters page of the largest selling national British newspaper, 'With all the cruelty and suffering brought to us daily via the media through wars, greed and callousness, we begin to get somewhat cynical and hardened to what is happening around us' (Chilton, 1992, p. 43). A Nobel prize-winner for literature puts it like this, 'As man gets used to hell, he gets used to the sacrifice of others' (Mahfouz, 1986, p. 97).

As was shown in studies of Greek torturers (Haritos-Faroutos, 1983), the first step for making a raw recruit into a fully fledged torturer appears to be training them in bystanding. Novices were usually required in the first instance to act as guards — observers — whilst others inflicted the torture. A lengthy process of desensitization was built on this foundation, from supervising prisoners forced to stand for very long periods, until they eventually participated completely in the atrocities. It is implicit in Williams' (1992) description that bystanding can be the training ground for moral corruption:

> Having acquiesced in *watching others* torture prisoners, or in beating prisoners, or in *denying them* sanitary facilities or blankets, it is difficult suddenly to protest the use of electrical torture. The recruit has been corrupted by *tacit acceptance* of earlier examples of torture, and it becomes difficult to backtrack and question its use [italics added] (pp. 306–307)

Our appalling capacity as human beings to inflict damage, death and torture upon other people, animals, trees and plants, and natural systems in general, has its roots in a profound and terrifying disconnectedness from ourselves as physical organisms:

> We feel and act as if we are in fact disconnected physically, spiritually, emotionally, ecologically and morally, from ourselves and from the universe. We behave *as if* we were each isolated and separate. We cut ourselves off from the roots and springs of life within us — our sensations — and therefore from each other and from all else that is. (Rinzler, 1984, pp. 231–233)

Apparently, if a plant is injured in the presence of another plant, the survivor resonates with the distress of its injured neighbour and subsequently even appears to recognise the aggressor (Watson, 1974). In human beings this phenomenon is referred to as *visceral empathy*, which means people feel the pain of others in their own bodies. Black South Africans have a word for this — *Ubuntu*. It means fellow human feeling — being able to feel as if the experience were happening to your own body.

Providing they have not become desensitized, as experiments show human beings can be, this visceral experience of pain in the presence of another's pain is an organismically healthy response. Babies can cry if other babies do. We can 'feel for' one another in community. Many people have experienced this visceral resonance in group situations, such as football crowds, rock concerts, religious and ceremonial occasions.

Freud (1912a), Berne (1972), Jung (1983) and Polster (1987) all understood that humans need to make their own dramas from their lives, but they paid little attention to how much others are needed to make the drama of their lives *for us* (Bataille, 1986). This is probably the major motivation behind the way the collective (i.e. large masses of the population) devours gossip articles about film or rock stars, presidential love and business affairs or even the British monarchy. The preoccupation with 'the famous' on pedestals makes it so much more fun to pull them off (Clarkson, 1994b). This is a very understandable human trait which requires understanding, compassion and investigation, not judgement alone. People bystand some way or other in a world which is overwhelming in its need for responsible engagement in the plight of those genuinely less fortunate than ourselves — and there are always those. 'We should incidentally be unable to imagine what goes on in the secret depths of the minds of the bystanders if we could not call on our own personal ... experiences, if only childhood ones' (Bataille, 1986. p. 16).

Vicarious Life

We also live vicariously. Sometimes living vicariously, as children do through vicious and bloodthirsty fairytales, is a kind of rehearsal for life as well as a participation in it. We feel with others and, in a sense, we can feel certain dangerous feelings most comfortably through watching others. Hare (1989) divides these into positive and negative vicarious *affects* (feelings):

I may experience distress because a child of mine is in pain, or fear because my wife is in danger, though I myself am in no danger or pain. These are examples of positive vicarious affects. There are also negative vicarious affects, when our own affect is the opposite of that appropriate to the other in his situation; examples of these are Schadenfreude, when we are pleased at the distress of another, and envy, when we are distressed at another's happiness. [From Sosa, 1979]. (p. 231)

Berke (1989) in his excellent work on malice, noted that the Tom and Jerry cartoons are:

... a study in persecution. And for their audience, children and adults, they are a focus of vicarious retribution. At any given moment either Tom or Jerry may be chopped, knifed, stung, shot, crushed, flattened, drowned, bounced, bombed, burned, chased, smacked, slapped or shattered. (p. 197)

This is also desensitization to the reality of violence and abuse, which supports bystanding. Rinzler (1984) writes that knowing and seeing (because the world is now in one communicative network) so much pain, so much hunger, so much violence, eventually can cause a moral bluntness, a coarsening of our sensibilities and a heightening of our threshold for outrage in a way similar to the training of torturers (Peters, 1985; Williams, 1992). In order for us to be able to inflict pain and torture and injustice on others, it seems we only first need to experience it ourselves. And even then, this may not be necessary. Experiments at Stanford University showed how quickly and comparatively easily middle-class students could become dehumanising and dehumanised in a mock prison experiment. The study of Haney, Banks and Zimbardo (1973) revealed the power of social institutional forces to make good men engage in evil deeds. It was anecdotally a woman's tears at the arbitrary humiliation she witnessed that brought this experiment to a premature but conclusive halt.

Wholeness

These ideas of our inevitable interconnection are very close to the conception of the human soul of the medieval Hildegard von Bingen whose work Fox (1983) is reviving. She saw spirituality as biological and inextricably connected with the nature which surrounds and penetrates our existence. According to von Bingen, our souls need to be moist and green and juicy. Fox (1983) derives inspiration from her to plead for human relationships with our planet on the basis of erotic justice (p. 295). There is academic support for this notion from all sides, for example, 'Donella Meadows notes that the nonlinear coupling of economic factors leads to the inescapable conclusion that "no part of the human race is really separate either from other human beings or from the global ecosystem. We all rise or fall together"' (Briggs & Peat, 1989, p. 178).

When we desensitize ourselves we destroy what is organismically valuable, whether this be natural resources or an intellectual heritage. It is only by cutting off a part of ourselves that we can claim that another part of the universe is separate from us. Later, in Chapter 9, it is shown how this is related to our biological sphere of experience, epistemology and processing of simultaneous levels of reality. Here other voices speak:

> Dillard explains that all the entire green world consists of chloroplasts. If we analyse a molecule of chlorophyll we see [that] ... human blood is *identical* to this chlorophyll, *except* that at its centre is a single atom of iron. Thus, our red power is a kissing cousin to the greening power all around us. These stories emerging from contemporary science are awesome; they are both mystical and scientific. They are part of our learning to live once again *in the cosmos*. (Fox, 1983, p. 352)

> Our physical organs connect us with millions of years of history; our minds are full of immemorial paths of pre-human experience. The intimate *rapport* with Nature is one of the precious things in life. Nature is indeed very close to us; sometimes perhaps closer than hands and feet, of which in truth she is but the extension. (Smuts, 1987, p. 336)

> Life is achieved by resolving the tension in responsive feeling and creative activity, in which having is not eliminated but is assimilated to being; in which one and another become I and Thou; in which science is integrated with metaphysics; in which autonomy [managing my own affairs] is transcended in liberty, which is participation; in which my body and the world with which it is consubstantial and which enlarges and multiplies its powers is the place in which I bear witness to Being; in which I work out my fidelity and my hope and keep my self open, fluid and ready to spend. (Blackman, 1961, p. 73)

World Soul

> The myth of interiority is over, or rather, the idea that interiority is confined to human persons is over. If we kill off the world-soul we actually kill off ourselves, since our souls do not exist independently of the world-soul. This is what true ecological sense is all about. The Australian Aboriginals knew that *only* by keeping the song-lines and the Dreaming tracks of the ancestors alive, could they keep themselves alive. Today, in secular and practical ecology, we are learning that what we do to the world we do to

ourselves. This reciprocal, interdependent view of 'physical' reality is the very first stage in an awakening of eros that will ultimately lead us toward a new cosmology and to an entirely new conception of the relationship between self and other, individual and the world. (Tacey, 1993, p. 281)

Our apparent control of nature, as tragically opposed to our connection with nature, is a deep but paradoxically reversible fatal malaise. Our human malaise of disconnection from natural sensation, our symptoms of violence on all levels, our lack of compassion for our home, the earth, our incomprehension of the connectedness among all the things of the earth, of the universe, are curable — if we are willing. (Rinzler, 1984, p. 236)

Perhaps a sense of totality is an indispensable fiction, a life-preserving lie as Nietzsche would put it, necessary for our sanity, for our continuing move-ment. But such a prospect, however necessary it may be, can no longer claim to provide access to a transglobal and transhistorical truth. That is why we find ourselves at the end of the establishment highway: not because its concern (with truth, knowledge, justice, freedom, equality) has dramati-cally terminated, but because the assumed link between our potential free-dom and the Enlightenment's abstract dreams of universal illumination (the totalising pretensions of the Encyclopaedia) has snapped. Today, in abandoning that highway for other, more modest roads there lies the final recognition of our responsibilities, where flesh, blood and bone, the hot body of mortality, triumphs over the cold light of an abstract reason. (Chambers, 1990, p. 99)

Reconnection

Does this mean that people should get involved in every single issue that they know about? We now really know too much. How can the injustice in the world then be resolved? Existentially, if you know about a problematical situation, you are already in it. By refusing to be involved, you are involved. To say you do not want to know is to take a very definite moral position that not knowing is better than knowing — that it is the higher good. The point of this book is not to posit a final answer to these intricate human dilemmas, but to ques-tion the lie (or the inauthenticity) that people can truly claim to be uninvolved, or that there is, in fact, any such position as that of *inno-cent bystander*. In using this phrase, I do not mean to apportion blame. Again, I would rather want to invoke responsibility.

It is, of course, not a question of meddling or interfering at every single opportunity. It is realising that any situation about which people have knowledge or with which they are in contact, necessarily means that they *are* involved. It is their business. For example, when people in psychotherapy start getting better, they often experience enhanced compassion for other people, for example, their parents, and an enhanced or renewed connection with the rest of the world, such as feeling concern for the rainforests.

Amongst other indicators of client readiness for termination of therapy, Bary and Hufford (1990) include 'a healthy respect for ... life in general' (p. 220). Maslow (1968), one of the very few psychologists who researched health instead of disease, put it this way:

> The state of being without a system of values is psychopathogenic ... The human being needs a framework of values, a philosophy of life, a religion or religion surrogate to live by and understand by, in about the same sense that he needs sunlight, calcium or love. (p. 206)

> A client recently reported: *'When I first came into counselling I was struggling with feelings of being a "non-person", powerless and in despair about ever changing my own life. I could not understand why anyone would get bothered about the possible extinction of rhinoceroses in Central Africa. As I claim my own power, my autonomy and begin to "own" my life and the repercussions of my existential choices, I begin to feel that those rhinoceroses are* my *rhinoceroses since they represent my response-able connection to the world'.* (Clarkson, 1989, p. 24)

Understanding and accepting personal responsibility for bystanding behaviour may be deeply uncomfortable knowledge. The questions raised by these issues tap into some very deep, primitive roots having to do with survival, archetypal rites of scapegoating (von Franz, 1986) and rewards for those who turned a blind eye to the excesses of rules in return for favours.

For example, a student on psychiatric placement in a mental hospital witnesses the systematic humiliation and abuse of patients and discusses this with the consultant psychiatrist. This proves a useless endeavour which could only result in her rejection from the placement. The fact is, she was involved. How can she exercise some response-ability in the situation at least for her own moral benefit, if not for that of the others? She feels there is nothing at all she can do about it and that no-one will listen to her. The rage and powerlessness infect the atmosphere of the ward and the patients see another caring professional reduced to impotence by a punitive system.

> A few years ago Sammy Davis Jr., a popular American entertainer, repudiated his Christian identity and became a Jew. 'As I see it', he said, 'the difference is that the Christian religion preaches love thy neighbor and the Jewish religion preaches justice, and I think justice is the big thing we need'. Here is the cry of a man who has suffered discrimination, and seen millions of other Negroes suffer, because people separate love and justice. (Fletcher, 1966, p. 91)

The Role of Time

An awareness of ourselves choosing our actions in a historical context can help us make choices that will bear the scrutiny of future generations. It is often effective to ask oneself and/or one's client, *'In 30 years' time, what will you wish you had done now? Would you be happy for your grandchildren to judge the commitments you are making or avoiding here and now?'*. *'What did you do in the war, Daddy?'* is not a simplistic question, but the voice of a child seeking meaning and purpose in the lives of his forbears and ancestors to sustain him in an increasingly complex and ethically demanding world:

> I find myself engaged along with others in a world which makes demands on me: I respond to others and undertake responsibilities to and for them. So far from my being myself the ground of my certainty in knowing and the motive of my constancy in willing, it is the existence of another that gives me my primary notion of existence and it is in so far as I believe in the existence of others and act on that belief that I affirm my own existence. (Marcel, 1952, p. 66)

History may change perceptions of who was the villain because of what seems right and fair in some ways and places may not seem so later and elsewhere. The backdrop of history moves in complicated ways. People may make genuine mistakes in their judgement on the basis of lack of information or deliberate misinformation, simple misunderstandings, fears, blindness, prejudice or jumping to conclusions which seemed *obvious* at the time.

As Sartre (1948) said, 'Man makes himself; he is not found ready-made; he makes himself by the choice of his morality, and he cannot but choose a morality, such is the pressure of circumstances upon him. We define man only in relation to his commitments' (p. 50).

In the final analysis it does not matter whether a person chooses the correct position first, even if it is changed later, because both the initial and subsequent changing can be honourable options. What is important is to be aware of choice in engaging in situations — since existentially a person cannot not be engaged. Even to decide not to choose, in Roberts' (1984) words, is to choose.

Relationship As Value

This view coincides with an idea that is frequently articulated in third-force psychology; that all actions or non-actions involve a commitment to implicit or explicit values (Maslow, 1968). 'Science' itself is reconsidering the effect of what we call values, of course, even the value of self-survival can also be a position of good faith — an authentic choice genuinely embraced and honestly acknowledged:

> The quantum world-view stresses dynamic relationship as the basis of all that is. It tells us that our world comes about through a mutually creative dialogue between mind and body [inner and outer, subject and object], between the individual and his personal material context, and between human culture and the natural world. It gives us a view of the human self which is free and responsible, responsible to others and to its environment, essentially related and naturally committed, and at every moment creative. (Zohar, 1990, p. 220)

One thing seems to stand out and that is that the *relationship* is the most important factor in all effective psychotherapies, and, indeed, in all constructive change in small or large systems and it is this relationship that, again, underlies the existential impossibility of the individual on an island being capable of being understood outside the web of human networks. I am reminded of a quotation (author unknown) drawn from a Social Services office wall which provides the genuine compassionate framework within which discussions and commitments from each individual about his or her bystanding responsibilities for the future can occur:

> Every single human being, when the entire situation is taken into account, has always, at every moment of the past, done the very best that he or she could do, and so deserves neither blame nor reproach from anyone, including self. This in particular is true of you.

White sheep of the family. Racial harassment interrupted

Odell Taliaferro, 83 at the time of this writing, has been an articulate activist for many years. The following happened a number of years ago while he was Chair of the local National Association for the Advancement of Colored People (NAACP). The position he held at the University, supporting the professors in their lectures and demonstrations, had increased both in time and responsibilities over the years. Odell Taliaferro was usually sought out by new faculty members for help and suggestions in designing their lecture demonstrations for the basic sciences courses.

In the months prior to the following incident, several of the new, younger faculty had advocated for his reclassification as faculty specialist, rather than the lower paid technical classification he held. This advocacy had elicited some opposition from several of the more conservative senior faculty. Although race was never mentioned publicly, he *was* the only black in the department and some others, non-black, in other departments, also without PhDs had already been reclassified as faculty specialists. Eventually the newer faculty won, he was reclassified as faculty specialist, receiving a substantial well deserved raise. However, several of the older men held some resentment about it.

This came out in subtle ways, and was sometimes insidious. For instance, one of Taliaferro's relatives, with the same surname, had gotten into considerable difficulty with the police. The local paper had carried the story on the front page. The following day, Odell Taliaferro happened to be in a crowded elevator with a couple of the senior faculty men.

'Oh! Tally!' one of them commented, in pseudo-friendly tones, 'That relative of yours ... he's in considerable trouble again, isn't he? That doesn't do much for your NAACP campaign for first class citizenship for colored people, now does it?'

The elevator arrived at Odell Taliaferro's floor. He turned to face his colleagues as he got off.

'Yes, he's in trouble again', he responded, just as the door was closing, 'He's the white sheep of our family'.

As told to Peg West, Madison, Wisconsin. (West, 1991, p. 65)

Chapter 3
The Dramatic
Structure of Human
Life

Nice Day for a Lynching
The bloodhounds look like sad old judges
In a strange court. They point their noses
At the Negro jerking in their noose;
His feet spread crowlike above these
Honorable men who laugh as he chokes.
I don't know this black man.
I don't know these white men.
But I know that one of my hands
Is black, and one white. I know that
One part of me is being strangled,
While another part horribly laughs.
Until it changes,
I shall be forever killing; and be killed.

(Patchen, 1971, p. 97)

The Function of Drama

It is probably impossible to trace the first burgeoning of drama in human consciousness or culture. But I have a fantasy that the first dramas were enactments of hunting tales or traveller tales, such as can be seen in the film *Quest for Fire* which represents the beginning of human culture in early tribes, with the language sounds createded by Anthony Burgess and the body language by Desmond Morris. The German word for bystander is *Schaulustiger*, which can translate literally as 'he who lusts after the show'. For most of us, this carries more truth than is comfortable. Blood, or its threat, draws the mass of people into the audience. Whether we like it or not, sex and violence are what most people find exciting and for their imaginal juxtaposition (as is witnessed by so many popular films of our time) most people find most exciting and are willing to pay for.

Human beings have engaged in dramatic productions for edification, entertainment and collective catharsis, since the dawn of history. For the Greeks, of course, drama was a major form of entertainment, education and — dare we say it? — group psychotherapy. Aristotle said 'tragedy is the imitation of an action ... with incidents arousing pity and fear, whereby to provide an outlet for such emotions' (Bywater, 1909, VI. 1449[b]).

There is also an immense, almost visceral, excitement and vicarious gratification when people can observe others (for example, Shakespeare's King Lear, Tennessee Williams' Brick or Bizet's Carmen) go through disaster, discomfort, despair while they sit in the audience feeling for, against or with the actors, but absolved from the reality of physical and public engagement. The Roman populace thronged to the spectacles of Christians being eaten by lions, Madame Defarge knitted whilst the guillotine was falling during the French Revolution, and now millions of people are the passive observers of violence, injustice and mass starvation on television news screens in every Western living room. This is in the continuing tradition of the thrill of participating in collective displays or tragedy, with the option of denying responsibility for any involvement. It is only when the spotlight falls on someone in the audience, when the comedian makes them the butt of a joke or the experimental theatre group create voluntary or involuntary audience participation (such as the actors' attack on the audience in *Marat-Sade* (Weiss, 1972)) that this culturally imposed, apparent separation between onlookers and actors breaks down and the fact and nature of our complicity is exposed to public view.

> The task of the therapist who is working from this [constructivist] perspective is to identify the plot that governs the patient's life and to see if a more positive one can be constructed — and believed, and lived by. Constructivist therapy is another sign of the times, one way that some people manage to take on the sometimes-frightening idea of reality as fiction and make it an approach to growth and moral responsibility (Anderson, 1990, p. 141)

The Archetype of the Theatre

Shakespeare wrote:

> All the world's a stage,
> And all the men and women merely players:
> They have their exits and their entrances;
> And one man in his time plays many parts (*As You Like It* II vii. 140–143).

The stage is a primary archetypal image that encapsulates within its space and within dramatic time the arena for engagement with the large themes of good and evil, the issues of involvement and responsibility, and the role of the bystander and others in the cast. In the theatre of life and history we play out, as actors or audience, the dilemmas of our world. In the consulting room we have the opportunity to re-view or re-enact the stories, re-shape our narratives, and tranform our lives. Moreno (1975) was one of the first psychotherapists or 'soul doctors', in the modern idiom, intentionally to use the dramatic format to act as both symbolic structural container and vessel for catharsis and transformation.

Predictable Dramas

Many professional and lay people are familiar with the notions of Greek tragedy where people are caught in destiny before transformation, before choice, indeed before the more modernist notion of individual responsibility was truly known. At the heart of our current dramas and the central story of many of the most popular films of our time (*Terminator*) are three distinct roles — the Hero, the Villain, and the Victim or scapegoat. These are familiar to some people as the Karpman (1968) 'Drama Triangle' from his paper in the idiom of transactional analysis. Karpman (1968) used the three role titles of 'Rescuer', 'Persecutor' and 'Victim' to capture the essence of the characters who enact them on life's stage in every person's life.

Berne (1968) introduced the idea of games — repetitive, negative interactions which we enact, often out of awareness and against our conscious will, with other people. Although much misunderstood and somewhat distorted, the general idea that 'people play games' was recognisable enough for the book title to become the title of a best-selling popular song. He suggested that in most negative human interactions or patterns there are these three roles which may be genuine positions or which may, in some way, be in bad faith or part of the unconscious repetition compulsion. The functions of control, vulnerability and helping are almost always present in any dramatic structure. The particular contribution of Berne (1968) and Karpman (1968) was to show how these roles can be assumed and enacted in repetitive and destructive human interactions. A series of such patterns can be said to form the individual scenes, acts or episodes of a life script — a tragedy, comedy or satire which is the existential situation of all individuals, from which they are to make the meaning of their life. The genuine function of the rescuer is that of helping and assisting, the persecutor that of structuring and controlling, and the victim represents the vulnerable and the injured part of the whole or role in the drama. Other people will fulfil the persecuting or structuring function in the drama — maybe the courtroom judge or the detective. The level of awareness, genuineness, authenticity, choice or intentional manipulation from any of these positions can vary enormously and an in-depth discussion of this is not relevant to our intention here.

Real victims are, indeed, people who are genuinely being victimised through no exceptional fault of their own. They are people who suffer from injustice, cruelty or oppression by virtue of their colour, their religion, their gender, their sexual orientation, their nationality and so on. Any group of people (or individuals) has some objectionable characteristics, because they are people like other people who all have some aspects or qualities which are more or less likeable, not particularly because they are black or artistic or Jewish! Any victim can be shown to have some characteristic or behaviour without which the victimisation may not have happened. A short dress or flirtatious behaviour does not deserve a brutal rape, such as dramatised on film by Jodie Foster in *The Accused*. Protesting against an employer's right to open your mail is not abusive. The prisoner who complains about prison conditions is a troublemaker and cannot be trusted to make 'reasoned' complaints — oh yes? A young woman teacher of disturbed children lost her job because she was homosexual. One of the primary reasons given for her dismissal was that she protested her dismissal. Yet, such constructions are frequently put upon situations.

Our complicated moral and ethical choices are made against the changing backdrop of history or the circumstances of the time. Of course, values are relative to our time and culture. What is accepted as just or right at a certain period in history or in certain parts of the world will not necessarily be accepted as good or true at other times or in other places. The Chinese practice of binding the feet of all girls has largely been abandoned; the practice of cliterodectomy has not. Homosexuals are still jailed and punished in certain parts of the world, but there have been many societies in history where they were welcomed and had honoured places. People who appear to be schizophrenic are medicated and locked up in certain parts of the world; in others they are accompanied on their journeys into the core of the fragmenting self and emerge as enlightened folk-doctors, capable of accompanying others and curing many ills of the flesh and spirit.

Of course it is difficult and perhaps sometimes even impossible to judge whether a person is being totally, unilaterally victimised or whether they are somehow also oppressing or victimising themselves ('granting the sanction of the victim') by not achieving in life what would, indeed, otherwise be possible. It concerns the woman who says, *'There's no point applying because they would only appoint men to the position of senior engineer.'* Yet, she never finishes her engineering degree to put this to the test. As Federer (1995) writes:

- Will comply
- Will adhere to
- Will cooperate

These phrases will certainly look familiar to most professionals who work with people with developmental disabilities. Much of our time is spent teaching our clients how to be 'socially appropriate'. We emphasize and reward 'compliant' behaviour, a choice which, in theory, is not necessarily wrong. We are, however, doing a great disservice to our clients if compliance is not tempered with the concept of personal safety. If we fail to combine 'social appropriateness' with the right to feel safe, we are teaching our clients not just to be good citizens, but also to be good victims! (p. 1)

The Role of the Audience

Karpman (1968) visualised this game role distribution as a triangle with the rescuer role in one corner, the persecutor in the other and the victim in the bottom corner. However, Karpman's Drama Triangle does not allow for the fact that the drama almost always has an audience. The audience is both affected by the play and has a profound effect on what transpires. At the simplest level, whether the play continues is determined by the audience; it may show displeasure by booing or leaving the theatre, or pleasure or acquiescence by applause. By their very presence, the members of the audience also agree, consent, and participate response-ably.

The presence of third parties, television cameras and/or verbatim recorders can and often does prevent secret abuses. When employers, police or governments refuse the presence of independent moderators or appropriate recording, genuine victims often have no recourse to justice, since the people with power may claim that the citizen 'resisted arrest', the employee was rude or the wife was exaggerating and he 'only pushed' her and then she fell and hit her head on the fireplace:

> The whites in the Deep South who resisted the civil rights demonstrations, and who resented the roles that the drama assigned to them, spoke often of 'outside agitators'. They felt invaded by hordes of radicals and do-gooders and reporters and photographers, people who did not understand them

and their way of dealing with things. But what was happening was not so much that outsiders were coming into the South as that the South was being taken to the world, ripped out of its old context and thrust by the news media onto the center of a global stage in which the drama was there for all to see. When demonstrators chanted, 'the whole world is watching', they were announcing the arrival of the postmodern era, in which time and space can be magically modified by media of communications, in which boundaries are not what they used to be, and in which ancient social construction of reality can wither in an instant under the bright lights of social scrutiny. (Anderson, 1990, p. 170)

Audience is another word for bystander, especially in its dictionary definition, 'a looker on' (Macdonald, 1972, p. 178). Just as any role in the drama triangle is an attempt to discount (minimise or ignore) aspects of self, others, or the reality of the situation (Schiff et al., 1975), so, too, can the bystander be considered a false drama role, involving the discounting which perpetuates offensive acts through people remaining passive. According to English (1992), it is equally possible to think of these and the fourth role of Bystander in terms of racketeering.

Rescuing, for example, usually means getting involved by giving help which is not asked for or needed, such as the story of the little boy who helped the old lady across the street even though she was fighting and protesting all the way. Once on the other side he asked her why she had objected so much. She explained that she had never wanted to be on the other side of the street anyway! Many psychotherapists and psychoanalysts have become phobic of rescuing or proselytizing or prescribing in the helping professions. In an effort to remain 'neutral' many have lost their humanity and their compassion, their capacity to be moved emotionally, physically and spiritually by the pain they witness and minister to. In particular, many have become immune to the plight of colleagues who may become scapegoats for the self-righteousness of others. The concept of responsibility may have become — like original sin — another form of using knowledge of the soul to oppress people and make them feel bad about themselves. Unfortunately, once people feel bad about themselves, they are much less likely to do things which may be good for them and good for others. Destruction or abuse is usually the outcome of some kind of unhappiness.

Bystanding, whether by a lay person or professional, is distinguished by the bystander accepting or claiming the ulterior contract (process justification) of passivity. Inauthentic victims can confuse themselves with punished bystanders when they get involved in ways which are more determined by their masochistic needs than by self-actualisation and social responsibility. Persecutors can positively exploit their sadistic needs when they are putatively not bystanding, but psychologically milking (for the gratification of their power or control needs) situations which call for compassion, understanding and correction. The bystander pretends to be innocent whilst avoiding responsibility. The use of the word 'innocent' here is existential — not intended as blaming.

There are, of course, real *controllers*, such as judges and traffic wardens, real *helpers*, such as doctors and nurses who mend broken legs, and real *victims*, those who through no excessive fault of their own, are persecuted for vague, often unquestioned or unconscious reasons, such as being young, being female, being observant and questioning. Sometimes the persecution is clear and viciously conscious, such as the genocide of the Tutsis in Rwanda. In a profound sense the authentic 'looker-on' can be 'the witness', as were, for example, some people in Nazi Germany who made drawings of the atrocities for posterity. Regardless of the option selected, one cannot *not choose*, because not choosing is still a choice. This 'variance and relativity' is sometimes used to excuse or justify what some people would call frankly immoral behaviour.

Drama As Creation

A more helpful model suggested by Physis (see Clarkson, 1995d) would be of a narrative which is not all present in one moment in time, a narrative which allows for the possibility of all the possibilities of time and allows, therefore, in that expanded time vista for creative decisions, licences, options, strategies synchronicities and chance.

> What the wise man prefers is the concrete world, *for it is this which manifests physis* .... Wisdom is not flight from but an engagement in the concrete world (as becomes especially clear with respect to the polis). The wise man prefers this. (Aristotle in Guerrière, 1980, p.115)

The model of narrative has both determined qualities as well as qualities of decision and free will. Narrative has respect for the narrator and listeners. The notion of the 'unconscious' denies the person the possibility of full self-knowledge in the present moment, whereas narrative allows full knowledge in time. The structure of time in the narrative contains many possibilities, including flashback, prescience, memories — things past narrative always selects from the field dreams of the future, different vantage points from which different characters can tell the stories coloured by their particular histories, aspirations and psychologies. Narrative undermines the idea that individuals are separate from each other in that a narrator binds within his or her narration many different characters, even atmospheres or places of interest, in which the narrator himself may be just one element. In a story it is possible to know everything — there is no mysterious factor which governs behaviour from a dark inaccessible place:

> The competition between different stories, whether based on religion or ideology, is far less critical to the prospects for peace in the world, and to the emergence of a global civilization, than the competition between different stories about stories — between absolutist/objectivist and relativist/constructivist ideas about the nature of human truth. A pluralistic civilization can only be built with a great amount of tolerance, and the kind of tolerance that comes from people who believe in the cosmic certainty of their truth (and theirs alone) is both limited and patronizing. You can only become truly tolerant of other people's realities by having found some new way to inhabit your own. (Anderson, 1990, p. 267)

Ancient legends carry the well-known story of the publicly acclaimed person who secretly knows that he/she is covering up a flaw which could well prove fatal. Achilles is one such story. Newspapers now also carry similar stories, such as the secret sexual vice of a priest, the hidden drug addiction of a family doctor. It may have been part of human consciousness since the time people first started reflecting on the meaning of their lives, and it is still with us. Studying these ancient myths can sometimes illustrate and help us in our lives today (Clarkson, 1994c).

Creating Our Own Dramas

> Our lives are both texts that we create, and texts created by the laws of others. This interplay opens the space for new reading, writing and speaking, for becoming other than what we are. Postmodern jurisprudence understands the law otherwise and reads the other in the law. The fixed oppositions that stabilised the modern world, left/right, black/white, East/West, state/society, have started to break down. As the communist edifice collapses, and state racism enters its last phase, all the great certainties of modernity are questioned. (Douzinas, Warrington & McVeigh, 1991, p. xiii)

Myths and stories have always presented humans with opportunities for engagement and inspiration with life. Sometimes they can provide us with images or metaphors which illuminate recurrent human dilemmas or problems. Learning from and thinking about life's problems through identifying with the characters in stories, legends and even today's films is a potent human way of trying to make sense and meaning of our lives and getting help in solving our dilemmas. Jung's ideas of archetypes are of this nature. Archetypes can be described as inherited patterns of meaning dating from our earliest ancestors, and supposed to be present in us as potential images or meanings which can be realised in individual lives. They are often carried in myths. Myths or ancient stories influence our everyday consciousness in very important ways. In such a way the archetype of the Roman amphitheatre, the shadow-play in the chieftain's cave and the drumming dance telling the story of the creation of the world on a high mountain:

> In a postmodern society we perceive life as drama, and our major issues involve the definition of personal roles and the fabrication of stories that give purpose and shape to social existence ... Public happenings have the quality of scenes created or stage-managed for public consumption. (Anderson, 1990, p. 108)

Although the roles of victim, persecutor and rescuer can all be taken on in bad faith or enacted unreasonably, these dramatic functions can also be authentically chosen responses to a given situation. All bystander patterns can masquerade as victim, rescuer or persecutor roles in psychological patterns. Bystander patterns are to be found in people in any or all of the other three roles. (Examples are intimidation by the persecutor, unhealthy narcissism in the rescuer, and the helplessness of the victim.) It is very important to distinguish a bystander role from other kinds of patterns in our exploration.

The Reciprocating Action of All Harm

Like other role behaviours, unaware or unquestioned bystanding behaviour interferes with full and complete integrated adult functioning. By avoiding autonomous goal-directed action, bystanding often does violence to very important aspects of a mature human being as well as limiting the scope, richness, range, and effectiveness of intelligent and responsible living.

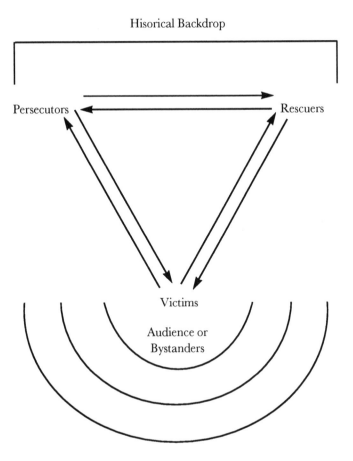

Figure 1 The Karpman Drama Triangle incorporating the bystander role in sociohistorical context. (Reprinted with permission from the author and the International Transactional Analysis Association)

He drives real reckless. Problem solving by a 10-year-old

John noticed me carrying a pile of books and papers into school one morning and offered to help.

'I had an Early Warning Sign last weekend', he confided quietly.

'Yes?' I encouraged.

'Well, I was feeling unsafe, and I used my Network', he continued. Like many third graders, he liked to be precise with words.

'Good for you,' I responded, 'How'd you do that?'

'I was at a big family party at my uncle's house, and my dad had been drinking so much that I didn't want to go home in the car with him. He drives real reckless when he's like that. So I got someone else to drive me home.'

'Good thinking!' I put my arm around him. 'Exactly what did you do?'

'Well, I asked one of my uncles first, but he said he thought it would be better not to make a fuss about it, and he didn't think my dad was *that* drunk.'

'But *you* did?'

'Yeah', John said ruefully, 'I did. I know. So I told my aunt that I was scared to drive with him, and could she just give me a lift — and not make a big deal of it with my father. So she did. I was kind of afraid he might be mad when he got home, and so was she.'

'Was he?'

'Well, I went right to my room and quick got ready for bed like my aunt suggested.

When mom came in to say goodnight, I pretended I was almost asleep, so she told my dad I was asleep. Later I heard them fighting again.'

'But you had kept yourself safe John. You took good care of yourself I think.'

John put his arm load of books on my desk and stood thoughtfully, straightening them.

'I wish he'd stop drinking so much, and they wouldn't fight.'

'Yes, me too. I know that's terribly hard for you. And maybe there isn't a lot you can do about them.'

'Mom doesn't like it either.'

'I bet not. Do you think any of them might be willing to talk to you and me together?'

'I dunno', he sighed. 'I could ask my mom.'

'You could say I suggested it, if you think that would help. We could talk to your mom about *her* right to feel safe all the time, too.'

'She feels scared when he drives like that.'

'I'm sure she does. I would. And you do.'

'Maybe I will ask her. Gotta go now, or I'll be late.'

'If you want to talk some more, come on back. Tell your teacher I said it was OK. I'll be here all morning.'

'I think I'm OK now. Thanks.'

'I'm glad you told me John. That was skilful taking care of yourself. Seems to me you've learned things that some grown ups don't know yet.'

'I sure wish they'd learn too. See ya.'

Incident at Schenk Elementary School, Madison, Wisconsin, November 1981. (West, 1991, pp. 74–75)

Part II
Bystander Patterns

Chapter 4
'And washed his hands'

> Therefore when they were gathered together, Pilate said unto them, Whom will ye that I release unto you? Barabbas, or Jesus which is called Christ?
> For he knew that for envy they had delivered him.
> When he was set down on the judgement seat, his wife sent unto him, saying, Have thou nothing to do with that just man; for I have suffered many things this day in a dream because of him.
> But the chief priests and elders persuaded the multitude that they should ask Barabbas, and destroy Jesus ...
> When Pilate saw that he could prevail nothing, but that rather a tumult was made, he took water, and washed his hands before the multitude, saying,
> I am innocent of the blood of this just person: see ye to it
>
> (St. Matthew 27: 17–24)

Bystander Patterns

The second part of this book reviews bystanding behaviour and analyses examples of 12 bystander patterns or slogans in personal, organisational and national contexts. It provides some explanations as well as suggestions for turning these kinds of patterns into opportunities for responsible involvement, intimacy and autonomy in our shared world. The listing of variations below is intended to act as examples rather than specific definitions, and to act as a stimulus for further development of the concepts.

This section explores the nature and dynamics of different bystander patterns and their motivations and possibilities for transformation, thereby extending the uses of game theory into a moral dimension concerning both the individual and the collective. *It is my hypothesis that, to the extent that people bystand or collude with bystanding in their personal, professional, organisational, national and global lives, they support the destruction of innate human biological responsiveness to the vicissitudes of others, their intellectual and moral connection with others and the planet.* We undermine our necessary existential obligation of remaining

51

engaged with others in terms of what we are doing in this world and in taking responsibility for our shared human condition.

Aristotle commented on passivity thus, 'The worst situation is when someone is with full knowledge on the point of doing the deed, and then leaves it undone. That situation offends our moral sensibilities' (Warrington, 1963, XIV. 1453[b]). And *The Bhavagad Gita* also stresses, 'Nor can anyone, even for an instant, remain really actionless; for helplessly is everyone driven to action by the qualities born of nature' (Besant, 1914, p. 47).

I do not believe that there are easy, permanent or entirely satisfactory solutions to the problems alluded to here. I wish to offer the bystander drama role concept and examples of bystander forms to explore and provide a theoretical and applied structure for how all people (clinicians, parents, managers, psychoanalysis and counselling consumers) can remain in the questioning process. Some bystanders choose to witness, some decide on passive collusion, and others turn the other way. At times all of us construct more or less elaborate defence systems to shield us from the full impact of knowing how our shadow selves are enacted on organisational, national, and global stages.

Just a reminder of the definition:

> A Bystander is considered to be a person who does not become actively involved in a situation where someone else requires help ... Where one or more people are in danger, Bystanders therefore could, by taking some form of action, affect the outcome of the situation even if they were not able to avert it. Thus, by definition, anyone who gets actively involved in a 'critical situation', whether we describe this choice as pathological (scriptbound) or autonomous, is not a Bystander. (Clarkson, 1987, p. 82)

All repetitive patterns have biological, existential, psychological and social advantages. For example, the biological advantage: the trainee on psychiatric placement did not need to hold back her feelings of anger, for she could find an appropriate channel to express her suppressed feelings. By being active in the situation she participated viscerally and potently in empowerment. Instead of reinforcing an existential belief that even victims can be empowered or activated in oppressive situations.

Avoiding the negative consequence of passivity, apathy, and helplessness is indeed a sign of mental health; for example, to be engaged in a struggle for what is good, or what a person believes to be good — even at the risk of danger to oneself (Boadella, 1987). To assume responsibility (including the risk of making mistakes) the individual can benefit from the enormously fertile opportunities for learning and increasing knowledge of how to be responsibly effective in the world. The Pre-Socratic Stoics occupied themselves with the active principle of Physis in such a way:

> A good bootmaker is one who makes good boots, a good shepherd is one who keeps his sheep well, and even though good boots are in the Day-of-Judgement sense entirely worthless and fat sheep no whit better than starved sheep, yet the good bootmaker or good shepherd must do his work well or he will cease to be good. To be good he must perform his function; ... in performing that function there are certain things that he must 'prefer' to others, even though they are not really 'good'. He must prefer a healthy sheep or a well-made boot to their opposites. It is this that Nature, or Physis, herself works when she shapes the seed into a tree or the blind puppy into a good hound. The perfection of the tree or the blind puppy is in itself indifferent, a thing of no ultimate value. Yet the goodness of Nature lies in working for that perfection.
>
> For the essence of Goodness is to do something, to labour, to achieve some end; and if Goodness is to exist, the world process must begin again ... Physis must be moving upward, or else it is not Physis. (Murray, 1915, p. 43)

A woman may receive genuine appreciation from her intimates: friends, family and lovers. Such recognition will be based on empathy and support for her genuine engagement in a struggle which costs her some trepidation, discipline, and the invitation not to respond at the lowest common denominator of the collective human being, but at the highest she can reach. Amongst friends and acquaintances, however, she risks opprobrium and criticism, particularly if the situation were to work out disadvantageously for her. This is likely, for example, if she were to be seen to have 'chosen the wrong side'. In a collusively bystanding culture (such as Western civilisation), the external social advantages are minimal, if not punishing, if it goes wrong. On the other hand, involving acquaintances as pseudo-spectators to provide applause or admiration for being, for example, the *buddy* of a person suffering from an AIDS-related disease, is also possible, although unusual.

However, the external social advantages (secondary rewards amongst acquaintances) may be enormously valuable if the end result meets collective desires or ideals. In the long run, it may be more important to participate in creating a culture in our world which is non-collusive in bystanding, even if this places people in a minority for a while.

Such minorities, which forgo enormous short-term positive external social advantages, risking losing friends or reputation for ideas or ideals which they believe to be good, find themselves in hallowed and honoured company in the long term. For example, people who made important social and historical changes (such as Florence Nightingale, Mahatma Gandhi, Martin Luther King, Emily Dickinson, Jean-Martin Charcot, Semmelweis) were all disapproved of by friends and intimates and faced much opposition, but as historical perspective shifted over time, the ultimate values of their involvement became more apparent.

Bystanding is also essentially an ethical issue. All social justice theorists have an intimate acquaintance with the problems and ramifications of bystanding. If people think something is wrong, when and how do they get involved? How will they act or take responsibility for it? Is it possible to respond effectively? The scope of the world's need is so overwhelming. Of course, it is very difficult to know in advance if one is going to be on the side of the right and the good. Usually, the choices have to be made while the story is still unfolding, and with necessarily ambiguous moral outcomes. Yet the existential responsibility is to choose how to be and do before the curtain falls and the last scene is played out. Waiting until someone wins may be profitable, but is morally dubious. It may even be clinically detrimental in so far as it serves passivity and destructiveness instead of autonomy and/or intimacy with the human condition. If people remain focused only on the product or the result, the process may become fatally poisoned and compliance and conformity reign.

Bystander patterns can be identified if they meet the criteria for bystanding behaviour:

- Something seems wrong in a situation.
- The person is aware of it.
- They do not actively take responsibility for their part in maintaining the problem or preventing its resolution.
- Existential bad faith or inauthenticity — they claim they could not have acted otherwise.
- It is based on minimising their capacity for autonomy, intimacy and potency in the world.

Since it is usually done out of awareness and not as a deliberate act of malice or neglect, the concept of bystanding should not be used to make people feel bad about themselves. It should be used creatively and respectfully, knowing that each person's life is basically valuable and significant. It is possible to invite and to educate ourselves and the people with whom we are in contact into more of the pleasures and satisfactions of taking more responsibility for the world in which they live, the animal world and the planetary system itself.

In the following section some bystanding patterns are presented with examples of the thesis, characteristics and dynamics of each, their respective advantages, and possible antitheses. This section is not intended to be comprehensive or prescriptive, but indicative of the likely dynamics in each of the different bystanding patterns. By bringing these repetitive, counterproductive interpersonal patterns to people's attention, others will grow more involved in identifying other bystanding patterns or variations of the ones mentioned here. In particular, it is hoped to energise and inspire people to find more personal, therapeutic, organisational and collective ways of defusing these patterns, refusing to join in with them and undercutting the destructive payoffs or results where possible.

I have grave objections against the use of psychological information to oppress people, so in general I disapprove of the use of diagnosis about people or calling patterns or names. Calling someone 'passive–aggressive', 'narcissistic', 'borderline' or 'anally retentive' is just another way of swearing at or diminishing them as people, with the dubious result of elevating the diagnostician to the level of expert or knowledgeable one. The use of game-names, diagnostic categories and any other psychological information in this way is morally reprehensible and an abuse of the healing aspirations of the so-called helping professions.

Diagnosis, particularly the one with a bad prognosis or little hope, such as alcoholism or psychopathy, is another way of blaming the patient or the inmate for our lack of skill, imagination or capacity to truly help. Frequently, such diagnoses are mere attempts at controlling the anxiety of the clinician, impressing the students and allaying one's own fears. It is invariably counterproductive — but not always. Diagnosis as an attempt to control is therapeutically ineffective and ultimately fruitless.

Although I have enjoyed and struggled with the intellectual excitement and emotional fit of naming the patterns, the point here is not about identifying the correct minutiae of the etymology of each. This contribution is not intended to make the reader participate in blaming patterns or names, but to make an offering which, given your goodwill, can act as a spur for the imagination, intelligence and compassion towards our own cowardly inaction as well as towards the lack of engagement and spurious justification of others.

For all 12 stereotypical bystanding patterns some examples and constructions are offered to help people scrutinise their own motivations and benefits. The slogans represent the colloquial expressions people often use as they prepare for withdrawal from a difficult situation in which someone may need their help. Of course, the phrases also crop up in retrospective justification for past inaction. The antithesis given as an illustration for any one identified pattern may apply to one or many of the examples. Naturally, these analyses and antitheses overlap and interlink and may be ordered otherwise.

According to English (1992), bystanding issues can equally well be separated into 'failure to act (paralysis; *freeze* reaction to danger) out of ignorance, cowardice (*flight* behaviour) ... where the basic intention or feeling is nevertheless one of "visceral empathy", versus non-action based on secret *"fight"* behaviour generating "thrill" ... or the vicarious affects'. It is not proposed that I, or indeed anybody, knows what is the correct way to think, feel or act in morally ambiguous situations. I am, however, profoundly identified with the serious questioning of any choice not to get involved.

'It's None of My Business' ('Pontius Pilate')

In this bystander pattern a person asks for help in solving a conflict, and is met with a refusal to mediate on the side of someone who may have some authority to act; often, *'Why don't you go and talk to John about it?'*. For example, an experienced and gifted teacher in a primary school goes to the headmaster for help in resolving a conflict. She complains that whenever a particular junior colleague teaches her class, he makes comments to the children about her stupidity. Obviously, this makes for difficulties in relating to her class. The children are turning against her and her colleague is not changing his behaviour in response to her pleas. (He also secretly wants her job and will benefit if her reputation of having a good relationship with the students is blackened.) When asked to intervene, the headmaster tells the teacher to take it up with her colleague again and blames her for not being able to control the children. He claims it is not his responsibility and anyway his intervention could be misconstrued. Perhaps she should speak to the school counsellor. The headmaster cannot be seen to be intervening in petty local staff disputes with his promotion looming.

By looking at the archetypal stories the lives and motives of ordinary people are often illuminated. Indeed, Pontius Pilate and Herod also gained substantial political advantage from sending Jesus to and fro to agree about who was to pass the verdict on him. Indeed, whereas before they were in enmity (according to St. Luke), after the event they became friends. The version of St. John also stresses the political benefits of disclaiming responsibility whilst delivering a scapegoat to the multitude baying for his blood. He writes that Pilate knew the charges against Jesus were essentially made to cover up the envy of the priests and scribes who experienced him as a rival. Pilate, in fact, repeatedly sought to release Jesus. He only decided to give up on trying to rescue him when someone threatened him, 'If thou let this man go, thou art not Caesar's friend: whosoever maketh himself a king speaketh against Caesar' (19: 12).

There is either no offer to mediate or a mediating role is refused, as did Pontius Pilate by washing his hands of Christ's crucifixion. It is often (too often for convenience) assumed that mediation interferes with or causes further riots in unstable civil situations. In organisations, employees or colleagues may experience a common confusion between the rights of privacy of the parties in need of help, and the abuses of privacy in the service of secrecy. By discounting the changeability of the situation, the bystander abdicates responsibility but does not leave the auditorium until the scapegoat hangs — metaphorically or actually. One workshop participant said it was like hiding in the toilet pretending that you are not interested in what happens when the curtain falls.

Stimulation and safety are some of the roots of this pattern. We can clearly imagine Pilate weighing up the political advantages and disadvantages as he went through the charade of crowd-calling, costuming and embarrassing Jesus, playing off his popularity with the Jews against his fear of Caesar; the advantages of friendship with Herod against displeasing his wife. The use of power for personal advantage and disowning it when exercise of this power can benefit some unfortunate who has fallen on the wrong side of the lynchmob is not unusual. Unthinking compliance or acceptance of or accommodation towards Nazi authority helped to explain the behaviour of some bystanders who engaged in neither general resistance nor in helping the Jews (Adorno, Frenkel-Brunswick, Levinson & Sanford, 1950):

> But, for most bystanders, failure to act appeared to have other causes.
> Despite their hostility toward Nazis, the majority of bystanders were over-

come by fear, hopelessness and uncertainty. These feelings, which encourage self-centredness and emotional distancing from others provide fertile soil for passivity. Survival of the self assumed a paramount importance. (Oliner & Oliner, 1988, p. 168)

Confirmation of the existential position can be achieved by proving that others are irresponsible and cannot be trusted to behave in appropriate ways. This can be accompanied by repression of the fear of personal involvement or risk-taking and the expression of vicarious pleasure in the discomfort of others. The external psychological advantage could be phrased as *'I don't have to make my own drama'*, or alternatively *'I don't want to get caught having made a mistake'*. The internal social advantage is a 'free ticket' to the circus of the other person's pain, with a good seat in the praetorium and a safety guarantee thrown in. Friendships and political alliances can be made. In conversation with others a certain moral superiority and cultural admiration for non-involvement may be implied, *'I tried my best, but that's what the majority wanted you see.'*

An antithesis to this kind of pattern is to take responsibility for mediating, informing, assisting realistic speculation, assisting de-escalating and/or learning how to do these in difficult situations. In particular, it means to exercise whatever power one has to rescue or safeguard one person or a minority against persecution by a crowd — often with a rivalrous agitator (a Judas, a Brutus or an Eurylochus of some description) in the background fanning the flames in secret. All one has to do is to avoid talking, to avoid dialogue, to avoid relationships. Contrast this with the poetic acknowledgement of Merleau-Ponty (1962):

In the experience of dialogue, there is constituted between the other person and myself, a common ground; my thought and his [or hers] are interwoven into a single fabric, my words and those of my interlocutor are called forth by the stage of the discussion, and they are inserted into a shared operation of which neither of us is the creator. We have here a dual being, where the other is for me no longer a mere bit of behaviour in my transcendental field, not I in his [or hers]; we are collaborators for each other in consummate reciprocity. (p. 354)

'I Want to Remain Neutral' ('I Don't Want to Take Sides')

In this kind of bystander pattern there is a conflict, injustice or cruelty and a third party is needed to mediate. This third party then exonerates him-or herself from real involvement by proclaiming a wish to remain neutral. In this case, the bystander pretends to mediate without actually mediating. He becomes a line of communication or a channel of access which the conflicting parties can draw into the fight. This is invariably useful to the aggressor, abuser or persecutor. The victim or scapegoat experiences the 'neutral' helper as another of the persecutor's instruments.

For example, a woman is beaten by her husband and turns to friends for help because she does not know what to do. They pretend to get involved, but avoid giving due recognition to the fact of abuse by saying that they do not want to take sides. The existential advantage of neutrality appeared to be used in this case primarily to confirm a false 'everybody is basically nice' position. It does not allow for the fact that there may be some real immoral, destructive or evil behaviour in the situation.

By default, the neutrals often support the abuse. Neutrality can often look good, or create good public relations, but usually supports the aggressor. Whatever one's judgement now, 'neutral' countries historically may appear as if they could have contributed to the consolidation of this role internationally, for example, the 'appeasement' policy of the 'Allies' before the Second World War.

This pattern is characterised by a lack of interest in an apparent wrong that is being done, or by a fear of public opinion. In this pattern people are more interested in appearing to be fair and getting recognition for this than in behaving in accordance with their conscience. Short term public relations benefits clearly outweigh the value of engagement in which the outcome is always uncertain. This kind of bystander uses the pattern to mask his failure to act by appearing to be wiser and fairer than anyone else in the situation. He does not leave the auditorium but continues to benefit from this so-called neutrality.

Neutrality is perhaps ethically only possible when there is clearly no personal benefit to be derived from the proximity to the injustice, the cruelty, the victimisation. And perhaps that is never the case? Not unless we are vagabonds or tourists in our world. Bauman, a postmodern ethical theorist developed the image of the vagabond and the tourist as encapsulating a moral position which denies moral proximity, and which moulds acceptable or popular moral position:

> One thing that the vagabond's and the tourist's lives are not designed to contain, and most often are excused from containing, is the cumbersome, incapacitating, joy-killing, insomniogenic moral responsibility. The pleasures of the massage parlour come clean of the sad thought about the

children sold into prostitution; the latter, like the rest of the bizarre ways the natives have chosen, is not the punter's responsibility, not his blame, not his deed — and there is nothing the punter can do (and thus nothing he *ought* to do) to repair it. (Bauman, 1993, p. 242)

One simple biological advantage of this pattern is safety. But what safety is being sought? Is it safety from being shouted at, safety from being ridiculed, or safety from having your children tortured? A moral decision is made accordingly. A social worker complained that no-one in authority would help her to protect a certain number of young children from ongoing Satanist abuse. Outraged, her supervisor asked why they had not succeeded in getting authoritative help in this case. The social worker said, *'Nobody believes in Satanist abuse and I didn't want them to laugh at me'*. Sometimes the penalty for involvement on behalf of a 'misfit', a 'miserable' or a 'misbegotten' is death, sometimes it is being laughed at.

But, even safety is bought at a price. Such internal repression of the natural human desire to satisfy curiosity and become engaged in situations which concern one takes its toll on the soul, even if at the same time it expresses a kind of vicarious sado-masochism which, in fact, favours the aggressor:

> Bystanders may witness parental abuse towards a child or be aware of mental or physical abuse of a psychotherapy client without taking action on behalf of the injured parties because of a misguided reluctance 'to rescue' or perhaps fear of becoming 'involved'. Often in our culture it is assumed that parents are more likely to be right than the child. (Clarkson, 1992a, p. 255)

Recent studies (Christy & Voigt, 1994) have shown that only one in four people witnessing a public episode of child abuse will act to intervene. The advantages of refraining from engagement, even the silent act of making your witness known, could include avoidance of involvement or entanglement with either or any of the main protagonists — often by discounting the seriousness of the situation. Sometimes people's fear of making a mistake can paralyse them morally. I think moral action is only possible knowing that we can, do and will make 'mistakes'. Certain social advantages include admiration for wanting to be 'fair' and wanting to give all sides the benefit of the doubt. This is fine unless the time taken for giving the benefit of the doubt is subtracted from saving someone in an emergency. People have commented *'how difficult it is to be put in a courtroom position where the opposing parties swing you from one side to the other'*. This is often a plea for understanding and empathy with bystanding. which may elicit the admiration of on lookers for such cool and considered rational objectivity, but violates natural justice.

The antithesis could involve taking an active interest in all the grievances that people have and how they came about. Sometimes to admit the failure is to decide what to do. It is possible in many if not all cases that one can be on both sides and actively support everyone. In this way the joint good of the opposing parties can be sought and affirmed. Neutrality, as pointed out before, frequently — if not always — favours the aggressor and, as such, neutrality is always against the oppressed. Neutrality is in this sense an act of oppression. St. Matthew put it like this, 'He that is not with me is against me; and he that gathereth not with me scattereth abroad' (12: 30). This is because if you do not challenge something wrong you admit by default that you do not see it as a wrongdoing. To the victim or the scapegoat your neutrality (for whatever reason) is abandonment or betrayal. A desire to be fair to both sides surely includes the necessity of pointing out where one of the sides may not be fair and working with all involved in relationship. And who is not involved?

'The Truth Lies Somewhere in the Middle' ('Six of One and Half-a-dozen of the Other')

This kind of bystanding situation exemplifies the fallacy of the statistical mean which is used to justify or rationalise bystanding. Of course, there is always a measure of good in the worst evil and a measure of evil in the most good. But sometimes there is more good on one side than on the other, not necessarily a matter of quantity or judgement, but maybe of education. As Ash (1985) noted in the context of the persecution of the Jews and Poles by the Nazis, the presentation of two intolerable facts does not imply moral equivalence.

Dynamically, in this pattern difficult judgements are dodged by applying the simplistic rule that the truth lies somewhere in the middle. For example, in a rape trial the victim claimed she was attacked without provocation. The accused claimed he was led on, and was therefore not actually guilty of criminal abuse. The jury concluded that the truth lay somewhere in the middle.

This pattern is often characterised by a notion that the truth is so relative that moral responsibility can be abrogated. There is a basic misunderstanding of what truth is, so that sometimes the person concerned feels unable to challenge the wrong. Basically this sort of bystander does not want to get involved with the difficulty of engaging any judgement and so applies a simplistic rule to obviate him from existential choice-making.

'We are seeing in our lifetimes the collapse of the objectivist worldview that dominated the modern era, the worldview that gave people faith in the absolute and permanent rightness of certain beliefs and values' (Anderson, 1990, p. 268). Unfortunately, in many cases, this has brought in its wake a cultural alienation from the task of ethical engagement at all and can easily result in this bystander pattern which claims the impossibility of making proper judgement as justification for avoiding responsible engagement with the plight of others.

The biological advantage of 'The truth lies somewhere in the middle' is equilibrium and homeostasis; and avoidance of cognitive dissonance (Festinger, 1957) by holding the mean. By confirming the *'I'm fine, there's something wrong with them'* existential position, a patronising façade can be maintained. Excitement is generated, but taking the public position, which can be wrong, is successfully avoided. Intimates offer appreciation and affirmation along the lines of *'It must be such a strain'*, whilst the public applauds *'How fair you are'*.

In a situation where there are two conflicting perspectives one could remain clear that the truth can be at least one of three cases:

1.   One person is right and the other is wrong.
2.   Both people are right from different points of view.
3.   Both people are partially right and partially wrong but not necessarily in equal proportions.

In philosophy this simplistic rule is called the *fallacy of the mean*. Truth (whatever that is) is not a mean between possibilities because, firstly, possibilities are impossible to average and, secondly, sometimes an extreme possibility is true. This is a particularly unpalatable 'truth' where scapegoating is the collective defence mechanism, for example. In any event, it appears that moral decisions are not usually decided by objective, rational or necessarily conscious means:

> Although this ... is not the place to consider philosophical views in any depth, I suggest that some of the paradoxes philosophers have encountered are due to a confusion of objective and subjective frames. Such confusion is common in philosophical essays on morality. G.E. Moore suggested that

good and bad must be defined by each person's conscious attitudes and feelings. Years later John Rawls stated that each person's rational decision in moral situations should be the criterion for morality. But both Moore and Rawls have implied that elements of consciousness participate in a moral choice. However, these philosophers, along with many others, also believe they are writing rules for morality in the objective frame. Their essays were persuasive pleas to the community to adopt into their consciousness elements of the scholars' objective arguments so that subjective and objective frames would be congruent. Unfortunately, the behavior of most people in situations with a moral choice reveals the futility of this aim. Many terrorists who kill feel highly moral in their subjective frame, even though we, in the objective frame, may regard them in quite the opposite way. By contrast, when a mother offers unconditional love to her child we are prone to declare her moral, even though her private, conscious motive may have been to win the child's affection away from an estranged father. Despite the fact that on occasion the two frames coincide, they are often discordant. (Kagan, 1992, p. 265)

'I Don't Want To Rock the Boat' ('I Don't Want To Raise a Difficult Issue')

The person who takes this position is usually one who acknowledges his or her connectedness with other human beings and is sensitive to issues of cruelty and injustice. However, he/she believes that 'Least said, soonest mended' and that 'It doesn't do to look too closely'. Such people may have a fear of conflict and confrontation, and hope that the appearance of social level harmony succeeds in avoiding the issue they sense at the psychological level.

Everybody may appear nice, compliant or in agreement with everybody else at a social level in this scenario. This prevents any of the genuine difficulties in the situation from being faced. Positive appreciation, promotion, referrals or favours are exchanged freely but falsely, or in an atmosphere of underlying tension. This is an artificial *'I, you and they are OK'* position which sometimes covers an inadequate sense of self, fear of reprisal or lack of confidence. Encountering existential aloneness or separateness, which is highlighted by any conflict, is avoided. Autonomy is abrogated, responsibility denied, but — trouble is avoided. Mostly the label of 'troublemaker' with all its attendant disadvantages is avoided.

Some research, reported to me but yet untraced, sounds plausible from both personal and clinical experiences. Small social groups of school age children were given various tasks. In each social group one child was secretly assigned to voice a minority or dissenting opinion whenever the rest of the group appeared to be in substantial agreement. Eventually, the group was informed (by the experimenters) that there were insufficient funds for continuing their educational programme and that one student would have to be deprived of the facilities. Guess who was chosen to be excluded by *democratic* vote? Are we adults any better at tolerating dissent, not to even think of valuing, treasuring and privileging the lone voice?

The penalty of 'rocking the boat' is social disapproval at least or permanent banishment at worst. Who would want to risk it? However, this particular bystanding pattern also suppresses the genuine excitement and enthusiasm of responsible engagement. The consequences of exercising personal power might be disturbing to the *status quo*. This is feared by the bystander whilst he expresses compliance, encouragement or support for the current distribution of power and disempowerment. This bystander avoids finding out that he can be a responsible and effective, if not always immediately successful, agent in the real world. Both success and failure are feared if either of these were to cause a storm of conflict, disagreement or war. Secretly these individuals may recognise the destructive dynamic. They might share their opinion with a trusted confidante, with the advantage of saying '*I knew it*' later, but they do not want to risk upsetting anybody publicly. And, bystanding is almost always a public issue where group norms prevail as we know from history, our own experience and even from experimental data. Individuals who thus avoid conflict in the significant social arena by have conversations with many friends about how they do not want to rock the boat. In a collusive group, they might be admired for this, as well as for expressing in the men's room or the cafeteria what is wrong whilst avoiding taking any action about it.

An example of an antithesis of this pattern can be to remember that the outcome of any communication is ultimately determined by the unsaid or unspoken psychological dynamics. The disturbing dynamic eventually emerges and takes effect. The antithesis of this pattern, therefore, is to express one's concerns even if they seem to instigate a disturbance; and then to remain committed to an effective resolution of such a disturbance, even whilst the storm rages! People will, of course, need support to do this — both internally (psychologically) and from others. And, often, this will not be forthcoming. As research has shown, people who feel part of a crowd — an in-group — are *less* likely to intervene on behalf of some persecuted or injured outsider. The greater the 'group cohesion' the more likely the possibility of scapegoating. Therefore relinquishing bystanding (from where there are often many others) frequently leads to loneliness. This loneliness is the existential assumption of our responsibility, and both our connection and disconnection with others the cost of refusing 'group collusion'.

Whose Hand Is This?

There's a story going the rounds: A woman, going home after a day's work, was tired, so she just sat down in the closest available seat on the bus. The man next to her immediately squeezed up against her. She pulled away. He moved closer, keeping body contact. She tried to ignore him, but he moved his hand next to her thigh, then on it. She stiffened and started to brush his hand away angrily. Then suddenly instead she grabbed his wrist, and holding his hand high above his head she stood up.

'Whose hand is this?' she loudly asked the bus at large. 'I found it on my leg.' And then she moved to another seat.

Told at a Chimera Self Defense Training, Madison, Wisconsin, November 1987 (West, 1991, p. 83)

Chapter 5
'And I did not speak out'

First they came for the Jews
and I did not speak out —
because I was not a Jew
Then they came for the communists
and I did not speak out —
because I was not a communist
Next they came for the trade unionists
and I did not speak out —
because I was not a trade unionist
Then they came for me
and there was no one left
to speak out for me.

'It's More Complex Than It Seems' ('Who Knows Anyway?')

The person involved in this pattern is aware of a problematical situation but claims that, because of its complexity, he cannot get effectively involved to participate in its resolution. So, there is an assumption that the situation needs to be simple, or fully understood, before the person can get involved. Too frequently human situations are not of the simple kind and to wait until they are absolutely clear and simple and obvious is usually the same as waiting until it is too late to help those being sacrificed in the complexity. An example would be those white people in South Africa who responded to reports in the foreign press about the South African apartheid regime press with comments such as, *'It's much more complicated than it seems'* or *'What can anybody know about South Africa who hasn't lived and worked there?'*. Such phrases were often used to justify the continuing financial, political and moral exploitation of the peoples of that country.

The person with this kind of attitude frequently contributes to the problem, if he does not cause or maintain it. Frequently he may benefit from its existence, or from not clarifying it to reduce its complexity to himself or to others. This attitude creates a type of psychological protection saving the individual from facing up to his role in a complex situation and serving the need to keep it complicated enough to avoid resolution. In this way the loss of benefits can be avoided. This kind of bystander uses the complexity and variety of life situations to undermine the idea that there are ethical, moral or humanitarian principles being breached or in danger, and that sometimes no amount of apparent complexity can justify non-involvement. He has the biological advantage of maintaining a safe and comfortable, non-demanding homeostasis. The existential advantage of the pattern is to confirm a position that the world is a complex place; so nobody knows enough to make an adequately informed judgement, to provide full justification for action or participation in the problem-solving process. Psychologically, the bystander may benefit from moral complicity or has an excuse for continuing to benefit from a problem which is oppressive to many and 'too complicated' for some.

The self-justification rests on an assumption of powerlessness to act on behalf of some disfavoured other in the face of ambiguity, complexity and possible misunderstanding. The loss of benefit is avoided, as is the discomfort of exercising judgement amid the ambiguities of life's existential dilemmas. Intimates and friends may give admiration for 'Doing your best', and acquaintances may appreciate or gossip about 'understanding that something is a very complex situation, but at least he has the humility to admit defeat!'

A simple antithesis to this kind of bystander situation is to say, '*I don't understand all that is going on, but it seems that Jorge may be doing something wrong. Let me talk to him about it*'. Amnesty International works on this basis, asking people to write letters to individual security policemen or government officials who are directly responsible for the incarceration and torture of political prisoners (English, 1979). I take it as an honour to be called 'a woman of letters'-even if those letters merely raise questions. It must be remembered that absolutely nobody has the entire facts of a situation before or even after they act on it. However, this gives no existential absolution from responsibility to challenge wrong-doings, or at least to establish that there is no deliberate wrongdoing. Amnesty International was started by two individuals in a hotel room who decided to get involved in the unlawful detention, disappearance and torture of political prisoners in parts of the world many of miles away in distance, culture and, sometimes, language.

'I Don't Have All the Information'
('Ignorance is bliss')

In this scenario, the bystanders are heard to say, *'Because I lack information all my judgements are completely unsound, so I can't make any'* or *'I don't have the full picture — therefore anything I do won't really be helpful, so I won't get involved at all'*. At a Board of Trustees meeting of an international psychotherapy association, the issue of sanctions against South Africa was raised. Several people claimed not to have enough information about the situation to judge whether they should support a particular action in favour of sanctions. At this point one Board member grew very angry, confronting the vacillators somewhat as follows, *'How dare you not have enough information to make a judgement? You need to inform yourselves sufficiently to get to a point of taking a stand'*.

Lack of information on moral issues is no historically justifiable excuse for bystanding. There are facts about any situation. A lack of facts is also a fact calling for further questioning, exploration and investigation. It is possible to obtain enough information to know that wrongdoing exists and that help is needed. One can never know if this help will in future be demonstrated to be correct or 'better', but it is part of our human condition that people are required to act in the present without guarantees for the future. As Whitehead reputedly said, 'Where attainable knowledge could have changed the issue, ignorance has the guilt of vice,' and Jung (1954) adds, 'And nature has no use for the pleas that "one did not know". Not knowing acts like guilt.' (p. 44).

This kind of bystander may believe his position is of blindness and powerlessness because the information held is invalidated by its incompleteness, not giving a picture of the whole, and is therefore meaningless. This pattern can provide a feeling of security and non-risk-taking, whilst confirming an existential position that *'I cannot get total security to support my actions on behalf of others'*. This pattern may also facilitate the repression of fear, discounting the information which is available. It may include the expression of halfhearted concern which masquerades as responsible caution. There is social and psychological advantage in avoiding the effort of getting more information, or at least enough information in order to be response-able from the position of awareness of the situation. Internal powerlessness and helplessness can combine with public protestations such as *'I don't have all the information'*, which invites friends to respond with reassuring 'strokes' to the effect of *'Of course not, and you should not "interfere" until you have'*. This pattern colludes with others' bystanding on the grounds of ignorance.

The antithesis of this pattern may involve accepting that *'What I do know is useful and what I don't know I can find out, or find out why I can't find out'*. There are many ways of being engaged in relationship. One way is to help to find the truth, or seek out where and why this is being blocked — for example, the South American mothers' initiative to find out what has happened to their 'disappeared' relatives. In healthy organisations and healthy countries information is available or feasible explanations exist as to when, how and to whom information is available. The fact that information is *not* available on request is all too often a clear signal that something is wrong. And this brings us again to the enormous normative power of the group:

> We have suggested four different reasons why people, once having noticed an emergency, are less likely to go to the aid of the victim when others are present: (i) Others serve as an audience to one's actions inhibiting him from doing foolish things; (ii) Others serve as guides to behaviour, and if they are inactive, they will lead the observer to be inactive also; (iii) The interactive effect of these two processes will be much greater than either alone; if each bystander sees other bystanders momentarily frozen by audience inhibition, each may be misled into thinking the situation must not be serious; (iv) The presence of other people dilutes the responsibility felt by any single bystander, making him feel that it is less necessary for himself to act. Each of these explanations involves different channels of communication among bystanders. The diffusion of responsibility explanation requires only that a bystander believe others to be present; he does not have to see them or they him. The audience inhibition hypothesis requires that the other bystanders see him but not that he see them. The social influence explanation requires that he see the others, but not that they see him. Finally, the interactive process requires full visual communication. (Latané & Darley, 1970, pp. 125–126)

'I Don't Want to Get Burned Again' ('Let Them Fry')

The core of this pattern is a sequence of events where something is wrong or someone is in trouble, but the bystander refuses to get involved because of an uncomfortable or painful experience as a previous result of engagement. Thus the person justifies his non-involvement in the situation. A situation which usually provokes this pattern occurs when someone is being bullied or physically attacked, either in the street or socially. In the Kitty Genovese murder case many local residents heard a woman screaming but took no action (Latané & Darley, 1970). Bystanders avoid doing anything to stop the violent or unjust event by telling themselves or others that the last time they tried to stop a fight or intervene when someone was being bullied, they were attacked. Of course people do get hurt when they get involved. This is always a risk.

This pattern is characterised by a complete withdrawal from active involvement because one previous strategy or intervention was ineffective or had negative results. It is also evidence of a lack of creativity in finding alternative ways of getting involved. The assumption is that the way a person was involved before is the only way to do it, and because it did not work or was unpleasant there is therefore nothing they can do. In future, therefore, they assume a simplistic moral solution — don't get involved.

The biological advantage of this pattern is a preservation drive — the natural human recoil from situations which, from learned experience, can be hurtful or damaging. It is only natural to protect ourselves at a biological level from the repetition of such painful experiences. However, it is also only profound moral and ethical questioning within the person's own heart that can help determine the extent to which such self-protective responses are ultimately useful or damaging. Sometimes people may choose to give up their lives in order to protect others. The how and the why of such decisions have to be determined in the deepest inner chambers of individual conscience and probably would not benefit from being imposed externally. On the other hand:

> What is more natural to banish one's fears than to live on delegated powers? And what does the whole growing-up period signify, if not the giving over of one's life project? ... man cuts out for himself a manageable world: he throws himself into action uncritically, unthinkingly. He accepts the cultural programming that turns his nose where he is supposed to look; ... he learns not to expose himself, not to stand out; he learns to embed himself in other-power, both of concrete persons and of other things and cultural commands; the result is that he comes to exist in the imagined infallibility of the world around him. He doesn't have to have fears when his feet are solidly mired and his life mapped out in a ready-made maze. (Becker,1973, p. 23)

Existential confirmation of the life position that *'I'll only get hurt if I try to get involved in correcting injustice, confusion or misunderstanding'* can be accomplished. Psychological advantages include a repression of either the desire for intimacy or fear of the penalties for involvement, such as exclusion, or the fear of bearing the brunt of someone else's rage at my 'interference', whereas socially there can be straightforward avoidance of both a potentially hurtful situation and the intimacy of engagement in a collective problem-solving process.

These participants may be appreciated for protecting themselves from repeated injury, and collect symbolic sympathy stamps for their past hurts in similar situations. Other people may say, *'You did your best and got hurt — what a hero! Of course you must be careful in the future'*. Of course, bystanders who get involved often get hurt and sometimes they die.

The antithesis (if one wishes to make one) may be to adopt the genuine helping role of the Good Samaritan — to switch healthily from bystander to true helper role instead of withdrawing. Previous attempts to get involved did not work, but the individual may have to see that there are other ways of getting involved; ways which need not invite disastrous fire. One needs to distinguish between individuals bent on suicide, exploiting a 'good cause' in an inauthentic way to kill themselves (as some terrorists do), and those making a genuine, existential life choice personally to offer to save the life or lives of chosen others, as many people did during the Second World War to save the lives of Jews, gypsies, homosexuals and others.

Everybody needs help from time to time in life. Many of us need genuine help many times. Frequently, the help required is not life-endangering, it may merely be uncomfortable, embarrassing, or make a person less popular for a time with a certain group, organisation or individual. There are often many more ways of being helpfully involved in a situation than people are willing to admit or to create:

> Take the situation of an exclusive department store that had a discriminatory employment policy, hiring minorities only for the most menial jobs. A community organization protested, but the store refused to negotiate. In response, the organization mobilized 3000 minority shoppers .... The shoppers would browse for hours, keeping the salespeople occupied. The store's regular clientele would enter, take one look at the milling crowd, and leave .... When the store managers learned of the scheme, they requested immediate negotiations with the community organization and quickly agreed to hire a sizable number of minority salespeople and executive trainees. (Ury, 1991, p. 120)

There are many life situations which require a person to be robust and to adopt the stance of the spiritual warrior. In Oriental cultures there are highly developed ideas about conflict, and the most gracious ways in which to engage in it. It is clear from these conceptualisations of the spiritual warrior that it is often unnecessary to be violent. One can be assertive in the defence of justice without having to resort to violence. As Lao Tzu (1973) taught, 'A good soldier is not violent. A good fighter is not angry' (p. 68). Recent work (Bly, 1990; Moore & Gillette, 1990) also bears this out, integrating the mythological with the psychological, by developing the warrior archetype in the modern male. Estés (1992) does something similar for the woman.

A schoolboy who was bullied launched a 'Kids' Watch' telephone hotline for other children who had been victims of bullying or other forms of extortion or crime. Instead of remaining a victim or passing by others in a similar position, he intervened, drawing in the support of a political party and neighbourhood watch groups. He said: *'I hope others will join me because there are so many children who suffer in silence and live in fear. It is not grassing — it is about being able to get on with life'* (*Daily Mail*, November 13, 1994, p. 15).

'My Contribution Won't Make Much Difference' ('Who? Me?')

This stance is usually characterised by the belief that the politics and power of an organisation, government or society are too great for an individual to have any influence on outcomes. Consequently, the individual assumes that his contribution is insignificant, for instance in not saving recyclable commodities, such as glass, paper or plastic, which represent saving the environment. This bystander position is demonstrated by an unwillingness to put oneself out and an expectation of expending too much energy, whether taking action is researching, recycling, spending money or whatever. These bystanders may be slow to acknowledge that any action of theirs would help. They are not sufficiently motivated to participate — maybe because there is no perceived reward. Apathy, self-depreciation and not really caring enough about the issue to take action are the hallmarks of this pattern.

For example, these individuals say *'The world will not be affected by my buying one can of ozone-friendly aerosol. It needs the big factories to stop using CFCs'*. They are, of course, right in a sense. However, this fact is used to justify doing nothing to solve the problem. This applies also to attitudes towards issues such as engagement with protests about nuclear warheads. These bystanders may say *'I don't think it will really help, so I'd rather do nothing'* (see Higgins, 1982).

These bystanders characteristically do not deny that there is a contribution to be made, but they present it as so small as to be practically worthless, 'so why bother doing anything?' They feel and believe that they have no power in the situation. The findings of Seligman (1970) on learned helplessness can be of enormous benefit here in understanding and liberating people from their experienced limitations. If challenged they may take a resentfully self-righteous position, blaming others instead of taking their share of communal responsibility. The recognition involved can concern all those connected with the person doing what he wants in a predictable way — be it indulgence in the material pleasures afforded by society or the freedom to deny personal accountability. Personal insignificance and discounting of personal ability to affect the situation can be affirmed.

The internal psychological advantages of this stance may concern the achievement of psychic stability by attributing responsibility to more powerful others and thereby avoiding the enormity of a situation for which there are no easy, convenient or foreseeable solutions. It is perceived that only 'the Government', 'God', 'management', 'the party' or some other force which is seen to be more powerful can affect the situation. This applies equally to the above global examples and the organisational or domestic situation where the axiom that *today's solution is tomorrow's problem* holds true. Human beings are often (and naturally) frightened of situations beyond their control. They can have some influence (which may be more or less decisive), but often they avoid testing this idea. An implicit request for more or renewed appreciation for humility frequently implies a false modesty at the cost of appropriate responsibility. There may also be repression of guilt at knowing that one could contribute, and that if everyone contributed the effect could be massive. The generations who will experience any benefit from our saving trees are far in the future and we may never know how our legacy would affect them.

There is substantial advantage in avoiding, for example, the anxiety-arousing situation of being a leader or role model, being the first one to take action in an ambiguous situation or to avoid risking either success or failure. To preserve the position of 'Little me' is non-threatening to the stability or perceived status of others; and presenting oneself as 'small' and ineffectual also invites contradiction, as in *'Of course you're not, you are very important'*, etc. Feeling helpless and insignificant has the advantage of claiming to feel guilty about being privileged so as to, for example, have food to throw away while other people starve. Yet people may still not quite find the time to go to the bottle bank, or the disposable income to make the donation to the world starvation fund. Sympathy for helplessness and liberal guilt-mongering can be expressed among like-minded friends without taking responsibility.

If people's contributions are really so small then they could join forces with others, pool resources and see them grow. The sum is greater than the parts. This bystanding attitude is an example of people's attachment to results. Unless they can have the narcissistic gratification of participating in the success, they are unwilling to engage in the struggle. Yet, most endeavours to improve the human condition take many years in order to achieve the desired social changes. The fact that individual contributions are small or that some may not see their outcome in a lifetime should not deter some active participation in the movement — if only so that future generations may benefit. Even if they do not, they can remember those who did try — like the Germans (including the Protestant theologian, Bonhoeffer) who attempted to stop Hitler, and who are honoured today.

Finally, it is possible to envision a world in which we do what is right whether or not we are rewarded with beneficial results in this life or the next. It may well be that some of our acts of truth, justice, or entreaty on behalf of others will be of no avail. Often, involvement fails because it is too small, at the wrong time, in the wrong place or just because the situation is not yet ready to change. But who knows if and when the small effort of the two-million-and-twenty-seventh person does not change the critical mass or become the single last flap of the butterfly's wing which effectively destabilises a system into the chaos from which renewed creativity can emerge? (Gleick, 1988).

I Went to Bed in the Bathtub

A young child who had been in one of the Protective Behaviors classes recently came running up to me in the playground.

'You know what?' she started, and continued before I had time to respond except non-verbally, 'Last weekend I had a sitter who tried to help me get undressed when I didn't want him to. Y'know what I did?'

'No, what?'

'Well, I told him three times to stop, I could do it for myself — but he didn't. So ...', she paused dramatically.

'So ... what did you do then?'

'Well, I grabbed my pillow, my blanket and my teddy bear, and I went in the bathroom and locked the door. I went to bed in the bathtub — it was dry and I didn't put any water in it. Then I just ignored him when he tried to get me to come out.'

'And then, when my Mom came home, she asked me why I was sleeping in the bathroom and I told her. She said we'd never have that sitter again. And she's going to call his mother.'

Journal excerpt, April 1979. (West 1991, p. 78)

Chapter 6
'Look behind you'

2nd Murderer:
Look behind you, my lord ...
A bloody deed, and desperately dispatch'd!
How fain, like Pilate, would I wash my hands
Of this most grievous murder!

(*King Richard the Third* I. iv. 266–271)

'I'm Only Telling the Truth (to Others) as I See It' ('Gossip is Juicier Than Responsibility')

The hypothesis of this pattern is that people jump to conclusions on the basis of limited information and take the opportunity to tell their version of the truth to others without checking perceptions with all the parties concerned. People with a preference for this form of bystanding may jump to early conclusions to justify non-involvement without checking all the available facts because it fits with their wishes, envies or fears. An essential part of the pattern, according to some of my clients, is the feeling of self-righteousness and the garnering of popularity votes based on a kind of bonding which exists at the expense of those *bonded against*. You can sometimes even see this phenomenon at professional conferences — people raising their eyebrows together or giggling conspiratorially like 11-year-old girls — as they share ideas about those who are different from 'people like us'. And the longer they do not act, the less likely they or others are to act — as Latané and Darley (1970) found in their experiments. Group cohesion and the fear of loss of popularity are apparently inversely related to the willingness of an individual to act on behalf of a scapegoat. Identification with group goals and norms is patently easier and much less demanding than identification and empathy with a marginalised 'other'. And, if nobody else is intervening — why that makes it only more likely that the situation is not serious and it is not necessary for anyone to take direct action and get involved.

This kind of bystander is characterised by not talking directly to the people concerned and deliberately avoiding taking action towards full understanding of the situation. They have an investment in taking an early opportunity to make someone bad, often to cash in old resentments or new fears. A very good way of doing this is for the bystander to interpret an ambiguous or apparently confusing situation in the direction of their own resentment or envy, rather than keeping all parties good enough and acknowledging the possibility that they may be wrong. Examples are the media defence of publishing 'the truth' (as it sees it) about personal relationships within the British royal family, the exposure of public figures thought to be homosexual, or the slandering of a colleague's reputation because it happens to increase your own if you demolish or undermine theirs.

These bystanders may *pretend* to get involved actively by talking to other people. However, they are careful to avoid confronting, or getting the help of a third party in talking to those most centrally concerned in this situation. They do not speak to the central players. There is usually some reason why talking would not help — but they rarely try and even more rarely genuinely persevere. They take a surreptitious stand by secretly spreading personal opinions to others (but not to the people concerned) as a way of avoiding compassionate and understanding involvement with those concerned. Often they benefit financially and/or in puffball popularity, based on having privileged access to 'confidential information' which they are prepared to divulge to privileged special friends or acquaintances in the hope that they will become friends. This all avoids fruitful engagement, based on the assessment (usually untrue or untested) that bystanding is the only possible option. People systematically under-estimate the degree to which they are influenced by other people. 'Moderate conformers to a man, we think of ourselves as sturdy independents. A study of the tactics people use to deny they are victims of social influence ought to be interesting and rewarding' (Latané & Darley, 1970, p. 125).

This kind of bystander can obtain appreciation and recognition for being informative, having risk-free 'inside' information or opinions, without being shown to be wrong for quite some time or getting involved in the actual issues of solving the problem. The bystander can confirm the existential advantage of this pattern with *'I'm the one who really knows what's going on without risking reality testing or personal responsibility for correcting what is wrong'*. The main protagonists can be blamed for their refusal to listen, understand or respond, but no real attempt is made to rectify, change or get help to influence the situation constructively. Perhaps they are 'not listening' for very good reasons. The internal psychological advantage often concerns a combination of the expression of sadism and envy:

> Creativeness becomes the deepest cause for envy ... envy of creativeness is a fundamental element in the disturbance of the creative process. To spoil and destroy the initial source of goodness soon leads to destroying and attacking the babies that the mother contains and results in the good object being turned into a hostile, critical, and envious one. (Klein, 1984, p. 202)

It also carries the advantage of the suppression of any genuine risk of failure or mistaken understanding in intimate engagement:

> The new neighbour who is invited for morning coffee is invited to play 'If it weren't for him'. If she plays, well and good, she will soon be a bosom friend of the old timers ... If she refuses to play and insists on taking a charitable view of her husband, she will not last long. Her situation will be the same as if she kept refusing to drink at cocktail parties — in most circles, she would gradually be dropped from the guest lists. (Berne, 1968, p. 52)

Internally, social benefits can accrue from sympathy strokes for the burden of the 'responsibility to the public' they carry (how much they know) and admiration for what they could do (if they wanted to) without the risk of being wrong, or risking genuine engagement with solving the problem. The social advantage is a variation of 'I told you so' — feeling smart and self-righteous after an event you have helped to bring brought about through lack of responsible or timely action. However, the telling does not get done in the presence of the parties concerned so that there can be no come-back if the prediction turns out to be wrong, which it often is. Internal information is used for external gain, for popularity bought at the price of intimacy and involvement. There are signs of concealed participation, talking about others, not about oneself or to the parties concerned. Many people may feel that they were singled out as the trusted confidantes of confidential and special information which they must keep secret as long as there is no genuine attempt to solve the problem with the others involved. Of course, 'confidential information' told within a slightly slanted context without the person being gossiped about knowing or having the opportunity to defend himself is easily manipulated. As Blake wrote, 'A truth that's told with bad intent, beats all the lies you can invent' (Keynes, 1991, p. 432).

The possible antithesis to this pattern is to take the position that if something is wrong, talk only to the people directly involved or responsible first. And keep talking. And then get help to keep talking. Keep people good. Challenge, and try to understand. If they have been in a position of having access to privileged information they are part of the systemic problem. Therefore they have a direct and authentic existential responsibility for their part in bringing about, and therefore resolving, the problem. Identify who is the aggressor. Help them too. Decline the temptation to use private information for personal advantage and devote it rather to collective problem-solving.

'I'm Only Following Orders' ('It's More Than My Job's Worth')

This is a case of moral bystanding where people claim to be unable to act in a situation because they are subject to a higher authority or popular demand. There is often a rigid *'I'm just following procedures'* element to this psychological pattern — a lack of empathic connection with others or a profound desensitization of such visceral empathic abilities. Well-known examples are the Nazi officers and soldiers involved in atrocities of the Second World War, and torturers active in Greece. However, this pattern can also be played out in support of the persecutors of the persecutors — insisting on rigid bureaucratic procedures and public humiliations for wrongdoings, punishing beyond apology or reparation, revenge without end even if the culprit has confessed, repented and (as far as human beings can) repaired.

In the words of Klaus Barbie on trial in Lyons, *'I was only doing my job'* (Williams, 1992, p. 308). The French word *Massuisme* refers to the 'argument that torturers may be responsible servants of the state in times of extreme crisis' (Peters, 1985, p. 177). It was born from General Massu's accomplished justification of the use of torture in Algeria. This is an idea that, according to Peters (1985), refuses to disappear, being 'a classic instance of one commonly used argument for the legitimacy of torture' (p. 177).

This bystanding pattern may be characterised by its convenient obedience to authority to avoid difficult moral or ethical decisions. These protagonists claim to lack the authority to intervene, ignoring the basic fact of their autonomy as human beings, and the many ways in which they do have power to change the outcome of a situation. Of course, authority has to be taken, it cannot be given. They may also benefit from the situation in terms of promotions or special privileges, as did, for example, the Greek torturers (Gibson & Haritos-Faroutos, 1986). They may also simply benefit from it financially (for example, multinational companies which consume rainforests) or in terms of status. Such is the case of 'cosmetic' surgeons, financiers and manufacturers (and those who support and recommend them) for exploiting the culturally induced feelings of inferiority and worthlessness of people who do not fit stereotypes of colour, cultural desirability or physical shape.

According to Wolf (1990), in 1989 130 000 American women underwent liposuction during which surgeons sucked 200 000 pounds of living body tissue out of them. Fourteen women died in the course of this procedure. 'Progressive dehumanisation has a stark, well-documented pattern. To undergo cosmetic surgery, one must feel and society must agree that some parts of the body are not worthy of life, though they are still living' (Wolf, 1990, p. 223). Minimising or ignoring salient facts seems a necessary aspect of all bystanding. Wolf raised a cry to stop the betrayal of the beauty of one's own body, of the preciousness of life, to the perniciousness of externally and commercially motivated standards of attractiveness. She also called bystanders to account:

> When is it appropriate to ... question the process that has women gamble their lives for a beauty that has nothing to do with them? ... Before this trend escalates any further until it can never again be considered appropriate, now is the time to stand back and notice fourteen dead bodies, real ones, human ones. (Wolf, 1990, p. 220)

There are substantial visible and invisible rewards for bystanding. Some of these concern physical safety, protection by authorities, as well as rewards in terms of financial or social status recognition. One of the particular advantages of this pattern is that you can participate as being one of the 'in-crowd' which has authority and special privilege in the situation. The existential advantage can be confirming that safety (or jobs) lie in obedience to rules. Of course, this also shields true persecutors, whilst hiding one's own sadistic impulses behind the façade that one is only doing this at the bidding of the persecutor. Psychodynamically, people can be using parents or authority figures as an excuse for avoiding autonomous decision-making. Vicarious identification with the scapegoat (for all our own ills and transgressions) is transformed into identification with the righteous action of the aggressors — the upholders of law and order and the prohibitors of exceptions — the people who, by adherence to the small print of regulations, prohibit exceptions and the natural creativity of the individual.

Externally, this type of bystander avoids making conscious, choiceful engagement, and so often avoids the victimised, 'bullied' person. In organisations employees who have been made redundant often experience that their colleagues (erstwhile friends) suddenly disappear or avoid them. They no longer get invited to parties, they are overlooked when credit is due. The person made redundant can frequently date this social ostracism from the time those colleagues found out that they themselves had been saved, but their friend had received 'the chop'. The people who are unconsciously 'dead-making' their soon-to-be ex-colleague may fear some of the contagion of misfortune — the way people sometimes desert friends in trouble or those who are ill or suffering from human immuno-deficiency virus. *'You're only doing your job'*, the wife of a Nazi officer may say, whereas acquaintances may reassure, *'It's not your fault really'*, coupled with exoneration from collusive culture by blaming 'them', whoever 'they' are, for the rules whilst not challenging or opposing the 'rule-makers' or the 'thought-police'. People may participate in this kind of bystanding because of fear for their own self-interest or guilt at their own survival of a discriminatory situation. One way of dealing with such survivor's guilt is to 'bad make' the people who did not survive; another way is to sanctify or beatify them.

One way to stop this pattern is to bend the rules, knowing that it can never be fair for everyone to be treated 'exactly the same', because they are not. It may be necessary to make special arrangements that meet the challenge of an ethical problem. It may be possible to protest. Authorities only have authority by consent of the people they represent. People in authority can only abuse power as long as others let them have such power. Many people in organisations cling to the myth that they are disempowered, and seek to experience empowerment as being given to them from the powers-that-be, as opposed to reaching for the strengths and freedoms which are within their own power. Popular opinion is rarely truly moral. As has been pointed out before, scientific evidence shows that bystanding is more likely to happen when there are many others in the group or audience who are not intervening, and that the longer no-one acts on behalf of the victim, the more unlikely it becomes that anyone *will* act.

Summing up the moral lessons of the Holocaust, Arendt (1964) demanded that:

Human beings be capable of telling right from wrong even when all they have to guide them is their own judgement, which, moreover, happens to be completely at odds with what they must regard as the unanimous opinion of all these around them ... These few who were still able to tell right from wrong went really only by their own judgements, and they did so freely; there were no rules to be abided by ... because no rules existed for the unprecedented (pp. 294–295).

Bauman (1989) suggested that:

Arendt's statement articulates the question of moral responsibility for *resisting* socialisation and any other pretenders to extra-individual adjudication on the ethically proper. What the Holocaust, that extreme manifestation of modern spirit and practice, brought to the surface, is the truth blurred and diluted under 'normal' circumstances: that morality may, and often should, express itself 'in *insubordination*' toward socially upheld principles, and in an action openly defying social solidarity and consensus (pp. 177–178).

Any rank-and-file soldier or employee has the power to withdraw his consent, as the Russian soldiers did in August 1991 when ordered to attack Yeltsin. The extent of the risk is always part of the equation of human responsibility. Another way is to use the position of being an insider to help make changes from within. Sometimes this works. Sometimes it does not. Without trying, without genuine creative experimentation, one will never know.

It is also necessary to face up to the idea that it is not only sadistic misfits who torture and end up willing and capable of perpetrating abuse in the name of moral bystanding. Anyone, given certain situational factors, could possibly become a torturer according to Williams (1992). Psychological research, such as that of Haney, Banks and Zimbardo (1973) and Milgram (1974), report that very ordinary people can be persuaded without great difficulty to become temporary torturers, inflicting pain on others in obedience to an authority they thought was legitimate.

The Spanish Inquisition, the committees for anti-American activities from the McCarthy era, and the punitive and over-zealous implementation of bureaucratic rules are usually conducted in absolute moral certainty of their correctness in the name of the greatest good. This is done on the instructions of the highest authority licensing those implementing the so-called laws and regulations, which are claimed to be inviolate and completely obedience-inducing. But just because the law requires it does not make it right. Laws may have to change, as they have over the centuries, when their practitioners or recipients questioned, challenged or overthrew them:

We ought to expose the shames and inequities which may be concealed beneath the law. But the rule of law itself, the imposing of effective inhibitions upon power and the defence of the citizen from power's all intrusive claims, seems to me an unqualified human good. To deny or belittle this good is, in this dangerous century when the resources and pretentions of power continue to enlarge, a desperate error of intellectual abstraction. More than this, it is a self-fulfilling error, which encourages us to give up the struggle against bad laws and class-bound procedures, and to disarm ourselves before power. It is to throw away a whole inheritance of struggle *about* law and within the forms of law, whose continuity can never be fractured without bringing men and women into immediate danger. (Thompson, 1979, p. 266)

Chiune Sugihara was a man who, in direct treasonable disobedience, refused to deny help to the Jews begging for his help in Kaunuas — the Lithuanian capital — in 1940. Three times he cabled his bosses in Tokyo for permission to issue the visas. Three times the answer came back: 'Absolutely not.' After consulting with his wife and two sons, at risk of dishonour and execution, he signed transit visas until his fingers became almost too stiff to move and his eyes were bloodshot from sleepless nights. It is estimated that his signature saved some 10 000 Jews from certain death. After he had to leave, an equivalent number who had not managed to escape were murdered within three days. He was once honourable, affluent and an international consul for Japan. He died in obscurity, poverty and disgrace, living outside Tokyo in a small 'wooden shack without water or even a gas stove ... shunned by his own government and neighbours who considered him a misfit.' (Willsher & Churcher, 1995, p. 48)

'I'm Just Keeping My Own Counsel' ('I'm all right Jack!')

The thesis of this bystander pattern is simply a refusal to risk one's sense of wellbeing by getting involved in a problem that does not immediately affect oneself. Typically, the refrain is *'It's not my problem'*. This pattern becomes apparent by a sudden change in behaviour and attitude as soon as the bystander sees that his interests are threatened. It is only then that he becomes involved. An uncaring atmosphere is fostered by this kind of bystanding, a failure to acknowledge that part of taking care of oneself involves taking care of others. It stems from being oblivious to the fact that everybody benefits from a more caring situation. There is a lack of the sense of vital connection between human beings and with what Fox (1983) calls erotic justice:

> An erotic justice means first of all getting in touch with our feelings about injustice. Do we have such feelings? Do we allow them to be? Do we have feelings towards unemployed people? Towards prisoners who become more violent in a violent prison system? Injustice is not an abstraction: it is about the draining away of Eros and joy from people's lives. (pp. 288–289).

A couple may regularly hear sounds of violent fighting through the walls of their semi-detached home. They know that the couple next door have financial problems — someone across the road told them. They do nothing because *'It's not our business'*, even when they hear the wife and children screaming. They do not want to interfere. Only when the police arrest the husband do they realise that events have gone too far. They are surprised to find how they are haunted by the sounds of the fighting and they cannot put the memories away. Soon they move to another area, but they still do not forget.

Oliner and Oliner (1988), in their analysis of people who intervened or not during the persecution of the Jews in Nazi Germany, describe the dynamic differences as follows:

> Involvement, commitment, care and responsibility are the hallmarks of extensive persons. Disassociation, detachment, and exclusiveness are the hallmarks of constricted persons. Rescuers* were marked by extensivity, whereas non-rescuers, and bystanders in particular, were marked by constrictedness, by an ego that perceived most of the world beyond its own boundaries as peripheral. More centered on themselves and their own needs, they were less conscious of others and less concerned with them. With the exception of ethnocentrics, their failure to act was less a reflection of a particular rejection of Jews or other outsiders than it was the expression of a tendency to distance themselves from relationships that imposed burdensome responsibilities on them. (p.186)

Bystanders often ensure predictable positive feedback for non-interference. They avoid the disturbing effects of self-questioning and genuine involvement with their connection with others. As long as Mr and Mrs Everyman maintain a distance from the couple next door, they can reassure themselves that they are living in a right way compared to others who do not. It confirms their, *'We're OK — They're Not OK'* position. Here is an attempt to avoid the existential responsibility for facing our own shadow. People have the potential to be violent to one another and our task is to manage that potential.

This bystanding position is one which suppresses 'badness' and projects it on to others. Those who take this role are also avoiding the

---

*Here used in a positive sense as helpers.

tasks of real involvement and intimacy, both with other people in the world and between themselves. Instead they can pass time with fake involvement and concern for the world's problems. Bystanders who take this position feel good about themselves as they reflect on the bad behaviour of others and how impossible it would be for them to act in that way; and they achieve respectable status, certainly in the UK, by being seen to mind their own business. They say, *'Isn't it awful about other people?'* and *'What is our society coming to?'*.

It is possible that the good of one can become the good of all. People who avoid this pattern use their own security as a base from which they help others with their difficulties. The only side to take is both, to stay involved, to adjust to changing circumstances, to get all the information appropriate and yet keep boundaries — difficult, but perhaps more honourable in the attempt. Beware, in particular, if you are in a position of moral righteousness when you pass over to the other side of the street.

And who is my neighbour?
And Jesus answering said, A certain man went down from Jerusalem to Jericho, and he fell among thieves, which stripped him of his raiment, and wounded him, and departed, leaving him half dead.
And by chance there came down a certain priest that way: and when he saw him, he passed by on the other side.
And likewise a Levite, when he was at the place, came and looked on him, and passed by on the other side.
But a certain Samaritan, as he journeyed, came where he was: and when he saw him, he had compassion on him.
And went to him, and bound up his wounds, pouring in oil and wine, and set him on his own beast, and brought him to an inn and took care of him.
And on the morrow when he departed, he took out two pence, and gave them to the host, and said unto him, Take care of him; and whatsoever thou spendest more, when I come again, I will repay thee.
Which now of these three, thinkest thou, was neighbour unto him that fell among the thieves? (St. Luke, 10: 29–36)

'Victim Blaming' ('They Brought it on Themselves Really')

The thesis of this pattern is that the bystanders (and others) assume, believe, or are convinced that the victims of the perceived injustice or cruelty *brought it upon themselves*. Somehow, the victims of injustice must have 'deserved' it. According to Equity Theory, people do not apply the same principles of justice and other moral values equally to all people. The bystanders comment that the victims probably

provoked or unconsciously ellicited what was merely an understandable (and perhaps forgivable) response to provocation. This is
another pattern in which bystanders and others collude with persecutors to allow injustice and cruelty to occur. This pattern also
conveniently covers the difficult role of 'casting the first stone' in an
act of collusive sympathy between bystanders and persecutors.
Indeed, this pattern appears to be inextricably linked to people with
a so-called authoritarian personality* who have a deepseated respect
and a longing for established authority. In the words of Fromm
(1991), 'He admires authority and tends to submit to it, but at the
same time he wants to be in authority himself and have others
submit to him' (p. 141). Fromm goes on to describe what may be
called 'closet authoritarian personalities' who seem to be 'against
authority' but consistently admire or submit to a set of authorities
perceived to have greater power or greater promises.

The most cursory study of history shows that people may always
have wanted to oppress certain sectors of society and have claimed
all kinds of justifications for doing so themselves or colluded with
those who were doing it, if not on their behalf, to their advantage.
People in unjust situations, such as political prisoners, have often
been punished for protesting their conditions, rather than for any
intrinsic fault of their own. Often, legitimate protests in these situations are labelled as abusive, rebellious or recalcitrant. This *label* then
provides further justification for the aggressor to injure or restrain
the protesters — whether they are innocent or guilty of the crime for
which they have been incarcerated. The audience can be fooled by
this and can then stop feeling any sympathy or empathy for the
victims as they rationalise the justified explanations for the violence.
Seeing persecution done by others, for apparently good reasons, can
raise a rush of secret approval and gratification in vindication of all
the times the silent observer felt the same punitive, sadistic urge but
lacked the sanction of the authorities or the approval of the mob:

> As a result of feminists' efforts to stop victim-blaming, many people who
> continue to regard women as bringing violence upon themselves no longer
> acknowledge their belief so openly. As long as people assume that women
> are masochistic, they will tend to seek the 'little thing' the victim must have
> done to bring the violence on herself. By contrast, this is not how the
> motives of male victims of violence are usually interpreted. For most audi-
> ences, the rape of a man by another man in the movie *Deliverance* was simply

---

*This is a term introduced in social psychology and was heavily influenced by psychoana-
lytic theory. (See especially Adorno et al., 1950).

horrifying and undeserved; no one said the guy loved it or really wanted it. Similar rape scenes with woman victims do not always elicit such responses. (Caplan, 1985, pp. 139–140)

Victim-blaming occurs when a woman wearing a short skirt is blamed by the judge for provoking a rape and the rapist goes free. It is victim-blaming when a lesbian loses her job, not for living with a woman but because she protests at being fired for 'being a third sexual role model'. The prisoner's protest of bad treatment is somehow construed as significant justification for further abuse. Victim-blaming may also happen when an employee is fired for objecting to sexual harassment or questioning of management policy. The rationalisation is that the person 'brought it on himself'. Victim-blamers may be more or less honest about it at a social level, but at a psychological level they are justifying their non-involvement on the grounds that if something went wrong for that person, they probably deserved it, and it therefore behoves the audience to stay out of the just retribution of the fates, governments or institutions. It is based on a psychological notion called the 'just world' assumption (Russell, 1961). This concerns the idea that human beings tend to cling to the belief (contrary to all experience) that, somehow, there is justice in this world and that the good will be rewarded and the bad punished by a 'just parent', a 'just God' or a 'just justice'.

These bystanders may have the predictable thrills from seeing, for example, an envied sibling being punished for disobedience or breaking the rules, but remaining safe themselves. This confirms the belief that there is something wrong with the people who are being treated badly by the 'parents' because, if the victims were not deserving of the cruelty, they would be treated better by the power holders. In this way, *'If I am not being punished, it must mean that I am all right'*:

> In the summer of 1944 Allied troops swept into a newly liberated Paris ... Many hungry French women had been tempted by the [German] invader. At best female collaborators had their heads shorn and swastikas painted on their bodies before being paraded through the streets. (Beevor & Cooper, 1994, pp. 30–31)

There is frequently some kind of relief or excitement at witnessing another person getting into trouble. One can perhaps vicariously identify with the aggressor in a partly guilt-free way. If Freud had never 'suggested that women are naturally and inevitably masochistic, we would be freer to find other explanations for women's suffering. We do not currently have such freedom, however.' (Caplan, 1985, p. 38)

These bystanders use victim-blaming as a rationalisation for non-involvement or spurious neutrality. They avoid taking responsibility for participating in social justice, in making judgements, or even taking risks overtly to condemn or to act in ways which may be construed as provoking punishment or cruelty. It is concerned with how to participate knowingly in the shame, humiliation and punishment of another person without risking oneself. Sympathy for the victim can be expressed quite often secretly and privately. Often, it is barely obscured by the glee or relief at not being the scapegoat this time. People may overtly or covertly support the belief that, for example, people who die of AIDS somehow deserve it. *Devaluation of the victim of misfortune is endemic.* 'Thus after police killed four students at the Kent State University campus, rumours circulated that the dead students had had syphilis and were covered with lice, and that the women were pregnant' (Williams, 1992, p. 307). Much material for conversation around dinner tables or elsewhere is based on clichés, such as *'She always had it coming', 'Any sane person would end up kicking a bitch like her', 'He was so paranoid he deserved to be hounded out of the Society'.* Those who have been hounded out of the relevant reference group or powerful establishment of the time make a long and honourable list (Galileo, Jesus Christ, Semmelweis, Irigaray, the frail suffragette on a hunger strike for the women's vote who died after being force fed), whereas the bystanders who fuelled or witnessed their destruction are long forgotten.

Bion (Grinberg, Sor & Tabak de Bianchedi, 1975) describes how the exceptional individual (genius, mystic or messiah) whether artist, psychologist or scientist, is often and intrinsically in tension with the establishment — an emotional configuration which repeats itself painfully throughout history in different forms. 'Establishment' is the term Bion used to designate those who:

> exercise power and responsibility in the State or in other institutions, or that person or force which expresses these functions in the personality or in the group. In a situation where envy is the main factor, the result of the combination of mystic–genius and establishment group is the destruction and stripping of both. (pp. 20–21)

Too often, the hounding of the creative genius to his death in poverty and ignominy by the group or the establishment could have been prevented by one or more people refusing to bystand. Too often the genius is blamed for 'arrogance', 'insensitivity', 'political naïvety' (otherwise known as honesty) or some personality flaw which in one of the members of the centre of the group would be tolerated, esteemed or indulged. Always, the group which has destroyed the disrupter, the revolutionary, the person whose creative task it is to 'bear the new idea for the group', suffers as well. Perhaps our world psyche has still not recovered from the millions of women tortured and burned not too long ago for 'being different'. Truly those women were mysterious and powerful in a world where the options for normality were very small indeed. And great their punishment. And profound our loss.

How to intervene or prevent more such slaughter? Perhaps attempt to search one's own soul. Maybe to try and get appropriately involved in protecting genuine victims, or finding and supporting structures or providers of structures for controlling genuine persecutors. Bring in genuine helpers if you truly cannot personally affect the situation. Write to newspapers, to parliamentary representatives. All counsellors and psychotherapists must be particularly aware of this facet of human motivation and interaction. Those in the helping professions have such potent tools for analysing patterns that we may be in danger of pointing the finger in a disempowering way, whilst absolving ourselves of the obligation to become involved socially or interpersonally on the grounds that we do not want to be drawn into the pattern.

Beware the isolate, the individual, the unusual, the different, the extraordinary, the abnormal, the child who 'just can't follow the rules' like Einstein, the stone the builders forgot — they may be only too aware of the emperor's dudgeons. Those individuals who cannot exactly fit into the norm often suffer the double burden of creativity and de-structivity (a necessary pairing). The 'group', the organisation, the establishment, the institution will easily perceive both qualities *in extremis* and may even persecute the individuals who personify them because of this difference. To participate in the destruction of the extraordinary individual (because of their disability or their unnatural abilities) by not intervening at the point of communal scapegoating may be, ultimately, as disastrous to the whole community as blaming Cassandra for her own tragedy. 'The establishment has, as one of its functions, to achieve an appropriate containment and representation of the new creative idea, partly limiting its disruptive power and at the same time making it accessible to all the members of the group who are not geniuses' (Grinberg et al., 1975, p. 21).

If all mankind minus one were of one opinion, mankind would be no more justified in silencing that one person than he, if he had the power, would be justified in silencing mankind ... The peculiar evil of silencing the expression of an opinion is that it is robbing the human race, posterity as well as the existing generation - those who dissent from the opinion, still more than those who hold it. If the opinion is right, they are deprived of the opportunity of exchanging error for truth; if wrong, they lose, what is almost as great a benefit, the clearer perception and livelier impression of truth produced by its collision with error. (Mill, 1992, p. 76)

J'accuse!

Of course we have romance. Everyone can see how useful romance is. Even the newspapers like romance. They should; they have helped to create it, it is their daily doses of world malaise that poison the heart and mind to such a degree that a strong antidote is required to save what humanness is left in us. I am not a machine, there is only so much and no more that I can absorb of the misery of my kind, when my tears are exhausted a dullness takes their place, and out of that dullness a terrible callousness, so that I look on suffering and feel it not.

Isn't it well known that nothing shocks us? That the photographs of wretchedness that 30 years ago would have made us protest in the streets, now flicker by our eyes and we hardly see them? More vivid, more graphic, more pornographic even, is the newsman's brief. He must make us feel, but like a body punched and punched again, we take the blows and do not even notice the damage they have done.

Reportage is violence. Violence to the spirit. Violence to the emotional sympathy that should quicken in you and me when face to face we meet with pain. How many defeated among our own do we step over and push aside on our way home to watch the evening news? 'Terrible' you said at Somalia, Bosnia, Ethiopia, Russia, China, the Indian earthquake, the American floods, and then you watched a quiz show or a film because there's nothing you can do, nothing you can do, and the fear and unease that such powerlessness brings, trails in its wash, a dead arrogance for the beggar on the bridge that you pass every day. Hasn't he got legs and a cardboard box to sleep in?

And still we long to feel.

What's left? Romance. Love's counterfeit free of charge to all. Fall into my arms and the world with its sorrows will shrink up into a tinsel ball. This is the favourite antidote to the cold robot life of faraway perils and nearby apathy. Apathy. From the Greek A Pathos. Want of feeling. (Winterson, 1994, pp. 13–14)

Carmen refers a friend

Carmen, an 11-year-old incest survivor, brought a classmate up to me in the school hallway one day.

'Peg knows all about my father', she said by way of introduction. 'And she helped me and my Mom. You can talk to her about what's happening to you.'

Incident at Schenk Elementary School, Madison, Wisconsin, February 1980. (West, 1991, p. 63)

Part III
The Retrieval of
Human
Relationship

Chapter 7
From 'Bystanding' to 'Standing By'

Clarence:
My friend, I spy some pity in thy looks;
O, if thine eye be not a flatterer,
Come thou on my side and entreat for me —
As you would beg were you in my distress.
A begging prince what beggar pities not?

(King Richard the Third I. iv. 261–265)

In the preceding section of this book we made a preliminary excursion into some of the common rationalisations (or reasons) which people use to justify or explain their bystanding behaviour — essentially a denial of relationship. As we have seen, bystanding is often not a momentary phenomenon but a pattern of response to morally demanding life situations. Like all other potentially destructive interpersonal patterns, those to do with bystanding can be identified, analysed and questioned in depth from any or all of the possible viewpoints. Here we can only point at some. Moral questions affect every life, no matter how young. A 5-year-old in the playground has to make a choice between being part of the gang and beating up the fat little boy with spectacles and befriending him (at the loss of playground status and risk of being persecuted himself). There was one single juror who tried to speak up for the alleged rapist-murderer, Brandley. They called him a 'nigger-lover' for protesting that they could not convict a man without evidence. Brandley, a black man in a white Texan town, was eventually found innocent after 10 years on death row (Davies, 1991).

Religious education in schools is a vexed question which is best left to others more qualified to pursue. However, ethical education cuts across attempts to engage with the meaning of human life and our relationships with others and the world.

All human beings are born into relationship and can only thrive in relationship. Studies have shown retarded emotional and intellectual development and even death in infants or children deprived of significant relationships (Spitz, 1945; Melzack, 1965; Riesen, 1965). This happens often in spite of adequate physical care. Our need for relationship as infants seems even stronger than the drive to live.

The ultimate punishment in many penal and concentration camp systems, short of physical injury or capital punishment, is solitary confinement. Even hardened criminals fear and suffer from this cutting off from human contact. Most of us seem to need relationship as a basic condition of feeling human. Children know the cruelty of 'being sent to Coventry' where no-one speaks to you. Many people who suffer misfortune, such as cancer or losing their job, have experienced the chilling loss of relationship as friends and colleagues withdraw their interest or care. 'Deadmaking' a scapegoat for the tribe is an ancient custom alive today for a 'redundant colleague'. There are many complex reasons for this. Some may be the irrational fear of contamination by disease or misfortune and embarrassment or shame at 'surviving'. One man who kept his job when all about him were losing theirs, phrased it succinctly, *'For no good reason, I was the one who missed the chop'*.

It is our close relationships — love, friendship, family, good colleagues — which provide for many people the greatest source of emotional nourishment and support in stressful times. Yet of course, it is also these close relationships which cause the most pain and distress when they are disturbed lost or distressed. There is no stress factor more challenging to the coping mechanisms or identity of an adult person than bereavement of a spouse, partner or child. These are rated as 5 or 6 on Axis IV of the *DSM IV* system of assessing the severity of psychosocial stressors. You are apparently also more likely to be killed or raped by someone within your family, or known to you, than by a stranger. Our greatest joys and satisfactions come from relationship as well as our deepest pain and suffering. It is those who love us who can and often do hurt us most — and vice versa of course. A threat of violence to the people we love — our partners, our children — is often experienced as more intolerable than threats to ourselves. The pain of those we love throws into relief the intense vulnerability of our sense of integrity drawn from our affectional relationship bonds.

Philosophical and Scientific Viewpoints on Relationship

During the Middle Ages, poets, painters and sculptors did not sign their names to their products. Although it is difficult, if not impossible, to be accurate about the inner psychological life of another era, it has seemed to some analysts that the idea of individualism as we live with it today, was foreign to the medieval mind. An icon was an utterance from the whole fellowship of monks, for example, and the relationship between self and the community appears to have been fundamentally different.

There are also some societies where words denoting self are absent from the language and the notion of an individual is abstract and unreal to the people of those groups. Many African tribes do not conceive of the individual as separate from ancestors who are alive in the here and now of that person's existence. The idea of the individual as separable — out of relationship — appears to be both an historical and geographical artefact.

Modern cultural theory, quantum physics and complexity theory drive our world view further and further away from the metaphor of a machine or clockwork mechanism which is composed of a multitude of separate parts, and towards a more holistic process conception — an interconnected, dynamic relationship system, including consciousness of this process. Einstein's theories concern relationship. Complexity theory concerns the relationships between chaos and emergent order. Wheeler (1993), for example, states that we are participating now in the creation of the universe — relationships of co-creation through the function of consciousness itself.

Of course, in terms of catching the 10.15 from Paddington and dropping a cup, the laws of Newton apply. However, it is possible that some of the difficulties and ambiguities of psychotherapy outcome research come about precisely because we are trying to deal with subtle chaotic and complex phenomena by the use of tools more suited to engineering steel bridges than the subtleties of human interaction and intention. In so far as there are levels of being human which are hospitable to causality and parts-analysis, the methodologies of old may be suitable. Insofar as there are levels of being human which are more amenable to the notions of process, holism, syntrophy and complexity the other tools may be more useful.

Not only in science but also in terms of epistemology — the

philosophy of what and how we know — it appears that the things we see (people, objects, etc.) exist only in relationship and, when analysed microscopically, they too are best viewed as relationships. It is no secret in physics (Capra, 1976; 1983) that the closer we analyse some 'thing' the less it appears as a thing and the more it appears as a dynamic process (things in relationship). Consequently, relationships become a primary source of our knowledge of the world. This can be taken to the ontological extreme by stating that things do not exist — that, in fact, things ultimately *are* relationships (Cottone, 1988, p. 360), and so are good and evil.

The response to a traumatic event is the response which can determine, alleviate or exacerbate the severity of the damage (Lowenfeld, 1988). There is no way to be out of relationship or even to have bad relationships — there is only relationship and the avoided, rejected or neglected relationship or projected relationship may be so much more potent for the very assumption of the shadow spheres. All we can do is influence to some extent the articulation of the relationship as it affects us and as far as the client allows us to respond and be in effect of their relationship to us — to be hospitable to their requirements which may include changing the therapist more than the client, or neither.

It is my experience that people of all ages are fascinated by the complexities of good and evil in human life and, from clinical experience, I know that even pre-verbal infants can have profound emotional responses to experiences of unfairness or injustice. Ethical education should be a part of everyone's life. It should not be kept just for those extreme situations where you have to decide to participate or collude in decisions concerning abortion, euthanasia, or risking one's life to save someone else.

These extreme opportunities do not come to us every day, but everyday life asks these questions of us in a myriad microscopic ways. Recently, in an incident that will never reach the newspapers or get a heroism medal, I saw a middle-aged white woman on a suburban street in her tweed coat and double row of pearls simply stand *watching* (in such a way that they knew perfectly that she was watching) when six police officers were bodily searching a young male Asian driver whom they had suspected of being over the alcohol limit. The style of their search or interrogation appeared to become much more respectful and restrained the longer the woman stood there watching. She was not interfering in any way, but stood at a sufficient distance to see everything that was happening as well as to let everybody know that she was witnessing whatever was happening. She only vacated her witness post when the police decided there was nothing that they could find to justify 'booking' the young man, and they departed. (Afterwards, the young Asian man came and shook her hand and thanked her — it was his Christmas present.)

All methods which can help to support and develop social responsibility for personal, organisational, national and global contexts are to be encouraged (Clarkson, 1986). They help us back to relationship with ourselves, with nature, with our world. *The retrieval of relationship has become perhaps the most important moral issue of our time. Of course, relationship is difficult, demanding, ambivalent, relative, de-centering, vertiginous, disturbing and disorientating as well as rewarding and delightful.* But it is only in relationship with others that I can begin to know who I am as a human being, and who I am and who I can be for others. Some object–relations theorists have even gone so far as to say: we *are* our others. Ancient mystical traditions of the Orient used the mantric phrase *Tat Tswam Asi* (that thou art). This spiritual discipline involves saluting the divine in all the forces and beings and things of the world, recognising always oneself in the other, the other in oneself.

We have given much thought to the 'good reasons' why one should wish to deny relationship. But there are profound advantages to giving up bystanding behaviours and attitudes. Genuinely authentic pattern-free involvement with the destiny of others is more likely to be to the person's Self-ish benefit, autonomy, empowerment and learning in an ultimate sense. There are even simpler benefits:

> As a consequence of their helping activities, extensive people are more likely to evaluate themselves positively, which further reinforces the original personality characteristics and behaviours that led to helping in the first place. As they continue throughout their lives to help others, they are also more likely to transmit such values to their children. (Oliner & Oliner, 1988, p. 251)

Psychotherapy often involves reliving traumatic involvements or non-involvements of the past. These traumatic experiences may need to be relived and worked through in the safety of the consulting relationship. Often, children who have been abused grow up with the belief that justice is not possible because they may never have experienced it. This contamination may inhibit appropriate processing of relevant environmental information in adulthood and prevent actions which support the work of Physis, of creativity and evolution. As one human rights activist said after a recent legislative victory,

'The world is not fair, but it is not necessarily true that justice can never be done. Sometimes the good guys win — even if only for a little while'.

Adults from morally depleted or 'perverted' backgrounds may need reparative therapeutic experiences in adulthood because their moral development has either been retarded or injured (Kohlberg, 1964). This is the idea of child abuse by 'perversion'. On the other hand, children who were allowed or encouraged to act out bullying or fascist behaviour themselves may bystand as adults when they cannot themselves put the boot in. They may still, covertly, identify out of awareness with other bullies and find gratification in the fact that others are the more obvious social persecutors. In this way they can have sadistic gratification but still appear to be socially acceptable, even popular.

There may even be a subtle sense in which these so-called aggressors (or villains) can be said to be psychologically exploited by people who unconsciously use these bystander patterns because many persecutors, whether on playgrounds or on the world stage, are indeed responsive to challenge. If we are all in relationship we all serve each other's purposes, no matter how convoluted the ways. Bullies are notorious cowards. Some may even benefit and be grateful for the confrontation and structure which prevents them from harming others further. This developmental need for structure is documented in the literature (Levin, 1974) as well as frequently encountered in clinical practice. There are also many anecdotes of criminals, particularly murderers, who want to be apprehended and contained and who express genuine relief when the rule of law and order is restored both in their external situations and intrapsychic experience.

There may also be deficits in a person's home, school or spiritual education, such as how to manage conflict, physical or psychological self-defence. Skills of complex or abstract thinking about ethical situations may be needed. It is difficult to develop or to shape the development of a sense of meaning-making in a universe where a mother can microwave her baby to punish it; where police roam the streets shooting street urchins who live in the sewers; where thousands sit in rows dying silently of hunger in the blaze of television camera lights; whilst elsewhere others bury their potatoes to keep prices up.

We have explored the negative (destructive or ultimately unhelpful) consequences and psychological and social advantages of bystanding at all levels. This is also true of the psychological and existential distress induced by bystanding behaviour to the individual and the collective. By problematising bystanding, it becomes necessary to find other healthier or ultimately more life-affirming ways of awareness, action, engagement, relationship. By knowing what the relationship needs are for the individual, the group or the organisation, it becomes possible to encourage alternative satisfactions of these needs. Indeed, such a replacement is probably necessary for bystanding behaviour to cease; or at least to be reduced from tragic levels to a lesser degree of danger (probably all that is ever possible in the world we know). If we had to wait for 'pure' motivation, nothing would ever happen because human motivation is always mixed:

> In the 1960s Nat Hentoff wrote an essay entitled *Them and Us: Are Peace Protests Self-Therapy?* in which he cited a particular act of protest — not particularly unusual for the times — in which 23 people stood up during a high mass at St. Patrick's Cathedral in New York City and unfurled posters showing a maimed Vietnamese child. Hentoff was a journalist of the Left, strongly in support of their cause — yet he found himself suspecting 'that their act's essential effect was to make *them* feel relevant, to make *them* feel that some of their guilt as Americans had been atoned for by this witness'. (Anderson, 1990, pp. 123–124).

Other Advantages of Not Being a Bystander

There are a number of other psychological reasons why people can feel better as they shake off apathy and become engaged or involved with the plight of others who are being scapegoated or punished for being less privileged than they (Seligman's (1970) important work on learned helplessness is a case in point). Many people in my acquaintance and in my clinical and supervisory practice report a particular sense of excitement and vitality, an enhanced sense of the preciousness and the vibrancy of life as they become engaged in its preservation or enhancement.

For other people, the avoidance of regret and guilt is an important motivation. When you think about facing yourself, your children or your grandchildren in the future, when they question you about your actions (or non-actions), which are the ones you would feel that, even if they did not obliterate all regret and guilt, at least would give you a feeling that you have done 'good enough' by yourself and by others in those particular emergencies?

Of course, there is a pride in being able to say *'I was there — I did that — I supported those people — I helped this person'.* This sense of bravery, achievement, autonomous choice, is an important and significant human motivator. The heroic, for all its flaws, is still inspirational.

Frankl (1964) was the particular psychotherapist of our time who, brutalised in several concentration camps in Nazi Germany, lost his parents, brother and wife in these conditions. Nonetheless, he undertook to create meaning from this kind of experience and developed a whole approach psychotherapy called 'Logotherapy' in which he centralised the *will to meaning*. In his own words:

> We had to learn ourselves and, furthermore, we had to teach the despairing men, that it did not really matter what we expected from life, but rather what life expected from us. We needed to stop asking about the meaning of life, and instead to think of ourselves as those who were being questioned by life — daily and hourly. Our answer must consist, not in talk and meditation, but in right action and in right conduct. Life ultimately means taking the responsibility to find the right answer to its problems and to fulfil the tasks which it constantly sets for each individual. (Frankl, 1964, p. 77)

This specifically has to do with helping oneself and others to create meaning from the impossibly distressing and psychologically devastating experience which life may offer us. Chung (1994) pointed out that Frankl's work '... may have given us some insights for the future study of those who have survived and used their trauma as a way to enhance personal growth' (p. 9).

To relinquish the dubious privileges of bystanding is to assume the risky benefits and advantages of autonomy — responsibility for your own life and your own choices. As we know from research, the political choices of most people are determined by their parents or other people whom they have held in esteem. As Fromm, amongst many others, pointed out, few human beings choose their values for themselves. Yet, some of those who do — often at great sacrifice — report that their lives are infinitely more satisfying than a life which is based on the upholding, maintenance and policing of other people's values.

To refuse to bystand is to initiate the process of empowerment, both for the person who refuses the bystanding position and for the person who may, from the position of the oppressed, be looking for a model and an example of how to become empowered. When people in organisations stop gossiping and start taking responsibility for the systemic problems which surround them, the whole culture of the organisation can change from one of passive victimisation to one of responsible empowerment. The vehement protest of the youngest of five girls, in a family where they were being systematically sexually abused over many years by their father, was all that was needed for him to stop. She broke the spell of silent compliance which had been the expectation from all female creatures in that household.

There is joy in action, excitement and pleasure in good work well done on behalf of others. Non-bystanding has its own intrinsic reward — not least participation in the making of history. There are also negative reasons why people get involved in acting against bystanding. One of them is some enmeshment in seeing the victim as pathetic, therefore different and separate from themselves. Examples of these are the images of starving, sick children used to raise funds for charity, which position themselves in:

> ... a dangerous area between sympathy, guilt and disgust. In abandoning the attractiveness of childhood these pictured children may well have sacrificed the indulgence childhood demands. Without the flattery offered by the appealing image they may arouse adult sadism without deflecting it and confirm a contempt for those many parts of the world which seem unable to help their own. (Holland, 1992, p. 154)

> Although these images remain prevalent, the predication of compassion on the representation of humble and submissive recipients makes it difficult for aid organisations to highlight project partners' *own* activities for reconstruction, and advertising campaigns which did this failed. (Black, 1992)

It is not always the sick and the bad who are scapegoated and in need of protection or someone to 'be on their side and entreat on their behalf'. It is also the exceptional individuals in any field whether scientific, artistic or religious, such as those whom Bion calls the mystic or genius.

Unfortunately, it is probably impossible to eradicate bystanding behaviour. This is partly because the need of the world is so great and partly because individuals have to make and re-make moral decisions again and again and again. These decisions do not operate from introjected rules about engagement or automatic assumptions about justice, but involve genuine and autonomous re-evaluation of each ethical choice here-and-now:

> Learning about such things, continually re-examining beliefs about beliefs, becomes the most important learning task of all the others needed for survival in our time ... We don't really know how to do such learning or such teaching, and it is likely that wherever people try to do such teaching they will be opposed — as the educators of 'moral reasoning' have been. (Anderson, 1990, p. 268)

What can people do? There is much that can be done. Studying those instances where bystanders have successfully intervened, like all good biographies, provides much wisdom for living life. One recent and superb book by Lattimer (1994) gives clear advice and many encouraging examples of how ordinary people can change society. It contains influence maps elucidating the primary power structures in society and where pressure can most usefully and effectively be utilised:

> Even the current environmental campaigns, which have redrawn our view of the world in which we live, started in the 1970s with little more than a man and a boat. Modern campaigning techniques make such disproportionate effects possible. In fact, as the welfare state contracts and the political parties fight for the centre ground, the future of social change will increasingly lie in the hands of pressure groups, charities and ordinary people. (p. 9)

The following section offers some questions related to five critical points at which people can choose to take effective action in 'bystanding' situations. It may also be a very useful educational tool in facilitating children and other learners in their understanding of and responsibilities to life's moral complexities.

Critical Choice Points in Bystanding

Latané and Darley (1970) cite five critical steps in the process of participation in bystanding situations:

1. *Notice* that something is happening.
2. *Interpret* the situation as one in which help is needed.
3. *Assume* personal responsibility.
4. *Choose* a form of assistance.
5. *Implement* the assistance*.

Based on a synthesis of these sources, the five following questions can guide appropriate self-questioning for both psychotherapist and client.

Am I aware of what is happening in my environment?

To notice that something is happening is to account for the existence of a problem, for example, *noticing* that a friend at a party is drunk enough to be potentially dangerous to self or others. Not confronting

---

*There is a significant correspondence between these five critical steps and the discounting matrix: (1) discounting existence of problem, (2) discounting significance of problem, (3) discounting solvability of problem, and (4) discounting own ability to cope with or solve problem (Schiff et al., 1975).

that friend as he or she leaves to drive home is to be a bystander (doing nothing relevant to solve the problem). 'We feel and act as if we are in fact disconnected physically, spiritually, ecologically and morally from ourselves and from the universe. We behave as if we were each isolated and separate' (Rinzler, 1984, p. 233). We are not.

There is increasing awareness of the psychotherapist's responsibility to invisible third parties to the therapeutic contract with a client. It is important to recognise the impact of problems such as long-lasting depression or severe anorexia on a client's children, spouse, students, or employees and to initiate appropriate action with the client and/or other relevant parts of the system with their co-operation if at all possible.

Is help needed?

The concept of Schiff et al. (1975) of accounting for the significance of a situation is equivalent to interpreting the situation as one in which help is needed. One example of this concerns assessing whether the child screaming in the flat upstairs is genuinely ill or is being abused. The potential bystander needs to decide whether this situation requires investigation. Therapeutic neutrality may be lethal, for example, as in the case of a promiscuous client who may not be aware of the need to take precautions against contracting AIDS.

Another example involves the woman who reveals in psychotherapy that her son beats her daughter to the point of unconsciousness. The woman fails to understand or acknowledge this as a potentially homicidal issue because it 'does not seem serious'. What should the therapist do? Similarly, a general practitioner mentions in passing that she has been giving her 5-year-old son antidepressant medication for the past year because the child is 'difficult'. In such case, non-contractual intervention by the psychotherapist as a professional and as a person is sometimes essential. It is frequently justified without being labelled rescuing.

Is it my responsibility?

To assume personal responsibility means to account for the existential fact that you are personally involved in a situation and are able to influence it. For example, how can people in oppressive situations claim they are not personally responsible for the surrounding injustice and persecution while continuing to benefit financially from the situation? If Jews, homosexuals, or blacks are being persecuted in my organisation or country, how can I sustain psychological well-being in that culture? If plants react at cellular levels when other plants are injured, how can human beings be exempt from visceral empathy? (Watson, 1974).

If a colleague is working 70 hours a week without rest, is it not my responsibility to discuss this with him or her? If a psychoanalytic training institute is propagating anti-homosexual prejudice, is it not my responsibility to seek ethical redress on behalf of the community at large?

What are the viable options for taking action to change the situation?

Possibilities for change can be developed by generating viable options and then choosing a form of assistance to a person or persons being threatened. For example, people in groups or crowds may participate collectively in bystanding even when one of their own is persecuted (for example, Nazi Germany). The fear for personal survival or the welfare of family may sustain their passivity. Bystanders in such situations frequently justify not intervening by believing that the situation cannot change, the problem cannot be solved, or that no other viable option for action exists. Similarly, many people claim that they personally have no ability to affect the likelihood of nuclear holocaust.

Assuming individual responsibility should not depend on a successful outcome to one's efforts. Personal responsibility constitutes a commitment to right action regardless of whether the commitment attains the desired short-term results. We have learned from Chaos Theory that the flapping of a butterfly's wings in South America could affect a hurricane over a Chicago airfield causing an aeroplane to crash. Large events are sometimes brought about by very small causes and vice versa. No one knows for sure if their one action may not be the critical flap of the metaphorical butterfly's wings snapping the fences of apartheid or the chains of hunger.

What action am I taking?

This question focuses on immediacy of action — the opposite of perpetuating and/or endorsing passive behaviour. For example, people may recurrently get into states of agitated depression about the nuclear threat without taking appropriate action related to the problem. Instead of using their biologically more appropriate anger to affect the situation, they become self-condemning and depressed while remaining passive. Incapacitation, such as fainting or hysterical amnesia, in the vicinity of someone abusing their power or authority is another example of bystanding as passive behaviour if no action follows either at the time or later.

Fighting the oppressor is one solution. Making a moral choice to withdraw and allow the interested parties to fight or negotiate their own battles is another. Human beings can develop many creative alternatives. For example, one South African artist recorded the historical events in her country through her painting at a time when emergency laws prohibited freedom of the press. Another South African wrote poetry, another dramas. Their task was to find a way of being an involved witness which was compatible with their survival *and* their conscience. Guilt is a phenomenon which offers us as human beings another opportunity to be in good faith.

Foresight, Midsight and Hindsight in Bystanding Patterns

One of the learning structures I have used for many years in teaching the constructive management and prevention of negative life patterns is the tripartite division between foresight, midsight and hindsight. Working with individuals, groups or organisations when engaged in repetitive, unsatisfying or destructive outcomes, I noticed people first develop the capacity for hindsight. *Hindsight* means *'Oh, I can see I've done it again'*. Berne (1968) links this to despair:

> In a successful therapeutic situation this may soon be replaced by humorous laughter, implying an Adult realization: 'There I go again!' This despair is a concern of the Adult, while in depression it is the Child who has the executive power. Hopefulness, enthusiasm or a lively interest in one's surroundings is the opposite of depression; laughter is the opposite of despair. Hence the enjoyable quality of therapeutic game analysis. (p. 48)

Of course, hindsight is usually perfect 20/20 vision. It is comparatively easy to see how a person could have behaved differently once the opportunity for doing so has passed. However, it is usually a necessary first step before the development of midsight.

Midsight is the awareness that we have become engaged in a sequence which will most predictably lead to negative consequences which we may (at some level) prefer to avoid. A person develops midsight on becoming aware of the predictable pattern before the payoff points are reached. Midsight prompts autonomous choice to abandon the set of transactions, refuse to play, or change the pattern so as at least to remove their share of the complementary transactions which could lead to the predicted negative outcome for one or both people.

Once people develop *foresight* they recognise their individual proclivities and understand their tendencies to engage in certain kinds of transactional patterns with others (whether these be of the victim, rescuing, persecuting, or bystanding kind). Such foresight is usually based on increased self-knowledge, in particular of the decisions made in childhood, often under parental or social pressure, as to how to behave in bystanding situations. Children who grow up in families where parents ignore the screams of a wife being abused next door, or nations which say that another's genocide is none of their business, may have learned how to desensitize themselves in ways which are ultimately extremely self-damaging.

The effectiveness of our foresight depends on how bound we still are, to the extent to which we can anticipate our future bystanding behaviours and get the information, achieve the insights, or make the redecisions necessary which will enable us to turn bystanding patterns into creative opportunities for responsible involvement, intimacy, spontaneity and autonomy in our shared world.

The foresight most needed to secure the creative survival of the planet includes the active shaping of the moral values, sensitivities and questioning of the children in our care and the trainees in our supervision. Oliner and Oliner (1988) described the kind of parenting which leads to what they call extensivity or its opposite, resistance to altruism (or bystanding). It is not as if those who involved themselves on behalf of others lacked concern for self, external approval or achievement, but they also had a capacity for extensive relationships — attachment, care and responsibility for the welfare of others including those outside their immediate family circles.

> It begins in close family relationships in which parents model caring behaviour and communicate caring values ... It is no accident that when the lives of outsiders are threatened, individuals with this orientation are more likely to initiate or be asked for help. More sensitive than others to violations that threaten their moral values, they may seek out opportunities to help ... Already more deeply and widely attached to others, they find it difficult to refrain from action. Already more inclined to include outsiders in their sphere of concern, they find no reason to exclude them in an emergency. (Oliner & Oliner, 1988, pp. 249–251)

We know from psychological research that human beings are more likely to learn or change their attitudes when they are feeling able and effective themselves. In studies researching attitude change which would be effective in changing behaviour, experimenters found that photographs of decaying lungs which were too gruesome, simply had no effect on changing smokers' attitudes. Apparently people do not respond effectively or learn adequately when the negative stimulus is too intense. In the same way many efforts at enhancing moral responsibility fail because they insist that people feel guilty and bad first and then they have to do something good, responsible, etc. in order to feel well and good enough again. When humans get involved in proving that they are blameless, they get involved in avoiding taking responsibility. Collect and teach examples of responsibility, involvement and engagement. Think through the inevitable mixture of motivation and the complexities of moral dilemmas that we face every day in buying factory-farmed chicken, in banking with members of the IMF, in ignoring a friend in trouble. Studying examples of non-bystanding behaviour is also a potentially rich source for reflection and inquiry. Whether one shouts *'Fire!'*, creates a distraction by innocently asking for directions, or simply make notes — all these are ways of intervention and there are many more. Research shows that ultimately relationship or engagement is not a rational act, and the likelihood that someone will systematically be going through the five critical choice points in an emergency situation is just about nil. However, preliminary exercises of this kind act as sensitisers, alerting us again and again to the fact that human beings and all living creatures are of the same fabric, no part of which can be torn without tearing each one of us.

> But where You is said, there is no something. You has no borders. Whoever says you does not have something; he has nothing. But he stands in relation. (Buber, 1970, p. 55)

Identify for yourself the actions you are currently taking or you have taken recently which were not bystanding, but some form of active and responsible involvement in situations of oppression, injustice or cruelty. Encourage other people to do the same. In wanting to be blameless, perhaps we avoid responsibility. Maybe we can then begin to learn how to move from bystanding to standing by, in the sense of acknowledgement of the inescapability of our relatedness.

> This ability to combine real individuality with definitive relationship is one unique and important result of looking at persons quantum mechanically.

Neither individuality nor relationship is lost. Neither is more primary.
(Zohar, 1990, p. 121)

Helpful Strategies and a Story

Finally, in a similar way that the St. John Ambulance Brigade runs
physical first aid classes spreading both awareness and skills to millions
of ordinary people in the population which inform them of risk
assessment, appropriate first aid and hone helpful reflexes in
conjunction with learned best strategies, we may conceive of *bystander
intervention training* — in every school, every workplace, every training
institution. Film clips, for example, could be shown for discussion
points on assessing situations, gaining information, acting appropriately in ambiguous situations. In the same way as physical first aid,
there would be no guarantee that the victim will always live or that
the helper will always do exactly the right thing, but the effort itself
may increase the chances that a more beneficial outcome is more
likely to happen.

In order to resource such efforts and for the sake of the research
itself, I plead for starting a *research project*, an archive, a collecting point
of all kinds of bystander and bystander intervention stories, histories
and researches. These can be collated at some central depot, perhaps
a university research project computer dedicated to such analysis, not
with the intention of blaming or creating unnecessary guilt, but with
the intention of raising awareness and improving education and sensitivity in ourselves and in others to bystanding issues — something
which could be called 'Bystander Witness' or another better title to
encapsulate the spirit of the work. This collection of incidents, documentation, strategies could involve bringing together the best thinking
of contemporary police practice to the best knowledge gained from
social psychology and psychotherapeutic psychology today.

To end this section included below is one example from ancient
Sumerian myth about how bystander intervention does not always
have to be 'have-a-go-heroes' as they are contemptuously referred to
in the UK — it could sometimes perhaps be the judicious use of
empathetic messengers:

> In the Sumerian poem Inanna decides to go into the underworld; she 'set
> her heart from highest heaven on earth's deepest ground', 'abandoned
> heaven, abandoned earth — to the Netherworld she descended'. As a
> precaution, she instructs Ninshubur, her trusted female executive, to
> appeal to the father gods for help in securing her release if she does not
> return within three days.

At the first gate to the Netherworld, Inanna is stopped and asked to declare herself. The gatekeeper informs Ereshkigal, queen of the Great Below, that Inanna, 'Queen of heaven, of the place where the sun rises', asks for admission to the 'land of no return' to witness the funeral of Gugalanna, husband of Ereshkigal. Ereshkigal becomes furious, and insists that the upper-world goddess be treated according to the laws and rites for anyone entering her kingdom — that she be brought 'naked and bowed low'.

The gatekeeper follows orders. He removes one piece of Inanna's magnificent regalia at each of the seven gates. 'Crouched and stripped bare', as the Sumerians were laid in the grave, Inanna is judged by the seven judges. Ereshkigal kills her. Her corpse is hung on a peg, where it turns into a side of green, rotting meat. After three days, when Inanna fails to return, her assistant Ninshubur sets in motion her instructions to rouse the people and gods with dirge drum and lamenting.

Ninshubur goes to Enlil, the highest god of sky and earth, and to Nanna, the moon god and Inanna's father. Both refuse to meddle in the exacting ways of the underworld. Finally Enki, the god of waters and wisdom, hears Ninshubur's plea and rescues Inanna, using two little mourners he creates from the dirt under his fingernail. They slip unnoticed into the Netherworld, carrying the food and water of life with which Enki provides them, and they secure Inanna's release by commiserating with Ereshkigal, who is now groaning — over the dead, or with her own birth pangs. She is so grateful for empathy that she finally hands over Inanna's corpse. (Perera, 1981, pp. 9–10)

That Just Doesn't Feel Like Loving To Us. Children Handle a Touching Situation By Themselves

My stepdaughter came up to me last month and told me she got an Early Warning Sign whenever she was around her grandfather, her mother's father. She said that sometimes he hugged her too long and kissed her sloppily. I was mad, and was ready to go and tell him off in no uncertain terms. But our daughter said that at school she'd learned that sometimes you could just tell someone to stop, and she wanted to try that. I reluctantly agreed, still steaming, with her agreeing that if it didn't work she'd let me know.

The very next weekend, we were at a family gathering at Grandpa's, and our daughter and two of her young cousins were there. I was watching closely, you can imagine. Grandpa came over to the three of them and started to hug one.

'Wait a minute Grandpa', she said, 'We don't like those hard hugs'.

'And we don't like the sloppy kisses, either!' chimed in the second cousin.

Then our daughter added, 'That just doesn't feel like loving to us, Grandpa'.

Grandpa looked thoughtful and a little embarrassed, as the three girls came running over to us.

'There! We told him', our daughter whispered to me.

A month later when I asked her, she said that now he hugs them 'sideways and carefully' and the sloppy kisses have stopped.

Told to [Peg West] PTA meeting, Kennedy School, Madison, Wisconsin, 1982. (West, 1991, p. 73)

Chapter 8
Bystanding in Counselling, Psychoanalysis and Psychotherapy

Queen Margaret:
Rivers and Dorset, you were standers by,
And so wast thou, Lord Hastings, when my son
Was stabb'd with bloody daggers.

(King Richard the Third, I. iii. 209–212)

Introduction

Counselling and psychotherapy are currently coming under increasing attack both from within the profession and from without. There are many articles being written in the popular press against psychotherapy, such as Weldon (1994), as well as from within the profession. For example, a delightfully provocative book title, *We've Had A Hundred Years of Psychotherapy and the World is Getting Worse* (Hillman & Ventura, 1992), encapsulates a gnawing uneasiness among both professionals and consumers that the 'helping professions' have failed in very important ways. As these authors correctly point out, psychotherapy has had 100 years with which to grapple with its role and function and at the end of the century we are in a position to assess its impact on the state of the world — and it does not look good.

> When religion and the meta-narratives of modernity have eroded, there appear no truths outside of man. In this relativist culture with no fixed and fundamental rules, the moral guide for life is sought in a scientific psychology. The new psychology took over religion's task of providing guidelines for human life. The priests as confessors were replaced by therapists as paid companions. With an economy of production being replaced by an economy of consumption, the Protestant work ethic is gradually replaced by a

psychology of need gratification and indulgence. With the erosion of a comprehensive frame of meaning, of traditional values and communal bonds, individual self-realization became the goal of life. 'In the United States, at least, psychology has become a new religion establishing an inner quest for self where before there had been an outer quest for God' (Leahey, 1987, p. 479). It should be noted that the religious roots of psychology are not confined to the humanistic versions. Thus Watson's scientific behaviourism was almost a literal translation of the Baptist theology that Watson studied while training for the ministry (see Birnbaum, 1964). (Kvale, 1992, p. 54)

Of course we cannot hold psychotherapy or psychology responsible for all social ills, but we can hold its practitioners responsible for their abuse of power as well as for their lack of involvement in social issues. An insistence on a spurious 'neutrality', a lack of appreciation for the role of values, the development of professional and regulatory societies and the preoccupation with competency all seem to be driving practitioners further and further away from dealing with real people in the real world and more towards a self-absorbed, overly rigid, somewhat hyper-vigilant kind of defensive practice.

Working on quite a number of professional investigation and ethical adjudication panels I am, of course, bound by very strict rules of confidentiality, but I can speak freely about certain general patterns which have emerged, not in single cases but repeatedly in different professional organisations. Rarely are these bad people doing intentionally bad things. Usually it is ignorance, fear, temptation, confusion and lack of support which lead to ethical problems. Anyway, the first resort should always be conversational, dialogic and enquiring rather than judgemental legalism, on the one hand, or pubescent tittle-tattle, on the other.

With the increase in consumer education and public awareness and the development of counselling and psychotherapy as a growth industry there has been a concomitant explosion of concerns about not making mistakes, insuring against client claims of damage, an unprecedented rise in complaints and ethics charges against practitioners. The increasing need for a professional psychotherapist to anticipate every kind of possible measurable outcome, professional audit or performance review may well result in a proliferation of contracts to be countersigned or even legal advice being taken before a client even starts to tell their story.

Unfortunately, among many practitioners there is seen a rather regrettable attempt to be more and more careful, more and more conscious of third parties listening, interpreting and judging on degrees of reality which can only ever be mediated by the two, or more people present in the confines of the consulting room. There seems to be increasing preoccupation with being 'error-free', with avoiding spontaneity and intuitive authenticity.

A kind of clinical practice is developing which may be called 'defensive psychotherapy'. This is my appropriation of the term 'defensive medicine' which is used in America to describe an ethos in which doctors and paramedics refuse to become involved, for example, with accident victims on the road. This is reportedly because they are frightened of, or protecting themselves against, potential lawsuits which may implicate them in malpractice or potentially lose them thousands of dollars and their reputation on the basis of an unpremeditated act of merciful intervention. If the doctor were to set a broken leg and the leg were not to heal properly or if additional complications set in, the risk now of being sued over this is simply too high for the doctor to take. The very fear of somebody else's reality being proved different from yours in a court of law or in the amphitheatre of public opinion prevents the *natural,* altruistic response to provide whatever help we can according to the best lights of our judgement and competence at the time. This avoidance of involvement, this denial of relationship, for whatever reason, is here called bystanding.

Clinicians are today often more concerned to practise in a way which is beyond the criticism of supervisors or vulnerability to misunderstanding by their clients. And, there is psychodynamic reason to anticipate such misunderstandings (Clarkson, 1995b). There is, on both sides of the Atlantic, a feeling that the joy and excitement of counselling and psychotherapy have abated and that the risks of experimentation and creativity are being minimised to a level of the kind of bland, self-conscious care-full-ness.

Of course, it is vitally important that these professions have grown up to question seriously its criteria for inclusion, membership, ethics and so on. Certain kinds of bad practice (for example, sexual relations with clients) are justifiably ameliorated or exposed as a result of these efforts of professionalisation. Going from free-for-all encounter groups led by unqualified practitioners to adjudicating five different levels of National Vocational Qualification (NVQ) competencies in terms of showing 'empathy' has solved some problems but has created and is creating many more. Whyte (1994) also expressed his disquiet about this in a recent issue of the *British Journal of Psychotherapy* (p. 568). In some circles the phrase 'the bureaucratisation of sadism' has been heard as a way of describing the ever-increasing professional demands for certification, qualification and documentation.

Much of the contemporary literature reveals an almost prurient preoccupation with an ideal, if not mandatory, hermetically sealed therapeutic relationship. Lloyd (1992), for example, refers to a 'dual relationship phobia' abroad in counselling education. Freud (1912a) advocated that the analyst should refrain from allowing his personality to intrude into the analysis and introduced the simile of the analyst being a 'mirror' for the analysand (p. 108). In 1912 he proposed that the psychoanalyst model himself on the surgeon, put aside his human sympathy and adopt an attitude of emotional coldness (Freud, 1912b, p.115). According to Greenson (1967) 'This means that the analyst must have the ability to restrain his therapeutic intentions, control his urge for closeness and "blanket" his usual personality' (p. 389).

However, these recommendations for emotional coldness and a mirror-like attitude must be understood in the context of the time. Perhaps Freud emphasised certain 'unnatural' aspects of psychoanalytic technique because they were so foreign and artificial to the usual doctor–patient relationship and the customary psychological treatment of his day. He prescribed mirror-like impassivity on the part of the analyst, who should not reciprocate the patient's confidences nor try to educate, morally influence or 'improve' the patient. In his own practice, however, Freud conducted therapy as no classically trained Freudian analyst would nowadays (Malcolm, 1981). He shouted at his patients, praised them, argued with them, accepted flowers from them on his birthday, lent them money, visited them at home and even gossiped with them about other patients! Recent research of some eminent psychologists, psychoanalysts and psychotherapists (Clarkson, 1994b) revealed that emotional coldness, absolute neutrality and total abstinence are more figments of the profession's imagination than the reality encountered by the average client.

Four major charges are being made against psychotherapy. These are:

Manipulation and Abuse

These are inevitably part of psychological treatment whether it is psychoanalysis or 'befriending' those diagnosed as having HIV:

> It might be argued that therapists, even if they are not more likely to show a sense of social justice, are not less likely to do so than any other professional. That there are individual therapists who feel outrage over social injustice I am certainly prepared to believe. But has any particular group of psychotherapists ever taken a stand against abuse? Did Freud? (Masson, 1989, pp. 44–45).

Certainly not many people from the anti-psychiatry movement and others, such as Smail (1987), Mair (1988) and Rowe (1990) Newnes (1991; 1994), have spoken out on many important issues. The founding of the organisation, Psychotherapists and Counsellors for Social Responsibility, in London in 1995 also heralds a new willingness for engagement in social relationship by British psychotherapists. Much of the current impetus for this movement can be credited to the work of Samuels (1993) who, in his major book *The Political Psyche*, opened politics as a legitimate issue for conversation and exploration in psychoanalysis and psychotherapy. Of course, Humanistic psychotherapists, from their grandfather Moreno (Greenberg, 1975), who first worked with groups of prostitutes and the latch-key children of Vienna, to the anti-psychiatry work of Steiner (Steiner et al., 1975) and the political anarchy of Goodman (Stoehr, 1991), have had quite a long and illustrious history of social engagement:

> The current emptiness and irrelevance of a psychological science to culture at large may be due to psychology's rootedness in modernity, in the study of the logic of an abstracted 'psyche', which is out of touch with a postmodern world. (Kvale, 1992, p. 52)

Neutrality or Non-involvement

The ideal of 'not imposing your values on your client' may be impossible, delusional and dangerous. Of course I do not mean outright evangelising. I mean the subtle and inescapable ways in which psychotherapists, like all other human beings, convey their values, ideals and aspirations through a myriad cues in their being, doing and not doing. The defence or rationalisation of innocent (or neutral) bystanding as 'professional behaviour' is wearing thin:

> While the counselor's moral and ethical standards may not be made clear to clients, or even to the counselor himself, they are influential in his reactions to the client's story, his emphases, his choice of objectives and counselling method, and in the techniques he uses to carry out the chosen method of interviewing. (Severin, 1965, p. 369)

Interiority or Unhealthy Narcissism

These notions of psychotherapy have led to a false and destructive rupture of the inevitable and morally and ecologically necessary interconnectedness between the individual, society and the planet. If neither therapist nor client are explicitly acting on their values they are being complicit with evil and social injustice despite the fact that they may, in other settings, claim to be against it.

> This is a staunchly political message: as people become more absorbed in the psychological life, they become on the average less concerned about social dramas. After all, the same sensibility that drives one to seek ever deeper layers of truth in the psychological sphere might as easily drive one to seek an understanding of social tragedies and attempt to remedy them. The same quest for growth that drives one to change one's psychological makeup might as easily drive one to struggle to change the social arrangements. But because there seems to be no public forum to accomplish the latter kind of change, and little hope for real social progress, many people turn their attention inward where real gains seem possible. Even the 60s generation of rebels and radicals has fallen prey. Many are just as committed therapy consumers today as they were activists then. As people get used to consulting therapists for help addressing more of their everyday problems — including unhappiness at work, problems raising children, domestic violence — they become less practised in social or collective solutions to these problems. And once we assume the unhappiness emanates entirely from a flaw deep within, we tend to seek more and better therapy whenever we experience more unhappiness. Clinicians are quick to devise new theories and new therapies. The endlessness of the quest explains the interminable nature of therapy. (Kupers, 1988, pp. 139–140)

Infantilisation in Psychotherapy

A number of socially committed psychotherapists, psychoanalysts and psychologists are seriously questioning the tendency to infantilisation in psychotherapy and psychotherapy training and supervision.

There is little doubt that childhood experiences can in many cases lead to adult disturbance. However, an increasing chorus of workers is beginning to question and criticise the infantilisation of clients, patients, trainees and even conference attendees. What is seen as an unhelpful and possibly even destructive and abusive over-emphasis on childhood and the unremitting use of developmental models predicated on the idiom of mother and child perpetuates a hierarchical and power-based patriarchal division of knowledge and expertise.

Furthermore, when this model is applied to adults, particularly in training and supervision situations, the capacity of autonomous decision-making, capacity for risk and ability to question and challenge can be seriously undermined. Where notions of 'holding', empathising and 'containing' hold sway and supervisors and therapists model themselves on ideal womb or mothering environments, the inner child runs a risk of being elevated to the overarching paradigm or archetype of our times. Titles such as *Rage for Utopia* (Conway, 1992) and *The Reluctant Adult* (Hall, 1993), and the poetic and iconoclastic tirades of Hillman (1992), all explore in different ways how citizens become babies when 'the numinosity of sex has been replaced by the numinosity of feeding' (Samuels, 1993, p. 274).

In the fable of the Grand Inquisitor encountering the returning Christ, Dostoyevsky (1955) had already come to the conclusion that human beings would always choose dependency rather than freedom. This is rather a sad vision of humanity but it corresponds with the fear of freedom as Fromm (1991) and others have articulated it.

> Thou wouldst go into the world, and art going with empty hands, with some promise of freedom which men in their simplicity and their natural unruliness cannot even understand, which they fear and dread — for nothing has ever been more insupportable for a man and a human society than freedom. But seest Thou these stones in this parched and barren wilderness? Turn them into bread, and mankind will run after Thee like a flock of sheep, grateful and obedient, though for ever trembling, lest Thou withdraw Thy hand and deny them Thy bread. (Dostoyevsky, 1955, pp. 299–300)

The blank screen psychoanalyst is for the patient or client a model of an individuated person as someone who is neutral and not involved. Therefore he is above the turbulent counter-currents of moral decision-making, and free from the ebb and flow of human relationships. Because we are never free from conflict, from ambivalence, from pain and fear, even when we are involved with other people, our love for others is the human creature's greatest vulnerability. It is the threat to a beloved spouse or kidnapping of a child which are the greatest levers for blackmail in our world. The pain of those close to us is often experienced as greater than our own pain. How often has a parent, watching a child die, not pleaded with God to let them take over the pain rather than to have to witness its ravages in the body of the other?

Rhetoric of 'Professionalisation'

Frank's (1973) argument that it has been impossible to show convincingly that one therapeutic method is more effective than any other for most psychological illnesses (p. 2), has been impressively substantiated by meta-analytic studies which further added an emphasis on

the success of placebo groups (Smith, Glass & Miller, 1980). There
are literally hundreds of other studies coming to the same conclusion
(Clarkson, 1995f; 1995g). Yet, in the face of a virtual avalanche of
such evidence, we still see a proliferation of counselling, psychotherapy and psychoanalytic training courses and training in institutes
which valorise single-model approaches and credentialing systems
which rely on 'theoretical adherence' or practice justified by congru-
ence with theoretical orientation whether integrative or not. This
professional situation of finer and finer theoretical differentiation
and accreditation procedures which rely on the replicated theory in
action can only exist when groups get together and label others as
outsiders — 'not people like us', for whatever reason. Then those who
do not meet the conformity criteria (such as heterosexuality) can be
excluded or allowed to be persecuted on the grounds that 'they do
not meet the standards'. A profession dedicated to neutrality can
then maintain a self-soothing rhetoric — sometimes on the flimsiest
of grounds.

Weigert (1970) explored the common characteristics of professional rhetorics:

> They include a rhetoric of affiliation by which the profession aligns itself
> with higher status groups and distances itself from lower status groups; a
> rhetoric of special expertise that includes claims to valid theories and
> distinctive methods; a rhetoric of public service that simultaneously plays
> down careerist motives; a rhetoric of social passage that identifies and justi-
> fies credentialing requirements; a rhetoric of self-policing that defends
> against 'interference' from others; and a delegitimizing of the rhetoric of
> outsiders, including 'pseudo-professionals', 'charlatans', 'popularizers', and
> 'cranks'. (Simons, 1989)

Values in Counselling, Psychoanalysis and Psychotherapy

> According to Taylor's [1954] definition of a value as '... an idea on which
> people act, or a principle on which they judge how to act' [p. 208], we
> cannot, since every choice and action must be based upon explicit or
> implicit acceptance of a value. (Severin, 1965, p. 368)

Counselling and psychotherapy are disciplines which emerged, on
the one hand, from religion and philosophy and, on the other, from
the scientific laboratories. The academic world attempted to think
through the issues of good and evil; in the laboratories they tried to
circumvent it by so-called objectivity. Three men are credited with

parenting the rivers from which counsellors and psychotherapists drink and from which we forge our ephemeral sieves for the sorting of psyche's seeds today (Clarkson, 1994a). These are the ones who shaped our attitudes and blindnesses, our hubris and our humilities, our engagement with or recoil from the regions ruled in previous times by the pastors, and the mythical and magical healers for whom the issues of right and wrong were divinely ordained and not the painful, wet, overheated clumsiness that we so often bring to bear upon them. Each one brought his own world view, beliefs about the limits and the reach of humankind, ideals and disappointments.

The originators of psychoanalysis and psychotherapy were not fanatics. Issues of respectability, status and economic concerns do not infect the regions devoted to the study of the forces of sex and death. Or might they? Can we tolerate the thought that Freud made interpretations about how a woman was transferring her hostile feelings on to him? Yes, but whilst she was actually rotting away from a suppurating wound in her nose, bandages gone septic, from an operation conducted by his friend because she masturbated too much? Was that not obsessively ridiculous, yet based on reason, indeed, psychoanalytical theory? What is to be said of Jung, who saw in Hitler a new Messiah for Germany? Of the analyst who treats a woman while she is engaged in a political movement against pornography but only confesses after many years that he really enjoys *Playboy*? The ones who keep taking the money while they use the couch for other purposes than Freud intended? The financial impossibility of serving any substantial proportion of the population except the most élite in the profession or the independently wealthy? The educational psychologist who supports the scapegoating and shaming of a homosexual teacher on 'theoretical' grounds?

Shallow ideas can be assimilated; ideas that require people to reorganise their picture of the world provoke hostility. A physicist at the Georgia Institute of Technology, Joseph Ford, quoted Tolstoy:

> I know that most men, including those at ease with problems of the greatest complexity, can seldom accept even the simplest and most obvious truth if it be such as would oblige them to admit the falsity of conclusions which they have delighted in explaining to colleagues, which they have proudly taught to others, and which they have woven, thread by thread, into the fabric of their lives. (Gleick, 1988, p. 38)

As Jung said, 'the fact that there are so many models of psychotherapy, taught by so many sincere and ethical teachers attests only to the perplexity with which we work'.

The fact that there are so many versions of psychotherapy reflects the disarray of the field and its inability after a century to find one single truth or best way of healing the human soul.

Human beings being what they are, it seems that the more we try to keep the laboratory clean and ordered, the more it also spews forth the unpredictable and the gruesome. The mould on the saucer which the assistant accidentally forgot to clean was noticed and gave us life-saving penicillin. The imaginative outbreak of the shadow fears of the mad scientist, *Frankenstein, Dr Jekyll and Mr Hyde*, the monstrous playing-out of our most macabre vision — the world destroyed in the brilliant light of a skin-searing, eyeball-melting, mushroom sun. These things were made by scientists who had no thought when they played of the havoc their objective scientific inventions would wreak.

Three Heritages and Their Position on Values

The ideological grandfather of the cognitive–behavioural therapy and rational–emotional therapeutic approaches which we know today is, of course, Pavlov — a white-coated scientist who apparently did not show concern for the dogs in his care driven mad by scientific experiments. He studied their psychotic terrors dispassionately, seeking to find principles which might be of value elsewhere. Explicit concern with social injustice in psychoanalytic schools is, as far as I can see, still substantially absent in cognitive–behavioural approaches. I found no mention of such issues in several of the major textbooks in this field which I have researched.

The second ideological grandfather, Freud, is directly in line with most approaches to counselling and psychotherapy which call themselves psychoanalytic, psychodynamic or similar variants. His prototype approach to human distress also emerged from scientific neurological studies. But Freud found himself enmeshed in the hysterical vicissitudes of *fin-de-siècle* middle-class Vienna, in which sexual desire and repressed fantasy mingled with the horrors of child abuse and professional respectability in almost indistinguishable ways. He tried throughout his career to find and keep an idiom of scientific acceptability for psychoanalysis. Arguably he failed in this quest. Even today it is most likely that practitioners and students from this school may resist implementation of outcome research measures and tape-recording of their sessions. Often, they are vociferous in questioning the validity of other attempts to quantify what is essentially unquantifiable and unmeasurable, for example, by claiming that shorter, cheaper more effective 'cures' are 'just' symptom substitutions. This may be true. Notable exceptions are many of the so-called Humanistic psychotherapies which have, since Moreno first worked with children and prostitutes at the beginning of this century (Greenberg, 1975), been actively, explicitly and often constructively involved with social justice issues. Humanistic psychology can claim to have an excellent record of concern with values in this respect.

Is it perhaps also true that issues of respectability, status and economic concerns infect the regions devoted to the study of the forces of sex and death?

The third ideological grandfather is, of course, Moreno — the doctor of souls who wanted as an epitaph that he brought laughter back into psychiatry. Most of the existential humanistic approaches owe a debt of allegiance, origin or familial affinity with his conviction, his methods and his vision. These include existential, phenomenological, Gestalt, Transactional Analysis, Integrative Arts and many group therapy and other integrative approaches. Moreno at least made no pretence of being 'objective' or free of values. He stated and celebrated the telling and enactment of stories, the freedom of spontaneity, and the energy of playfulness as major values. Moreno (1953) also entitled a major work around a crucial ethical question: *Who Shall Survive?*

Perhaps Jaspers (1963) is a joint grandfather with Moreno. At approximately the same time he was describing human pain and madness phenomenologically — without psychiatric or psychoanalytic diagnosis — and significantly pairing interpretation with empathy. This theme was later picked up by Rogers (1951) and later still by Kohut (1959). Early on, Jaspers was signalling the cross-fertilisation of practitioners concerned about value as an unavoidable aspect of any psychotherapeutic encounter, whether willed or not; whether 'conscious or not' as being capable of being in what Sartre (1969) later called 'good or bad faith'.

Did this conscious approach to values change the realities of being human — the inevitable dual nature of our existence? No. Consider Perls, whose indiscriminate sexuality may have been a sign of his times, but a travesty of the doctor–patient relationship in terms of the timeless Hippocratic oath. Add to this the excesses of many of his followers who taught more by *insemination* than *dissemination*, and the adoption of 'encounter methods', by leaders of religious cults and business organisations which have traduced the original values and parcelled them in the most cost-effective, feelgood packages for easy consumption. These 'products' are often devoid of ultimate ethical concerns, empty of aesthetics, and suffering mutely from the loss of soul.

Of course I do not speak of all people in all approaches. However, I think we *all* stand in the shadow of the goodness of those from whom we inherit and pass on this complicated legacy in a similarly double-edged way. When we talk about values, no one approach has emerged as *better* than any other in alleviating human pain, providing for all who need help, keeping itself free from the corrosive discarded acid of the very chemicals with which it sought to cure. Is this failure an embarrassment or a liberation? An omen to throw it all away or an invocation to think and feel and question again for ourselves?

Psychology as Value-Free Science?

Interestingly enough, as psychology continues to seek a scientific logical positivistic objective kind of validation for itself as a science, science has moved well away from objectivist delusions, the hope for a constant reality, the simplistic modernist notions of the Enlightenment Project. Physics (once the stamping ground of Newton and the wellspring for Cartesian dualism) stands open-mouthed before its own progeny: asserting that one particle is in two places at the same time; that light is both a particle and a wave, two mutually exclusive entities, depending on how and when you look at it; that the cat in a cage filled with cyanide gas is dead or not, depending on the moment of opening; that the objective, impartial observer always interferes with the field; that there are currently eight different authoritative scientific versions of the nature of physical reality, all of them 'weird' to common science and positivism (Herbert, 1985); and that the places at the edges of imbalance, disorder and chaos are often the optimum conditions for healing, creativity and evolution on earth (see Gleick, 1988; Briggs & Peat, 1989; Zohar, 1990).

> The methodology that distinguishes modern psychological practice is explicitly designed to circumvent the potentially biasing influence of values. A large body of social psychological research has demonstrated a pronounced tendency for individuals to interpret and recall information as consistent with their social hypotheses (see Fiske & Taylor, 1987, for a review). Rosenthal's research on 'expectancy effects' has delineated the same tropism in social scientific investigation (1963; for a review of the confirmation bias, see Greenwald, Pratkanis, Leippe & Baumgardner, 1986). Because interests and values can taint the integrity of scientific exploration, they are justifiably controlled through methodological safeguards and professional attitudes. Nevertheless, despite the pretensions of modern psychology, no inquiry is devoid of valuational influence. Gouldner (1970) points out that Parsons' structural–functional theory of society legitimises the *status quo* because it implies that if one social institution falls,

the functional interdependence places the remainder in jeopardy. The organizational psychologist studying personnel selection implicitly endorses the capitalist venture and proliferates class distinctions between management and labor. Even in cognitive psychology, one of the most resolute bastions of experimental rigor in the sociobehavioral sciences, the ideology of American individualism shapes questions, forms methods and couches interpretations (Sampson, 1981). For the purposes of our analysis two points are salient: (a) no science, at least no social or Behavioral science, can proceed without some valuational influence; and (b) this influence typically goes either unnoticed or unmentioned. Here the early positivists' explicit value commitments provide a potential model for contemporary psychologists: valuational influences that are explicit can be better understood and evaluated than those left tacit. (Bailey & Eastman, 1994, p. 518).

At about this time we also have to cope with the thought that, despite the fundamentalist convictions of the different theoretical schools of counselling and psychotherapy, none of them has been found to be better than any of the others on most measures. The very proliferation of approaches (some 450 at last count) seems to spell out more a desperate search than a certain, solid rock. There is research indicating that theoretical orientation makes no difference to the effectiveness of outcome in counselling and psychotherapy, (Smith, Glass and Miller, 1980) that training makes no difference; a beginner may well be as effective, if not more so, than an experienced practitioner; even that personal psychotherapy makes no discernible difference to successful outcome! The fact that we can hold as firmly to our convictions of what 'works' in the face of all this scientific objective evidence, and continue to promote our version of this discipline, is a credit to our faith in the ineffable, the unsaid and the unproved — hardly a thorough scientific positivistic or rationalist basis from which to operate. The jury is out, but it seems as if neither the marketplace vendors nor their customers have heard the verdict yet.

A brochure for a respectable psychotherapy training organisation states that 'It is expected that the trainee will come to share the theoretical orientation of their training analyst'. Well, this is quite clear. The Humanistic and Integrative Section of the United Kingdom Council for Psychotherapy is also quite clear about the place of values in its combined approaches. An approach which specifically adheres to Buddhist values sits next to those of a more specifically Psychosynthesis persuasion in the Transpersonal grouping of schools in this section.

In contrast, most of the commonly available and read books on psychology, psychoanalysis and psychotherapy deal with the issues of values, social justice and ethical questions either by simply ignoring them (check the indexes of your favourite textbooks!) or by referring to agreed codes of ethics and professional practice — all of which are shot through with unanswered ethical dilemmas and profoundly serious questions to the profession (see Thompson, 1990).

However, even when we acknowledge the shaping and influencing role of values in the work of counselling and psychotherapy, probably the most frequently heard admonition (with which most training schools would agree) is the dictum: *'Do not impose your values on your clients or patients!'*. To do so is a grievous and probably unforgivable professional sin, leading to charges of exploitation, zealotry, missionary urges and the like. It is very unprofessional. Yet what else are we doing? And can we truly deny that we do so? It seems not so much a matter of *'Do not impose your values'* because you obviously do, (at least in implicit ways), but rather *'Be aware of what values you are indeed imposing and become conscious of this importation of the world of ethics and aesthetics, which you inevitably do when you engage in a healing encounter with any other human being'*.

Merleau-Ponty (1962) wrote of a social universe in which we participate and co-create each other.:

> Once the other is posited, once the other's gaze is fixed upon me has, by inserting me into his field, stripped me of part of my being, it will readily be understood that I can recover it only by establishing relations with him, by bringing about his clear recognition of me, and that my freedom requires the same freedom for others. (p. 357)

The Ubiquity of Values in Human Life

Scientific findings indicate that we hardly ever perceive any stimulus without experiencing it as better or worse, more or less beautiful, more or less important, more or less valuable than another. Just look at a sharp corner or a rounded one — which do you prefer? Perhaps you cannot say which, or why. To be human is to make value. This finding corresponds with our own common sense and everyday subjective experiences. Some kind of constantly changing selection according to criteria of value is clearly the only way in which the central nervous system switchboard can keep some kind of prioritising in process; especially given the bombardment of a multitude of competing demands for our perceptual and emotional attention. Whenever any one stimulus becomes figure, another inevitably becomes ground and is thus less important than the first one for a while.

Whenever my first psychoanalyst, safely ensconced behind me (out of my field of vision) made a note, I heard the scratching of his pencil on the paper and knew in that moment that my particular utterance had special value. I may well have been wrong, but I felt that I had just said something very important. Of course, I sought to replicate the stimulus which made him move. Many people have since told me similar stories from their own experiences. Clinical lore tells that Jungian patients have Jungian dreams, Freudian patients have Freudian dreams and Gestalt patients, Gestalt dreams.

The principles of operant conditioning explain how, when the Rogerian counsellor says *'Uhm'* after a particular expression of emotion but sits still during an intellectual exposition, it is more likely that the person will repeat the expression of emotion. So, the *'Uhm'* of the Rogerian counsellor, the interpretation or the shuffle of the psychoanalyst all give constant selective reinforcement to the patients in the position of supplicant. *'This is what makes him yawn; if I do this she goes to sleep; if I do this I can hear his breathing increase and his body animate with feeling — I can smell his fear'*, and so on. I can have these effects on my psychoanalyst or psychotherapist and in this process condition and be conditioned not too dissimilarly to rats who learn to stabilise certain learning best when intermittent reinforcement schedules are implemented. The occasional sympathetic 'hum' is more indicative (and more powerfully so for long-term learning) about how to be the client the psychotherapist wants than are regular and predictable 'pellets' of attention of movement or interest.

This is not really very strange. Who has not dreamt of the movie seen the previous night, the office dispute the previous day, the family problem upon which we were racking our imagination just before we went to sleep? Of course we are influenced by, and influence others, in the selective attention paid to some aspects of an interaction and not to others. And each one carries a statement of value, even if implicitly. Indeed, each statement carries a value charge more powerfully the more implicitly its value messages are hidden or embedded out of conscious awareness.

It seems that experimenter expectation apparently even influences the speed at which rats learn mazes (Feather, 1982); we know that children perform better academically if their teachers (even if falsely) believe them to be more intelligent (Rosenthal & Jacobson, 1968), we know the measurements of atoms are influenced by the presence of the physicist (Gribbin, 1984). Do we really think that in the close and intimate space of the therapeutic consulting room we can keep a value-hygienic environment which no-one has been able to successfully and repeatedly accomplish anywhere else in the universe?

At the very least each communication message in human interaction carries with its overt content a covert content — a meta-communication which is a statement about the relationship between sender and receiver or a message about the context in which the communicative message is being delivered (Satir, 1967). Apparently, 85% of the meaning of a communication is visual — the words alone count for a measly 15%. It is the context of the question, '*Where have you been?*' which makes it either friendly interest, a genuine enquiry or the restart of a long-smouldering marital fight. It is not the words of mother saying '*I love you*' which declare the emotional truth — it is the look in her eyes, the gentleness or roughness of her hands, the willingness to be attentive or neglectful when others and other things are calling that fundamentally conveys the value of the person enfolded in in the message.

Avowed and Enacted Values

Of course, there is a difference between *avowed* and *enacted* values. A true value is enacted as well as avowed (Severin, 1965). This is one of the biggest problems faced by schools of thought, psychotherapy or pastoral counselling which are willing and able to enunciate their values explicitly and which do not rely on their covert transmission. Fletcher (1966) explores this as situational ethics. Freud prescribed the importance of the analyst being a blank screen, yet shouted at his patients, lent them money, and gossiped to them about other patients. Melanie Klein treated her own children (how blank can you get?) and some Kleinians currently alive have been known to touch their patients, allow between-session phone calls, and participate in conferences where patients and analysts, supervisors and trainees engage in politically sensitive, ethically delicate and controversial decision-making meetings. How do you reconcile what you say with what you do? Do the discrepancies between your walk and your talk outweigh the congruencies? The explicit statement of values immediately (and necessarily) moves the ethical debate to another level of questioning. Not only are there values in here, but which are those values? And if these are they, how do they work in the everyday living, teaching and practice of this work?

In humanistic and existential psychotherapies there has always been an open and espoused position about the importance of values and their exploration in counselling and psychotherapy. A tradition which began with Moreno has continued through the radical psychiatry movement of the 1960s (ably assisted by many transactional analysts), to recent involvement with eastern European problems today by several members of the Gestalt, Group Analytic and Psychosynthesis communities in the UK. Gradually, there is an awakening to the issues of social responsibility, moral relevance and responsible engagement. Mostly this is tentative so as not to challenge the avowed legalistic (but perhaps spurious) supremacy of the *'Don't impose your values on your clients'* caveat.

A theoretical door from psychoanalysis opens when we consider the issues in terms of countertransference. Surely we bring to the analytic encounter our prejudices about men and women and what they each can achieve in our society? Our discrimination against the disabled, the black, the different? Of course these countertransferences are affecting the treatment, but how, if we do not own them as values ready to change or grow as all ethical systems do and continue to do over time and place?

The Communication of Values in Counselling, Psychoanalysis and Psychotherapy

Of course, you should not berate, preach and exploit clients to adopt your religious, political or psychotherapeutic beliefs. Of course, you do impose your values even when you try not to. And, to the extent that you are unaware of this, it is probably most dangerous. Saying it out loud may be fairer, because then a client may be in a better position to give informed consent to working with a counsellor who believes that a gay lifestyle will always show genital immaturity. Any helper models a certain way of dressing, of speaking — it is not too difficult to change an accent and intonation. This is the way of speaking you have valued above all others. You could pretend to be class-deaf or colourblind. You could deny or overly emphasise the difference in experience, you do not comment on it. When the client asks your position on homosexuality or mothers who give artificially assisted birth past their menopause you can speak or you can explore what these issues mean for the patient. Whatever you do you are complicit in supporting or suppressing values or value-clarification in yourself and your client. You may think you are truly neutral, your clients know you are not.

You either have or do not have certain pictures in your room. Your furniture proclaims a whole cultural world of values reverberating as strongly around the psyche of your client as the living rooms of their childhood (Rowan, 1988). Are there flowers there or is it a bland beige and brown space so as not to interrupt the transference? Is what will be 'counter-transferred' in terms of blandness, poverty, clinical white, what makes transference the higher value? Or is it like the consulting room of the person who first suggested this 'neutrality' — a riot of a fantasy space imbued with ruby-red and terracotta Persian carpets, lusciously shaped, sensual Egyptian figures and ancient evocations of the past in sculptures, pre-historic rocks, much-loved books, the traces of ongoing intellectual labour, and figurines which hark back and forward, above and below?

> After several months of fruitless endeavours to establish a mutually satisfactory supervisory relationship a supervisor asked the trainee (who was from Asia), *'Please tell me what the matter is — I know I may be doing something wrong for you to block your learning and growth — please tell me what it is.'* She replied shyly, saying that in their culture they would never criticise a teacher and now she was being asked to do so. This was already too difficult. After much more prevarication she said that it was the books. What about the books? *'The books in your office. They make me feel inferior. They make me feel stupid. I can't think with those books in your bookcase sitting there judging me.'* Another value confronted, another lesson learned, another adjustment to be made, another awareness to metabolise.

Of course we impose our values. But how? And which ones, when? Where do we learn to investigate this imposition, this teaching by example, this conversion through the adoption of the particular way of talking of the person in 'authority' (the person being paid)? Farrell (1979) pointed out some years ago (in a comparative study of different approaches to training groups and organisational systems) that a person is often declared as having 'insight' when they have adopted the 'WOT' (the *way of talking*) of the consultant. Is this very different from the way oppressed nations learn the language of the conqueror, but the ruling class rarely learns the language of the slaves, the victims or the blatantly needy of the vanquished country? Is this metaphor too strong or can we honestly say that a meta-narrative based on the white, male, capitalist, Eurocentric, able-bodied, heterosexual storyteller (author) of the history of our professions leaves a full, free voice for alternative narratives? For other stories equally possible, equally privileged, equally worth listening to and being silent for? And when we do not explicitly say this, what are we saying by our silence? A woman told me that when she told her first counsellor that she had attacked her husband, the therapist simply ignored it — not once, but several times. In this way we write our stories, give our lives meaning and the applause, catharsis or denial of the others define and rework these values. In the end, since being human is such a value-constituting enterprise the conduct of counselling or psychotherapy without meaning giving values is impossible.

That is inside the consulting room — but what about the profession as a whole in the outward-turned profile of its Janus head? Clinical psychology has been accused of 'ethical irrelevance'. Masson (1989) said that the non-abusive practice of counselling and psychotherapy is impossible. Hillman and Ventura (1992) charge the profession with interiority, narcissism, self-absorption; Olivier (1991) sees a falling between the stools of privatisation and professionalisation. Samuels (1993) called us to face the need for political development of the psyche and mature involvement in the affairs of *polis* and state. He reckons this is the work of analysts and counsellors. Fox (1983) exhorted us to look to our organismic oneness with the whole of the living planet — its plants, its stories and its rhythms of coming into being and dying, again and again. I have written and spoken (Clarkson, 1995b) about the incursion of 'defensive psychotherapy' (*How can I prevent being sued by my client or their family, challenged by my supervisor, criticised by my colleagues?*).

Legitimisation in this profession has moved from the hand-on-the-shoulder 'knighting' by founders or second-generation followers to legitimisations by groups of people — none of whom really own the responsibility for deciding who is in, who is out and who is in charge, but all of them guardians of standards and ethics — as long as these are their own. I take our profession to task in its commitment to, and complicity with bystanding in clients, colleagues, the profession and our culture as a whole. Bystanding is an active choice of non-involvement in a situation where someone else is in danger or being treated unjustly. The major bystanding rationalisation of counsellors and psychotherapists is their much-avowed putative scientific neutrality. Yet, neutrality always favours the aggressor — and can we not see it in the distribution of resources within our society? In the practice of our laws? In the genocide around us?

> Any resurrection of community values is bound to depend upon a shared morality. In contemporary society, no such shared morality exists. I know that this is an unpalatable opinion and I am saddened to have to state it so bluntly. The conventional view of today's Britain is that the overwhelming majority of its citizens agree about morality but for some mysterious reason they are prevented from getting what they want. We are told that nearly everybody has the same view of the crime of murder. Similarly there is a

shared opinion about the institution of marriage, the obligations owed to parents, the need to show uncomplaining fortitude and the importance of putting social duties ahead of personal gratification. Life would be simple if all of this were true, but one only has to look around to see that it is not (Walden, 1994).

In effect, members of any institution or organisation of psychologists or psychoanalysts internalise their proto-therapists simultaneously with a whole world view. However neutral the therapists feel, they are spreading a very specific message about the proper conduct of lives. Firstly, the therapist confirms there is a flaw deep within that explains one's feelings of alienation and also calls for a course of psychotherapy. Then the therapist, in conducting the therapy, presents the client with this prescription: analyse actions and fantasies; search for meanings instead of acting out impulsively; try to be in touch with feelings, or, if the problem is a tendency to be overwhelmed by feelings, always remember to think things through and be confident there will be no falling apart. Whatever the particular words therapists tailor for specific clients, the therapist's maxim is always to give the inner life a place of priority in one's conscious ruminations. Wisdom does flow from this way of thinking, and for many the message is quite compelling.

These conversations all rely on a universe of discourse where values can be articulated, explored, clarified (Smith, 1977). It is the task of counselling to do so whether these values are explicit (counselling in a pastoral setting (Catholic, Adventist or Buddhist)) or implicit (psychotherapy in a Brixton refuge for battered women or psychoanalysis in a middle-class home in a leafy North London suburb); whether these are the values we bring to the enterprise, the values the clients bring, or those the circumstances impose and with which we comply. Where the explication and exploration of these values are hedged, dodged or excused, they exist nonetheless — probably more virulent in neglect than in the careful monitoring of their pervasive potency for good or ill.

It is this duality of good and evil, the good and the bad, the Christian and the un-Christian, the ethical versus the unethical practice, which designate these discussions as predicated on a duality where the world is one and the soul another, a left hand and a right, shadow and light. And, in most human affairs these are the battles fought in the name of love, country, the flag, the cause, *'For England, Harry and St. George'*. It is in the name of such value divisions or disputes that entire tribes are wiped out. The names change, the story of brutality, starvation, torture, rape by one group or another in the name of a 'higher good' does not. In Miller's (1941) words:

> And as long as human beings can sit and watch with hands folded while their fellow-men are tortured and butchered so long will civilization be a hollow mockery, a wordy phantom suspended like a mirage above a swelling sea of murdered carcasses. (p. 177)

This applies to the 'helping' professionals as well. Psychology, psychoanalysis, even psychotherapy and counselling have attempted to become sciences, modelling the discipline on that of old-style physics since Freud's Newtonian dualistic division into the conscious and the unconscious realms of the mind, the blind positivistic dedication of clinical psychology and the desperate devotion to neutrality, impartiality and objectivity which are still held as ideals in much of psychology teaching at university and much of psychoanalytic and psychotherapy training outside in the practice of the professions.

> With the death of God, proclaimed by Nietzsche at the turn of the century, man came to be the measure of all things, and psychology became the secularized religion of modernity. In modernity the loss of belief in an absolute God had been succeeded by the modernist declaration of faith: 'I believe in one objective reality'. Religion as a truth guarantee was replaced by the new sciences, the priests as truth mediators were substituted by the scientists (Kvale, 1992, pp. 53–54)

> We will have to come to terms, as we stagger into the postmodern era, with the hard-to-avoid evidence that there are many different realities, and different ways of experiencing them, and that people seem to want to keep exploring them, and that there is only a limited amount any society can do to insure that its official reality is installed in the minds of most of its citizens most of the time. (Anderson, 1990, p. 152)

I think that psychoanalysis, psychotherapy and counselling psychology have much to learn from post-modernism, chaos and complexity theory and quantum physics. All of these disciplines implicate the individual as indivisible from their context, and the responsibility as shared co-creation and an alternative to dualistic, linear, causal, Newtonian–Cartesian epistemologies and moralities. Trainings which privilege enquiry more than dogma, critical analysis more than compliance and responsibility more than a collectively agreed consensus are rare and risky. In the Dieratao (Learning by Enquiry) programme at **PHYSIS** we are conducting experiments in the education of psychotherapists, counselling psychologists, organisational psychologists and supervisors who will predicate their work on the new paradigms — even whilst continuing to include the old modernist paradigms — to reach for a richly articulated intellectual, professional and moral endeavour (Clarkson, 1995h).

Somehow I Did Persist!

Looking back on it now, it doesn't seem like such a big deal, but at the time it was. I'm 30 years old, manic depressive, and sometimes I get crazy. Not just manic acting, but very fast inside, too. Like I can't think straight because my brain speeds up and too much is going on all at once.

At first it feels sort of good — I have lots of energy, I don't need much sleep, and I feel like I can do most things more easily. It's like a natural high. But then it gets to be too much, too fast and if I don't get some help, then it all snowballs and I end up in the hospital. Sometimes I haven't gotten into the hospital until after quite a while of being very crazy on the streets.

I'm very responsible about taking Lithium when I'm not manic — but when I start getting manic, I honestly don't know what I do. Perhaps sometimes I forget to take it, or sometimes I take extra. Time just gets different for me then, and it's hard to keep track of even simple things.

I haven't been able to figure out yet why I break through and get manic sometimes even when I'm taking my meds regularly. And the doctors don't seem to be able to figure it out either.

When I'm manic, I don't think anyone else knows anything, I don't want any advice, and I don't think anyone is trying to help me, even if they are. When I start to get manic it feels so great that I just like to be that way for a while. And like I said, sometimes then I start to feel like other people are just interfering in my life and I get annoyed even with the people who I usually know have my best interests at heart. It doesn't feel to me like help at that point, it feels bothersome, and I just want them to go away and leave me alone to run my own life. And I tell them that.

I've been dealing with this condition since I was 19 — I'm 30 now — and I've learned a lot about myself. I can tell you now when I start to go up — there are signs, if I can let myself notice them. It's hard, like I said, because it feels so good to have lots of energy again. But when I start sleeping less, that's an early sign, and so is the feeling that my brain is speeding up. But that's hard to notice sometimes, because at first I just think I'm having an especially good day. And another and another ...

Well, this last time when I started to get manic, I did something different. I hadn't been sleeping, and I was speeding up inside fast. I was getting very short tempered with people around me. And I realized that I needed to get some attention, and I needed it fast. Sirens in my head. Well, I called my Doc for an appointment, and the receptionist said, 'Next week'.

I just hung up, mad, because I needed it sooner than that, and somehow I didn't have the patience right then to explain to her.

Now other times when this has happened, I've just gone off and been mad. Let myself feel that no one wants to help me, and then pretty soon I'm thinking that no one *can* help me, and then I get farther into the manic and think I don't *need* any help.

But this time I didn't do that. Somehow I did persist — and I realized that I didn't have much time. It was an emergency for me. More sirens in my head. I realize now, looking back, that I was already thinking skewed — I never even considered going to my social worker. But never mind — I did what I needed to do as I saw it then.

So I went to my Dad's office and he was out just then. He was in town, and that was lucky — because he travels a lot. So, I just paced around in his office, and waited until he came back. I told him I needed to be in the hospital and he seemed to agree because he made some phone calls and got it arranged for me. I guess it was simple for him — but it didn't seem simple to me at the time, it seemed an hour, and I couldn't stay on one thought for more than a short time.

As it turned out, I *was* right, I did need to be in the hospital — and it took a while to get back in balance again. Looking back, I feel like I made a good decision, to decide that I knew what I needed, instead of waiting until I got so crazy-acting on the streets that the cops would take me in. Now I think I'll probably be able to take care of myself just as well the next time — and maybe sometime there will be a way to cure manic-depression. I sure hope so, and I hope it's soon.

Dave R. West as told to [Peg West], June 1988 (West, 1991, pp. 62–63)

Chapter 9
Beyond Bystanding

If I am not for myself, who will be for me?
If I am for myself only, what am I?
If not now — when? (Talmudic Saying, Mishnah, Abot)

In this book, we have remembered or disagreed or imagined how and why people bystand when they are aware that others are being abused, tortured, excluded. We have considered the changing requirements of history, the characteristics of our time. We have incorporated the archetypal dramatic narrative structure of the human story — its roots in ancient sacrificial rituals, its contemporary form in the soap opera. We have made some catalogue of the rationalisations — the justifications that people make to explain or excuse their bystanding. We have respected the infinite diversity and complexity of human motivation, the ineradicable difficulties of judging or understanding another being's inner world of meaning. We know that no amount of empathy or insight into another's dynamics can make the starved corpses disappear, bring a battered and broken child back to life, restore trust to those who have been spiritually violated in the name of Love. These are works of different levels, different kinds of responses, coming from different worlds of human experience.

> [The] quest then is not for solutions to issues of good and evil, but rather for increased problematization. To solve problems of good and evil in any instance is to freeze meaning at a given point and thus to silence voices and segment the social world ... To the extent that the dialogue continues and constructions remain open, local meanings may ramify and people may come to share or absorb each other's modes of life. In this outcome lies perhaps the greatest hope for achieving human well-being. (Gergen, 1994, p. 114)

And relationship. We have ranged far and wide, but neither far nor wide enough, over the issues, themes and concerns that impinge upon the human phenomenon of bystanding or the denial of our relational similarity and connectedness with others. We have hardly touched on the heart of human relationship. In some ways I am very sorry that I have not been able to find true, lasting and generic answers to the moral and ethical implications of bystanding in our personal and professional lives. But then Jung (1983), too, felt the complexity *and* the imperative:

> The meaning of my existence is that life has addressed a question to me. Or, conversely, I myself am a question which is addressed to the world, and I must communicate my answer, for otherwise I am dependent upon the world's answer. (p. 350)

In different ways I know that many others whom I cherish, respect and admire have grappled even more intensively with these issues, achieving but similar outcomes. How are we to act then? I do not really know, neither am I infused with trust for those who claim to know for sure. I notice that *being human* is more adequately honoured when its complexity is acknowledged and the many exceptions nuance the easy answers and the clear-cut simple solutions which are trotted out by the 'majorities'. I have but small ambitions now. I would want a person to feel and to think and to ask questions and to choose their actions rather than respond with knee-jerk reflexes essentially borrowed from others, whether those in the past or those currently in power.

It appears to me at the moment that binary systems are rarely sufficient, neither are dialectic integrations. Yet sometimes something is simply right or absolutely wrong in this moment. It is clear that what is taken for granted as a truth of today about exactly what is right and wrong may be different tomorrow or in different circumstances. Historical, social, geographic, economic or philosophical changes often bring turnabouts which then appear as self-evident to us as their opposites were before. I hope I have succeeded in making it clear that I am pleading for engagement, for dialogue, for relationship, for interaction and intercourse, for proximity and involvement, for responsiveness and responsibility, for a kind of honesty in facing the choices we make when we turn away, refuse, reject and pretend. *I am pleading for the recognition that we are already in relationship.* After research enquiry in the form of writing (Richardson, 1994), I now believe even more that it is an organismic denial to hold that the pain, distress or confusion of another human being in my vicinity 'has nothing to do with me' or 'does not fall within my brief'.

Despair, nihilism, and abdication of our responsibility seem less fashionable now than they were in the 1960s and less of an answer to our world condition now. For many people our world seems to be teetering on the brink of either physical self-destruction, immolation of the world soul — the *anima mundi* — or a blinding and terminal moral malaise. 'But if we are in as bad a state as I take us to be, pessimism too will turn out to be one more cultural luxury that we shall have to dispense with in order to survive in these hard times.' (Macintyre, 1985, p. 5). For others a new dawn is beckoning. The complexity of ethical and moral problems which we face at this time demands a complex range of responses devoid of a putative inno- cence — a calibration of sensitivity and sense which attempts to account for at least our *physiological, emotional, linguistic, socio-cultural, rational, theoretical/ metaphorical and transpersonal* dimensions of experi- ence and knowledge. These are seven designated universes of discourse, planetary orbits of conversation which can help to plot the paths of certain excursions into the unknown. Their pluralistic juxta- position is intended to refract the problem of bystanding through multiple lenses in order to enrich our understandings of it and to increase our possibilities for committed action.

Of course there are other grappling hooks. The model which follows has been valued enough for me to be encouraged to offer it here. It has evolutionary implications in that:

> A document of our past bifurcations appears in our embryos as we pass through stages where we resemble fish, then amphibians and reptiles. Enfolded in all the shapes and processes that make us unique — in the chemical reactions of our cells and the shape of our nerve nets — are thou- sands upon thousands of bifurcation points constituting a living chronology of the choices by which we evolved as a system from the primordial single cell to our present form. (Briggs & Peat, 1989, p. 144)

Or in other more famous words: ontogeny recapitulates phylogeny. But the whole is encoded in each part, even the tiniest, earliest part. This does not mean that the earlier levels are less important or less evolved. Only that they may be manifest earlier, even as they are all equally present from the beginning. It should be noted that this is somewhat different from Kohlberg's (1964) sequen- tial, hierarchical and developmentally based stages of moral development and closer to that of Gilligan (1982), but not at all the same. It could be implicit in the work of Stern (1985).

The seven levels mentioned are part of an epistemological model of ordering the complexities of psychological knowledge, experience and practice. They can also be seen as identified layers of value. This model is thus not meant to close the conversation, but to begin it. It is meant to provide another tool for the clarification of values, not for the termination of the meeting. These are seven conceptualised universes of human discourse, experience and behaviour which together are seen as constituting a pluralistic perspective on the person as a whole, yet forgoing the temptation to unify the responses in a false synthesis. For example, a client is in general support of abortion until she relives in her own therapy the full force of the terror and pain she experienced as a foetus when her mother tried to abort her. Then she knew viscerally that it is indeed murder, not termination. Yet she would support 'therapeutic abortion' in the case of, for example, a Bosnian woman who was pregnant as a result of rape. The facts are comparatively simple. They are accessible to measurement, to a scan, to the technical and medical experience — about which there is little dispute. How long since the foetus was conceived? What is its heart rate? What is the structure of its DNA? In how many ways can one kill it?

Yet, at another level, stories and explanations exist for this act which, by their very telling, their rhetoric, their images, can devalue or valorise the event of an abortion into a transformative elegy of grief and regret, or into a doctoral treatise on the sociological importance of 'a woman's right to choose'. And at a transcendental level? Who knows why or how a soul comes and goes, and by whose hand it comes into being or is snatched away?

This attempt is an illustration of an attempt to hold multiple levels in consciousness at the same time on one particular issue. Sometimes no reconciliation is possible. Sometimes what is required is living with unbearable contradiction. Sometimes binary simplification procedures just fail. The animal self, the emotional self, the self of *Logos* — the speech-maker — the cultural self (the one belonging to a group) are reasonable, logical, a secondary-process self, a myth-making self — the teller of theories, the maker of dreams. These, with the Self which surpasses all understanding, coexist, equally demanding of our attention, our validation and our action.

Our experiences are often contradictory, mutually opposing and mostly drawing energy from irrational wellsprings of our personal and collective being, as we have seen in the foregoing explorations of the bystander phenomenon. The seven levels discussed here also may be used as foci for psychotherapeutic theory, strategy or interventions. This is one of many maps found useful for the conceptualising and organising of levels of attention in psychotherapy or human experience. All psychotherapists, whatever their approach, probably develop maps or organising frameworks such as these as they develop and refine their own individual models of thinking about and practising psychotherapy.

I developed the seven level model some 21 years ago as an attempt to construct a thinking tool or organising matrix (or conceptual protractor) for myself and my psychology students. My aim was to provide a meaningful reference framework which could help us to deal more manageably with the explosion of knowledge and the resounding increase in the complexity of experience and psychological, philosophical and epistemological worlds which are bombarding us (Clarkson, 1992b). It has been used elsewhere to offer the means to obtain an *holistic view of the patient as a person* in most aspects of human functioning, *as well as a comprehensive, pluralistic view of psychotherapy* with its multiplicity of emphases and applications to the person in the wider context of their existence. Here, holistic does not mean a peaceful and harmonious integration. It is more a co-existence making space for all the paradoxes, contradictions and ironies of human life.

This model has substantial application to the areas which we have been considering in this book. Time after time, it seems important to acknowledge the co-existence of multiple levels of reality and multiple levels of understanding (Clarkson, 1995e). What is often 'true' at one level, can be experienced as 'untrue' at another. At a physiological level (Level 1) taking an EEG of the brain will indicate that certain odour sensations have been registered in the cortex, whereas the person may have no response at an emotional level (Level 2), lack words to describe the sensation (Level 3, the nominative) or even have a culturally conditioned bias to devalue by ignoring certain kinds of smell sensations (Level 4, the normative). Yet, consensual validity at Level 5 (the rational) shows up without argument on the technological machinery. How we explain such things, in theories of psychophysiological contaminants of olfaction, in the poetry of legendary fragrances ('the prayers of saints in golden vials of revelation') or in the role of 'experimenter' effects, will depend on a multitude of factors and an which criteria we use for such 'theoretical' or 'poetic' explanations — beauty, elegance or Occam's razor. And, at another level, the discussion is superfluous and unnecessary.

These separations of epistemological domains can be useful in exploring and conceptualising ethical and moral questions and differentiating the many demands for responsible action. All seven levels are seen as co-existing but, so to speak, different 'truth values' apply to the different levels. A binary or dualistic Aristotelian form of deciding 'truth' is merely one aspect of a whole spectrum in which my intuition of impending danger is as real and true at one level as the conviction that autonomy and freedom are good for people is at another.

This seven level model is not in the mode of the 'grand narratives of the past' (Lyotard, 1984). It does not set out to be a meta-theory that will include and surpass all that has gone before, nor does it seek to obliterate conflict and difference. Rather, it seeks to provide a frame of reference with which to scan one's present situation, whether theoretical or clinical, and to sharpen one's perception of the balance of figure and ground across the many varied areas of interaction.

In particular, the seven level model can help to clarify confusions about the boundaries between the various levels. In this sense the model functions on Level 3, as a notative tool useful to address some of the following issues.

Level confusion

A form of category confusion indicating a wrong identification of levels, for example, when a statement that expresses a group norm is taken to be a rational definition of fact. Imprecise language use supports many level confusions. This will occur when one or more categories are confused or conflated in unhelpful ways. To mention only a few examples:

> When *'I think'* is used for Levels 1 or 7.
> When *'It is'* is used for Levels 2, 3, 4, 5 or 6.
> When *'I feel'* is used for Levels 1, 3 or 7.

It may mean something as obvious (and unfortunately ordinary) as *'I don't like them, therefore they should be excluded from our group, our crowd, our training programme, our party'* (Wolf, 1994, p. 183). Level 1 is *'I physically don't like them because I feel stupid and small when next to them'*, and Level 4 is *'... therefore they are bad'*. Other examples concern the conflation of Level 4, *'I believe that human life is valuable and should be preserved'*, with the language games and the conceptual universes of all the

different stories at Level 6. That is, the normative or consensually
'agreed to be good' is not clearly separate from the fact that this is
one of many narratives, any or all of which may have ultimate
explanatory value.

Level contamination

When the functioning of one level is impaired by the controlling
influence of another level. For example, during an infant's toilet
training a sense of guilt and shame may be encouraged in order to
reinforce anal sphincter control. The integrity of the bodily function
at Level 1 is thus interrupted by an excessive and unnecessary influence from another level — the normative spectrum of Level 4.

Conflict

This exists when one or more levels are in opposition and, in fact,
they usually are. The seven level model can be useful in identifying
which particular facets of a person's experience are in conflict. This,
of course, can only happen once the different levels of experience
have been clarified. Many dramas (in life as in the theatre) are
concerned with the embattlement of one or more of these levels
against another. For example:

> The traditional definition of sanity and mental health involves as a funda-
> mental postulate a perceptual, emotional and cognitive congruence with
> the Newtonian–Cartesian image of the world, which is seen not only as an
> important pragmatic framework of reference, but also as the only accurate
> description of reality. More specifically, this means experiential identifica-
> tion with one's physical space and irreversible linear time as objective and
> mandatory coordinates of existence, and the limitation of one's sources of
> information to sensory channels and records in the material substrata of the
> central nervous system. (Grof, 1985, p. 396)

Knowledge or wisdom derived from different models is often in
conflict with Level 5 Newtonian–Cartesian models. There are different styles of bystanding and working with bystanding.

Cross-level Displacement

This occurs when a condition pertaining to one level cannot find
expression on that level and manifests on another level in symbolic
form, perhaps as a symptom. Movements of libido through sublima-
tion, compensation, etc., could be understood in this way.

The model also provides a warp on which to weave the many strands of clinical praxis, a method of structuring and analysis which supports the therapist in responding creatively to the needs of the client. It places attention to phenomenological precision over theoretical correctness and thus allows one to think more clearly about and work with material that does not fit into any particular theoretical model. Thus, it supports an approach which is open, self-critical and explanatory rather than closed, self-justificatory and deterministic. Its use lies in supporting inquiry, not in confirming hypotheses.

The Degree of Permeability

The degree of permeability between the different levels changes over time. In the language of Gestalt there is a contract boundary between each level, with the same interruptions to contact that are found in interpersonal interaction. The needs of one level cannot be truly satisfied by direct action on another level. Although there is a systemic spread of satisfaction and dissatisfaction across levels, level-specific needs require satisfaction on their own level. The different psychotherapy models have their own preferred entry points into the seven levels. Every level can be seen as having its own procedures which are level-specific and appropriate, but when they are contacted and changed by level-specific interventions the total systemic field of the individual is always influenced in the same way as the alteration of any part will always affect the whole system.

At no point is it conceived that one level is necessarily higher or better than another. It is thought that the healthy human being will be functioning well on all levels simultaneously, with the biological at least as significant as any other. It is postulated that these 'universes' of discourse are frequently confused in the theory and in the practice of psychotherapy, leading to category errors, apparently irreconcilable differences, and spurious contradictions, some of which have been mentioned above.

As pointed out before, it is unlikely that the concept or problem of bystanding is one that is morally soluble along the tracks of enquiry normal to modern reasoning. The seven level model is used here not with the intention of effecting such a moral reduction but in order to help clarify the various categories of complexity and moral decision-making. When making decisions about issues or situations where the diversity of the problem has to some extent been realised, it is necessary to have some kind of map or bearing if we are to avoid bewilderment and inaction.

The model is epistemological in the sense that it implies different analytical techniques which define boundaries for the processes of knowing (Bateson, 1979). However, by the ordering of knowledge (and ways of obtaining knowledge from the world in this way), different kinds of 'language games' (Wittgenstein, 1967; Lyotard, 1984) played in these different universes of discourse can begin to be differentiated and evaluated.

The seven level model is concerned with knowledge in two major ways. Firstly, it can be used to differentiate how we obtain knowledge about the world by use of different levels of conceptualisation, different universes of discourse and different criteria for establishing validity, sense or 'truth' (epistemology in a philosophical sense). It is epistemological for the psychotherapist or psychoanalyst in the sense that people can sort their experiences in these different categories. Psychotherapeutic areas of knowledge, theories and procedures can also be discriminated by this means and therefore it can be useful to guide the choice of concretely specific operations. Here, the model is used to consider the issues of bystanding in summarising and concluding our explorations.

The seven level model is naturally a map, not a territory — a grid that can assist the psychotherapist practising in complex territory created in the face-to-face encounter of psychotherapist and client, and the life experiences brought by each into the psychotherapeutic arena, and help each of them to respond to life's demands for involvement, complicity and responsibility. It is important to emphasise that it is a sorting device, or a kind of protractor, to be used as a guide and measure of thoughtfulness rather than as a directive to dictate the right answers. It separates universes of discourse in a way which can retain respect for all, acknowledging the reality of the co-existence of many of our spheres of being and doing in the world. It will probably never remove the imperative to act, but it may make our actions more profound.

Since readers may not be familiar with it, a summarised explanation will be woven into the following discussion. To reiterate, at no point is it intended to have it conceived that one level is necessarily higher or better than another. It is thought that the healthy human being will be functioning well on *all levels* simultaneously, with the biological at least as significant as any other. It is living life on all tracks or in stereo which is represented, not the elevation of any one domain above all others. There is no one privileged discourse — theories all have their own kind of truth, all of which co-exist anyway whether we want this or not. It is postulated that these 'universes' of discourse are frequently confused in the theory and in the practice of ethical investigations, value exploration and psychotherapy and lead to category errors, apparently irreconcilable difference and spurious contradictions. Such differences, of course, are also the root causes of war.

The Seven Level Model

The seven levels are currently identified as: (1) Physiological, (2) Emotional, (3) Nominative, (4) Normative, (5) Rational, (6) Theoretical and (7) Transpersonal. Under each heading below follows a brief, and by no means exhaustive, synopsis of possible aspects of experience and the psychotherapeutic approaches which may be emphasised at each level.

Level 1, the Physiological

This concerns the person as an 'amoeba' or 'body' with biological, physical, visceral and sensational experience, temperament, body type and predispositions. It concerns body processes, psychophysiology, sleep, food, physical symptoms of disease, the physical manifestation of anxiety and general sensory awareness. It provides a rough container for all ideas which concern the human being as of the same substance as plants, of the same vibrational field as crystals, of the same substance as the living material which constitutes the living organisms of our world.

When discussing bystanding, this is the level of our organismic involvement with the rest of the biological, organismic universe at a cellular level. It has apparently recently been discovered (!) that the foetus feels pain when it is aborted. New evidence now leads doctors to think of anaesthetising the foetus during abortion. Our sense of outrage and participation when hearing this information is sufficient evidence that we are connected (that we can and perhaps should 'feel with') at a viscerally empathic level. This is the sense in which we are part of the rivers which the factories pollute; we breathe the air which our cars foul, and we share in the distress and despair of all the animals, human and otherwise, who are in pain and fear as part of the living organismic whole which is our world — our Gaia.

Jan Smuts was the South African philosopher-general who was an originator of the League of Nations, which became the United Nations. His ideas were the dominant, and perhaps one of the only philosophical and intellectually interesting cultural influences in

Level 1 **The Physiological**, concerns the person as an 'amoeba' or 'body' with biological, physical, visceral and sensational experience, temperament, body type and predispositions. It concerns body processes, psychophysiology, natural sleep rhythms, food, physical symptoms of disease, the physical manifestation of anxiety and general sensory awareness, proprioception, 'first nature'. Physiological processes may be 'measured' in some instances such as brain waves patterns on EEG but it is probably impossible to ever know a physiological level whether another person's sensation of the colour red is similar to or different from one's own.

Level 2 **The Emotional**, concerns the person as 'mammal'. It is essentially a pre-verbal area of experience and activity. It concerns those psychophysiological states of electrochemical muscular changes in our bodies we talk about as feelings, affect and/or emotion in psychology. Emotions are essentially subjective, experiental and felt states. Our knowledge concerning emotions seems to be essentially existential, phenomenological and unique.

Level 3 **The Nominative**, concerns the person as 'primate'. Under this heading are included the awareness and labelling of experiences and the validation of experience through naming. It represents the verbal part of communication. Since at least the earliest biblical times, people have known that the 'giving of names' develops dominion', ownership and the feeling of mastery over the existential world and the transformation of human experience. There can be some agreement or disagreement within groups, with dialect or language or disciplinary groups for example about 'what things are called'. Within any common set of language rules the fact that certain kinds of words are known to stand for certain kinds of objects can be agreed, debated or disputed.

Level 4 **The Normative**, concerns the person as social animal. It refers to norms, values, collective belief systems and societal expectations. This level tends to deal with facts, knowledge of attributes and practices regarding people as 'cultural beings' – the tribe, the group, the community, the church, the political party, and the organisation. Values, morals, ethics are not always subject to logical tests of truth or statistical rationality – it is a different realm of questioning or knowing.

Level 5 **The Rational**, concerns 'Homo Sapiens' – the person as a thinker. This layer of knowledge and activity includes thinking, making sense of things, examination of cause and effect, frames of reference, working with facts and information of the time and place. It covers science, logic, statistical probabilities, provable facts, established 'truth' statements and consensually observable phenomena. It is characteristic of level 5 discourse that it is possible to establish truth values.

Level 6 **The Theoretical**, throws into relief a 'storyteller' – as a meaning-maker, making sense of human experience through symbolism, story and metaphor. This is based on the notion of theoretical plurality and relativity. Theories can be seen as 'narratives'– stories that people tell themselves – interesting, exciting, depressing, controlling, useful and relative, but no one forever true. 'Theories' are in a different logical category from that of facts. Both in psychological theory and individual experience, it is important to separate these where possible. The hypotheses, explanations, metaphors and stories that humans have created in order to explain or test why things are as they are and why people behave as they do are included at this level. Theories e.g. can be more or less elegant, economical, valid, reliable, explanatory or practical. If a theory becomes fact it enters into the non-disputable level 5 area.

Level 7 **The Transpersonal**, refers to the epistemological area or universe of discourse concerned with people as, for example, 'spiritual beings' or with the world of soul. Beyond rationality, facts and even theories are the prescient regions of dreams, 'direct knowing', altered states of ecstatic consciousness, the spiritual, the metaphysical, 'quantum chaos', the mystical, the essentially paradoxical, the unpredictable and the inexplicable.

Figure 2 Characteristics of the Sevel Levels of Epistemological universes of discourse. Version of table taken from: Clarkson, (1995a).

South Africa. As he (Smuts, 1987) said:

> This is a universe of whole-making, not merely of soul-making, which is only its climax phase. The universe is not a pure transparency of Reason or Spirit. It contains unreason and contradiction, it contains error and evil, sin and suffering. There are grades and gaps, there are clashes and disharmonies between the grades. It is not the embodiment of some simple homogeneous human Ideal. It is profoundly complex and replete with unsearchable diversity and variety. It is the expression of a creative process which is for ever revealing new riches and supplying new unpredictable surprises. But the creative process is not, on that account, issuing in chaos and hopeless irreconcilable conflict. It is for ever mitigating the conflict through a higher system of controls. It is for ever evolving new and higher wholes as the organs of a greater harmony. Through the steadily rising series of wholes it is producing ever more highly organised centres whose inner freedom and creative metabolism transform the fetters of fate and the contingencies of circumstance into the freedom and harmony of a more profoundly co-operative universe. But though the crest of the spiritual wave is no doubt steadily rising, the ocean which supports it contains much more besides the Spirit. Enough for us to know that the lower is not in hopeless enmity to the higher, but its basis and support, a feeder to it, a source whence it mysteriously draws its creative strength for further effort, and hence the necessary precondition for all further advance. (pp. 337–338)

Level 2, the Emotional

This level concerns the person as 'mammal'. It is essentially a preverbal area of experience and activity and concerns affect, feeling and emotion in psychology. The theoretical and experiential foci here are bonding, attachment, nursing, and deprivation, not only in a physical but also in a cyclical sense (Bowlby, 1953; Winnicott, 1960; Rutter, 1972). At this level are included the experiencing and expression of affect over and above physiological presence; the animal's or person's fear, anger, sadness, joy, rage and despair. 'Resonance' phenomena and hypnotic induction procedures would probably be emphasised at this level of experience. We are close to our animal cousins here. The dog feels something which could be sympathy and concern when there is a marital fight or someone is grieving; one whale supports another when they are stranded and in danger of dying. In ethical and moral issues, this sense of emotional connectedness with the rest of humanity, if unimpaired, binds us through empathy with our fellows and can prevent us from inflicting pain because of our emotional capacity to imagine what that would feel like. It is only when relationship is denied and kindness is refused; when the kidnapper places a paper bag over his prisoner's head;

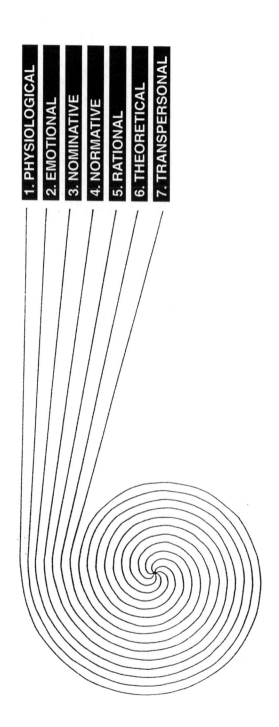

Figure 3 The seven level model (Clarkson, 1975; Dryden, 1992). (Reproduced with permission from the Open University Press.)

when the Argentinian Jew is dehumanised by shaving and cursing; when 10 million women are called witches, that they can be beaten, broken and have rats forced up the cavities of their bodies. And this brings us to the role of language.

Level 3, the Nominative

This concerns the person as 'primate', as animal which can speak. Under this heading are included the awareness and labelling of experiences and the validation of experience through naming.

Since at least the earliest biblical times people have known that the 'giving of names' develops 'dominion', ownership and the feeling of mastery over the existential world and the transformation of human experience. The naming of events, people, political parties, feelings and sensations, are relevant to this level. Whether the name of the Korean leader is 'Our Great Leader' or the 'world's worst dictator'; whether the IRA are freedom fighters or terrorists; whether armies are said to liberate or to occupy; whether individuals are partisans or traitors; whether Philby or a great train robber was a cult hero or a coward and a crook, this is the endlessly complicated world of manipulation by intentional propaganda or unintentional collusion with an advertising culture (perhaps equally effective in achieving compliance). The archetypal novel of this domain is perhaps *1984* by Orwell, wherein the plasticity of reality in the face of what things are called, and who defines it, is laid bare.

The naming and labelling of experience according to philosophical orientation would also come under this heading. As Williams (1992) describes:

'When you shot at someone you didn't think you were shooting at a human. They were a Gook or a Commie and it was okay.' (Vietnam Veteran, *Amnesty International Report on Torture*, 1973)

This dehumanisation is an aspect of another strategy: the creation of in-groups and out-groups. Tajfel (1981) has demonstrated that the minimal conditions for the development of in-group bias and out-group prejudice may be as insignificant as a preference for the paintings of Klee over those of Kandinsky. In fact, these distinctions are established even when subjects are told that allocation to groups will be random.

For the torturer, the training fosters in-group bias: Gerard and Mathewson (1966) have demonstrated that having to undergo strenuous initiation rites makes group membership more desirable. Torturers are encouraged to see themselves as an élite group, and the strength of their identification with this group may result in what Zimbardo terms de-individuation: that is, they cease to think and act as individuals, but instead are carried along by the group will. (p. 307)

Level 4, the Normative

Level 4 consequently concerns the person as social animal or archetypal member of the primal tribe. It refers to group norms, shared values, collective belief systems, societal expectations which are held in common by the herd, the group, the family, the nation, the professional society, the collective. All discussions which deal in important ways with norms and values handed down by tradition, inculcated by teaching, holy books (whether the *Koran* or *The Interpretation of Dreams*) or convention, belong in this domain. The Values Clarification movement (Simon, Howe & Kirschenbaum, 1972) also provided major contributions to psychological thinking and intervention at the normative level. This level attends to the relation between the individual and the group, and how culture is built and value ecologies are maintained.

Shaw (1991) alludes to it quite clearly in *Caesar and Cleopatra*: 'Pardon him Theodotus: he is a barbarian, and thinks that the customs of his tribe and island are the laws of nature' (pp. 209–210). As we saw in Chapter 8, the tribes and churches or psychoanalysis and psychotherapy are not always that different. Level 4 usually concerns dualities of good and evil, of good and bad, the Christian and the infidel, the kosher and the non-kosher, where the world is one, the soul another, a left hand and a right, a chosen people and a fallen one, shadow and light. And in most human affairs, these are the battles fought in the name of love, the country, the flag, the cause. It is in the name of such value divisions of disputes that entire tribes are wiped out. The names change, the story of brutality, starvation, torture, rape by one majority group in the name of a higher good, does not. It is essentially the psychology of the group, the culture, the consensus, the majority, the establishment, the profession:

> We resisted Rieff's contention that psychotherapy is a form of secularised moral proselytizing. We argued that, rather than espousing any particular set of substantive values, psychotherapy tries to expose the psychological mechanisms which underlie different moral alternatives, and so help the patient to choose between them. In this it is congruent with the liberal conception of individuality. Liberals place great value on individual choice and autonomy. Believing in the worth of autonomy is itself espousing a

value. However, liberals are opposed to forcing particular conceptions of a good life on people. Thus psychotherapy and liberalism do have a moral viewpoint — that individuals should be free to make their own choices, at least to the extent that this does not harm other people's chances of doing the same. This may put psychotherapists in the ethically dubious position of forcibly telling their patients to 'be autonomous', or of imposing what they see to be their own truth on to patients. (Holmes & Lindley, 1989, p. 136)

Both statistical and cultural norms are included at this level. It refers to the measurements by which we assess some of the 'oughts' of our belief-systems, how to do things, what things mean in our culture, what is the 'usual' and what the 'unusual'. What exceptions can be tolerated and which should be punished, who belongs and what they have to do to belong to 'people like us' and what we would do to them when they do not. It provides a category for looking at norms in terms of their appropriateness, usefulness and application in specific circumstances. Although acceptance of some norms may be useful in certain circumstances, psychotherapies differ in how much they emphasise aims such as autonomy, integration, growth, responsibility, awareness and self-actualisation. These can challenge and transcend many cultural and societal 'norms'. These are, of course, the very norms that enshrine who belongs and who does not: the oppression of blacks, of women, of homosexuals, of the disabled, of the elderly, of the genetically 'impaired', and so on. It is essentially concerned with identifying those as different from us from those who are the same as us, because of their colour, gender, religion, what they do in bed, which society they belong to, which party they vote for. And, it is clear from even the most cursory study of these kinds of phenomena in society, that the greatest oppression is often internalised oppression of the oppressed — if not their outright sanction or plea. Wolf (1994), for example, shows how women, often in the absence of experienced autonomy and power on their own behalf, emerge in indirect and sometimes insidiously vicious ways of exerting normative powers over others — particularly other powerful women:

> Her dominion is the world of social relations. With her children, she can withhold herself emotionally. With her husband, she can withhold herself sexually. And with her female peers, she can use censure or disapproval. Since her primary weapon is the guest list, her primary power is to include or exclude others. Her most familiar retaliation against a world that displeases her is to stop speaking to it. (p. 182)

Level 5, the Rational

This concerns *Homo sapiens* — the person as thinker. This layer of knowledge and activity includes thinking, making sense of things, examination of cause and effect, frames of reference, probabilities, statistical significances, working with facts and information, and reading skills. 'Reality testing', developing rationality, experimentation (for example, Kelly, 1955), form the ways by which knowledge is gained or experience differentiated on this level. All approaches to ethical and moral decision-making which have appeal to reason, logic and mathematical formulae belong in this category, like Fletcher (1966) mentioning about adding up on computer what is the greatest good for the greatest number. Indeed, reason and logic have their place in moral and ethical considerations of bystanding — assessing the situation, considering risk, exploring options are all functions of reason which can be clouded, improved or clear.

Psychotherapists can also make a difference by teaching and modelling by example. The use of reason and questioning in the moral and ethical domains can be demonstrated through their own clarity of thinking and their willingness to be explicit about their criteria for bystanding for those who want or need to discover for themselves.

As Bauman (1993) writes about the difference between *the moral universe of discourse* (Level 4) and *experience of the reasonable one* (Level 5):

> Morality is not safe in the hands of reason, though this is exactly what spokesmen of reason promise. Reason cannot help the moral self without depriving the self of what makes the self moral: that unfounded, non-rational, un-arguable, no-excuses-given and non-calculable urge to stretch towards the other, to caress, to be for, to live for happen what may. Reason is about making correct decisions, while moral responsibility precedes all thinking about decisions as it does not, and cannot care about any logic which would allow approval of an action as correct. Thus morality can be 'rationalised' only at the cost of self-denial and self-attrition. From that reason-assisted self-denial, the self emerges morally disarmed, unable (and unwilling) to face up to the multitude of moral challenges and cacophony of ethical prescriptions. At the far end of the long march of reason, moral nihilism waits: that moral nihilism which in its deepest essence means not the denial of binding ethical code, and not the blunders of relativistic theory — but the loss of the ability to be moral. (pp. 247–248)

Level 6, the Theoretical or Metaphorical

This throws into relief the person as 'storyteller' — as a meaning maker, making sense of human experience through symbolism, story and metaphor. This is the arena of narration. Its being is based on the notion of theoretical plurality and relativity: theories can be seen as 'narratives' — stories that people tell themselves — interesting, exciting, depressing, controlling, useful and relative, but no one forever true.

'Theories' are in a different logical category from that of facts. Both in psychological theory and individual experience, it is important to separate these where possible. It is, for example, quite likely that the psychological theories or explanations we have developed to support the empirical evidence science has accumulated at Level 5, may be 'mistaken' and, in time, replaced by other (better?) theories (Kuhn, 1970). The history of science can certainly tell many such tales. The theories, explanations, metaphors and stories that humans have created in order to explain why things are as they are and why people behave as they do are included at this level.

The many and varied psychotherapies each provide their own narratives or stories to explain people's behaviour and to create ways of changing it. Moreover, the Oxford philosopher, Farrell (1979), pointed out that each story in psychotherapy tends to manufacture material that will fit it. The 'group' is trained when it has accepted and complied with the leader's Way Of Talking — his WOT.

Psychoanalysis has several stories (Freud, Klein, Winnicott, Lacan, Kohut). Each of these has their value-laden universe of discourse carried by the dominant images, for example, that of containment and holding in the field of object relations. As Samuels (1993) questions, 'Is containment even the characteristic of the mother–infant relationship that it is sometimes claimed to be? Does society "contain" its individual members? Should it?' (p. 274). Behavioural Therapy has others and Humanistic Psychotherapy has yet several others. Within these are further stories or metaphors which may be very different or very similar, overlap or interface, but all of which attempt to make some sense of our human experience and *ipso facto* try to tell us what is the good and how is the better way to act. Theories are to be judged by criteria other than facts or normative beliefs.

Even Freud acknowledged the mythical status of theories — and science — as we see here in his correspondence with Einstein: 'It may perhaps seem to you as though our theories are a kind of mythology ... But does not every science come in the end to a kind of mythology like this? Cannot the same be said today of your own Physics?' (May, 1991, p. 11).

An examination of the epistemology that explicitly informs most of the theoretical systems we know shows that:

> ... they were conceived prior to the developments of cognitive science and its constructivist implications. Freud and Jung wrote as if they were providing descriptions that accurately reflected the actual inner workings of the psyche; Rogers, as if he were describing the actual operations of a substantial self; and Skinner, as if the mechanisms of learning he presented were precise descriptions of real human dynamics. Within a postmodern epistemology, these systems are reinterpreted as models of metaphors that can serve as heuristic devices or as possible cognitive templates for organising client experiences. (Polkinghorne, 1992, p. 155)

Proulx (1994) writes in the *Journal of Analytical Psychology* that the ethical problem is not one that can be answered from a purely intellectual level (Level 5), 'but one that reaches down to the centre of one's own myth, one's picture of the world. What is needed is not science, but "the creative resolve to entrust our life to this or that hypothesis. In other words, this is where the ethical problem [level 4] begins, without which a *Weltanschauung* [Level 6] is inconceivable" (Jung, 1969, p. 381).'

There are even stories which problematise the individual's responsibility and so-called 'free will':

> If the notion that a good society depends on the proper exercise of free will by separate and stable individuals is sufficiently problematic that some reject it as a useful idea, what are the alternatives for creating a morally sound society? And what becomes of the autonomous individual who rationally and morally decides? In a sense he disappears. In his place a new conception of the human being is emerging from various theoretical domains. This self is construed as relational — as a temporary, partial, and flexible emergent identity created within the social interactions among persons (Gergen, 1992). Human activities become regarded as 'joint actions' produced with others within social networks (Shotter, 1984). From the perspective, identities 'circulate' within the networks ... In these relational formulations, individuals do not act on the basis of their own 'free will'. They act in ways that are defined in the historical context as moral or immoral by virtue of the part(s) they play in the ongoing action. There is also no final determination as to whether or not an action is good because there are no foundational axioms on which to rest the case. How an action is judged depends on the ways in which the consequences of the action are played out and defined over time. In this sense the meaning, value, purpose, or exactness of an action or a person's moral status is always open to an inconclusive negotiation process. The social order becomes disordered as a result of this transformation; all is in flux. (Gergen, 1994, p. 20)

Level 7, the Transpersonal

This refers to the epistemological area concerned with people as 'spiritual beings'. Beyond rationality, facts and even theories are the prescient regions of dreams, altered states of ecstatic consciousness, the spiritual, the metaphysical, the mystical, the existentially paradoxical, the unpredictable and the inexplicable. Religion both experientially and theoretically impacts psychological perspectives. It is represented in several approaches to psychotherapy and human development, for example, the influence of eastern philosophies (Fromm, 1960), and the creation-centred spirituality of Fox (1983). Also included at this level are those experiences which may be described as the surreal, the transcendent, the numinous, the sublime and the synchronous:

> Soulmaking follows no program; we can only await the appearance of the transforming image, that messenger from the unknown, which, unheralded, makes a sudden entry into our lives, like the annunciation of the crimson-robed archangel Gabriel to the Virgin. (Cobb, 1992, p. 29)

This level refers to the transpersonal — the spiritual or inexplicable — dimensions of relationship in psychotherapy, and its uneasy historical and present relationship to science, causality and the new physics. It essentially concerns the conditions of creation of the *temenos* (sacred space), or the *vas bene clausum* (the beneficent container) which Adler (1979) wrote about and draws on psychology's roots in mysticism and religion.

At this level belongs Jung's work on archetypes and the collective unconscious (1954), much of his approach to dreams and symbols (1964), as well as transpersonal psychotherapies, such as psychosynthesis, and many others which include a spiritual dimension within their parameters. Perhaps even included are tools for human healing and evolution derived from the *I Ching* (Wilhelm, 1988), the tarot, transcendental meditation, yoga, Taoism and T'ai Chi.

The physical, body-process considerations of Level 1 may *seem* unrelated, but what links these and all the other levels is that they are precisely the levels at which we experience ourselves, our bodies and our environment, and the relationship between them. And always inevitably, the physical meets the sacred. Such an holistic approach to bystanding is essential to our integration — or the maintenance of simultaneous fractures. All aspects of our human experience can find inclusion under these seven levels (if not, we need to find other means):

... throughout recorded history the power of a symbolic dimension has
always been recognized; people saw themselves as being threatened by the
tremendous, the awesome, the fey. This dimension not only set boundaries
to the power of the king and the magician, but also to that of the artisan and
the technician. Indeed, Malinowski claims that no society other than ours
has allowed the use of available tools to their utmost efficiency. Until now,
recognizing a sacred dimension was a necessary foundation for ethics.
(Illich, 1975, pp. 161–162)

Two Universes of Discourse Primarily Relating to Values

There is, however, another universe of discourse which concerns
itself with ultimate values, but it is of the kind where duality, causality
and sequentiality would not make sense. This is the sense in which
the world in all its beingness is God (or whatever other name), in its
becomingness, and there is nothing worse or better, more or less
worthy, more or less an aspect of this cosmic consciousness, the great
spirit, the Atman, the gnu. And, any or all of these names is not what
we are referring to in this dimension, because it is beyond thought,
beyond naming, beyond understanding — particularly beyond our
conceptual grasp. This is the realm of mystery, the space for grace,
the finger pointing toward the echo of an archetype dimly glimpsed,
yet surely apprehended, the miracle room, the palace of simultaneous contradiction, the chaos of a teacup in a universe of creativity,
the disorder fragmenting into a dark night of the soul as well as infinite bliss and peacefulness in the face of the forces of darkness seem-
ing again only one of the hand of God, one aspect of illusion, one
with all there is and no matter while it is all present, all now, all
whole. This is the view that there is at one level no conflict between
that which is good or has soul, and that which is bad or lacks soul, a
conflict between culture and nature, between man and woman,
between progression and regression, God and the devil, life and
death. The seventh level way of grasping is that there is nothing
which is not Physis — no aspect, peculiarity, thread or moment of life
which can be separated from the world soul itself whatever the
names or secrets we use.

I have distinguished between these seven kinds of universes of
discourse. We can argue differential values at Level 4 (the normative)
and, indeed, people, couples and nations do. We can use other
names for the categories. It depends on our values at Level 4.
Wheeler, an archetypal psychologist, for example, also differentiates
between the myth of the wronged soul ever in conflict with 'unsoul-

like phenomena' and the myth of the omnimorphic soul where 'There are no enemies of the soul because nothing can block the soul from the world' (Wheeler, 1993, p. 293). The soul is also the world. At Level 7 (the transpersonal) there is no need for argument and, if one tried, it would dissolve in a meaningless chatter since the nature of that story is its intrinsic ability to be speechless, unarguable, beyond articulation. Indeed, whenever we succeed in a postulation it itself becomes a contradiction. It is so well captured in the saying that the Tao which can be talked about is not the Tao; the tale of the rabbi who saw the real face of God could not live, and in the experience of the Christian contemplative who falls perilously and permanently silent.

The story continues in a forthcoming book, *On the Sublime* (Clarkson, 1996).

Human Matter

And you in the dark night who've opened your eyes and risen.
You've gone to the window and looked out.
The city at night. What do you see? Everyone far away.
Everyone near.
Everyone so close together in the night. And all and each one in windows, singular and many.

If you move your hand, the city feels it for an instant, and a wave begins in the water.
And if you speak and look, everyone knows you're watching, and they wait, and the city receives a pure wave of substance:
The whole common city ripples and the whole city is all one substance:
a single wave where everyone is, where everything is, and where all exist; they arrive, their hearts beat, they come alive.
A pure material wave where you find yourself immersed, to which you too gave life, and which has reached you from a long way off.
There, humanity expands and breathes, extended in space, almost limitless.

You have such a huge body!
All that matter rising from the depths of existence,
which pauses in you a moment and then goes on, generating you and inheriting you and giving your existence meaning.
It's all your own immense body, as it is his body, and another's body, and that old woman's,
as it is that warrior's who doesn't know himself, there in the depths of the ages, beating along with you.
With you the emperor and the soldier, the monk and the hermit.
With you the pale courtesan who's just finished painting her sad, spent

cheek. There in the endless centuries.

But here she smiles with you, she swims in the swell of the pure matter, and
    her heart beats inside the virgin.

Like that calm governor who coldly condemns, there in the far-off
    night, and breathes now in the pure mouth of a child.

Everyone trusting the single vibration which sums them all up, or
    better, supports and saves them, carries and makes them, and there,
    still whole, is losing itself in the future.

Everything's present.

A single wave spread out which begins in time, and continues and has
    no age.

Or has one, yes, like Man.

(Aleixandre, 1979, pp. 202–205)

You'll Have to Ask Her

'And what does the little girl want?' asked the waiter, addressing the 4-year-old's father.

    'I don't know', he answered as he settled back to read the newspaper. 'You'll have to ask her.'

Appendix I
A Socio-cultural
Context for
Psychotherapy

(Bystanding Issues in the Five Kinds of Therapeutic Relationship)

Historical Context

This book on the bystander will be published 10 years after my first publication drawing attention to the social responsibility of psychotherapists and the necessary interlinking between mental and physical health, psychotherapy and the condition of our world. Indeed, *Peace and the Social Responsibility* (Clarkson, 1986) appears to be my first piece of published writing in the field of psychotherapy. The first. It found me my voice.

I remember it. It was the piece I felt 'had to be said' at the time. The threat of nuclear extinction lay vividly around us every day in the global news. There was also the heartrendingly poignant drawings of Hiroshima survivors which I had arranged — with considerable difficulty — to show at a small psychotherapy conference in San Francisco.

I was aware of published work at the time showing two polarities in the stances of psychology, psychotherapy or psychoanalysis. Put simplistically, on the one hand there were the extremes of *'I am not in the world to live up to your expectations'* brigade and, on the other, the extremes of the *'absolute neutrality is good practice'* faction. The tension in me of trying to articulate a more complex and vital and interdependent relationship between person and world, between psychotherapy and social action, even between different approaches to psychotherapy and analysis, broke through what had been a 10-year total writing block. (Since then, to date, have followed 10 books, 90 papers translated into 10 languages — I am still trying of course.)

157

Researching the Therapeutic Relationship

As a teacher and supervisor, I was puzzled by the proliferation of approaches to psychotherapy and counselling psychology. How to account for this in the face of the empirical, scientific, anecdotal, phenomenological and subjective personal experience of 25 years of consumption (not to mention training) to the effect that theoretical differences seem to have little or no effect on determining effective or successful outcomes of psychotherapy? There were also indications from many authorities that the relationship between psychoanalyst/psychotherapist/psychologist and client/patient often was the most important factor in therapeutic effectiveness (see Smith, Glass & Miller, 1980, for example). Based also on my extensive experience of constructing the original designs as well as leading and supervising several validated therapy training and supervision diploma courses, I released what was in effect a pilot document called *A Multiplicity of Therapeutic Relationships* (Clarkson, 1990).

In this paper (published in the *British Journal of Psychotherapy*) I identified five kinds of relationship potentially present in all psychotherapies. Five kinds of *therapeutic relationship*. Relationships potentially present in *all* therapeutic work. These were found to be: the working alliance, the transference–countertransference relationship; the developmentally needed or reparative relationship; the person-to-person relationship; and the transpersonal relationship.

Psychotherapy training could thus be defined as training in the intentional use of relationship. This conceptual structure has formed the spine or basis for several 'so-called' integrative psychotherapy trainings in this country and abroad, whether fully acknowledged or not (Sivyer, 1996). It has also been well received by exponents of more singular approaches (for example, Hinshelwood, 1990; and Barnett, 1995).

My survey of more than 1000 specific named texts in the fields of psychoanalysis, psychotherapy and counselling psychology over the period of study seemed to show (usually mostly) that it is the therapeutic relationship which determines its benefit to the client as judged by the client. A long-term qualitative research project culminated in a book called *The Therapeutic Relationship* (Clarkson, 1995a).

My research hypothesis that all five of these kinds of *therapeutic relationships* are at least theoretically potentially available in most approaches to psychotherapy and that aspects of each actually appear in most of the major approaches studied was confirmed. It could also successfully and effectively be used as the basis for the training of psychotherapists and counselling psychologists by skilled, creative and effective teachers and supervisors who had been supervised by and/or trained with me and as an approach to integrating the psychotherapies — and it has. (Details of the methodology of the qualitative enquiry are available in Clarkson (1995f; 1995g).

Bystanding Issues in the Five Therapeutic Relationships

Hauke (1996) from having clearly read and understood my book The Therapeutic Relationship (Clarkson, 1995a) wrote:

> Petrūska Clarkson's book is timely and sits very well in the current *zeitgeist*. It is presented primarily, but not solely, as a teaching text — one that can be viewed from, and used from, different angles. For instance, from one position it suggests a range of different approaches to psychological and emotional treatment in the psychotherapies; viewed another way, the book suggests how *all* these different approaches may be found in any *one* psychotherapy treatment. Or rather, all are present sometimes and some are present every time; this is not an eclectic view — the 'best of' — but a truly pluralistic view — the 'inclusive of' approach (p. 406).

This is also my notion of the place of social responsibility and questions about bystanding or not in psychoanalysis, psychotherapy and counselling psychology. *Inclusive.* These themes of cultural relationship are in the blood and marrow of any encounter which claims to be therapeutic. (Social responsibility may be an inadequate term but at least it points towards the issues.) I believe these issues cannot be divorced in any but an arbitrary way from the reality of their intermeshing with every human life in every situation wherever and whenever we are. I have tried to show this again in this book on the bystander.

According to two counts, 9% of the book *The Therapeutic Relationship* (Clarkson, 1995a) specifically and explicitly addresses themes related to social responsibility and (non-)bystanding. Careful reading of the subtext would substantially increase this percentage. My intention was both an interweaving, a context, as well as a complete section explaining how all actions, all professions, even all perceptions are imbued with our values and prejudices or cultural injuries and reinforcers.

The therapeutic working alliance, of course, can be used to focus on issues of social justice, client/therapist matching, choice of treatment, equal access to services, availability of information, cultural biases in testing and diagnosis, rights and responsibilities, differential confidentialities and so on, as in the example of the black man who was given ECT in South Africa for 'psychotic aural hallucinations' until some young psychiatrist discovered that the 'voices' were those on the intercom in the mental hospital (Dobson, 1969).

The therapeutic transference–countertransference relationship can highlight particularly issues of prejudice, including the psycho-physiological or emotional/olfactory bases of intuition, judgement, attraction, repulsion and culture-based assumptions. For example, the process of projective identification in an analyst's subtle rejec-tion, shaming or minimisation of the sexuality of a person who is paraplegic or homosexual.

The developmentally needed or reparative therapeutic relation-ship has been used to emphasise the 'tyranny of theory' and the many ways in which developmental theory can be used in therapy and in the training of therapists to support the *status quo* and delegit-imise dissent or difference to the extent that junior trainers on humanistic psychotherapy programmes, for example, complain that their 'readiness' to teach or supervise should be decided by their 'elders' on dubious, unknown and undisclosed grounds.

The therapeutic person-to-person relationship can be used to explore the inescapability of valuing as part and parcel of every ther-apeutic moment, every perception, every intervention or non-inter-vention, every disclosure as well as every non-disclosure. I have attempted to show here specifically in Chapter 8, as well as the fundamental meanings of 'working with difference' — the unavoid-able 'otherness' of another any other.

The therapeutic transpersonal relationship implicates the nature of the universe and our place in it — the creative order found at the edge of chaos, the way in which every thing *is* relationship, the inter-penetration of observer and observed; of I and Thou; *Physis* rising *and* hiding, as living and dying, the paradoxical identity of wave and particle, self and other; the culmination of *antimonian* thought; the mystery of a quantum universe; the *coniunctio* of responsibility and freedom, justice and mercy, passion and compassion.

The 'Social' is in Every Therapeutic Relationship

Indeed, there may be no 'response-able' place for the psychothera-pist to posit social responsibility or cultural and ecological awareness different or separate from therapeutic work (Samuels, 1989). In my way I have tried to say, whether explicit or implicit, they are the same. *Because*, being human, we are in relationship — with each other, the rhinoceroses in Africa, the billboards, the planet itself (Clarkson, 1989). Context is everywhere. In some particular ways, we can never be truly separate from each other, never *not* talk to each other, never disengage from relationship — as long as life perhaps.

Social justice issues should ideally not be seen as being an 'add-on' to any of the therapeutic relationships, but an intrinsic and inextricable part of every relationship, *including* the five I identified (Clarkson, 1990). As soon as 'culture', for example, is subject to such a state of 'apartheid' the distance may increase — and we know from personal experience and psychological studies that proximity can sometimes even help to reduce prejudice. A separation of content and context on these matters may be seen as equivalent to tacking on 'a module' on race or ethics in counsellor education or organisational development — instead of inviting such awareness to scent the very air we always breathe together.

The social is not an additional relationship, it permeates all our relationships — particularly each one of the five the therapeutic relationships. My plea is exactly for inclusion, not an artificial separation. I know, of course, that I do not succeed in this. I want to learn as well as teach. I hope for recognition that such theoretical and professional separation often reflects both the origin and the continuation of the problem of denial of human relationship. The recognition of our *inter*-relationship could begin to restore and enliven the dualistic Newtonian–Cartesian fractures in our sensibilities as well as in our professional lives.

It may be tempting to view the socio-cultural-planetary context as a relationship mode in its own right. However, this view is philosophically flawed. This is because the purpose of isolating the five different therapeutic relationships is primarily to assist the practitioners in the relationship in identifying the task or the work to be done. It is often not possible or useful to isolate the socio-cultural context in this way *separate* from the people in the relationship, since no clear indication of what is to be done with or about it emerges. The functionality of distinguishing five separate relationships does not extend beyond the question that arises in psychotherapy and psychoanalysis of 'what is to be done?'.

Of Category Errors and Love

My five-therapeutic relationship categorisation should also not be confused with separating out universes of discourse or epistemologies about human relationships. It is different in *kind* from the ways of knowing or thinking about our work or our world as I did in the conceptual Seven Level Model (Clarkson, 1992b) where, for example, Level 4 (the normative) circumscribes the cultural and the collective universes of discourse. (See also Hauke, 1996, and Chapter 9 of this book.)

Confusing apples with oranges; the practice of psychotherapy with the philosophy of psychology; or relationship types with levels of differentiating epistemological truth values; or phenomenologies with theories — these constitute what the philosopher Ryle (1960) would call 'category errors'. We are, of course, at liberty to commit them — as well as to bear the emotional, ethical and intellectual consequences of such logical confusions. But, again:

> Despair and empowerment work, therefore, is consciousness raising in the truest sense of the term. It increases our awareness not only of the perils that face us, but also of the promise inherent in the human heart. Whether we 'make it' or not, whether our efforts to heal our world succeed or fail, we then live in so vivid a consciousness of our community that the obvious and accurate word for it is love ... (Macy, 1983, p. 164)

Appendix II
Bystanding: A Block to Empowerment

Here follows a short summary for convenience of some of the salient points of the book which has been used successfully and effectively in consultancy, training and management development work specifically with organisations:

> *'It's none of my business'*
> *'This situation is more complex than it seems'*
> *'I do not have the all the information/am not qualified to deal with this'*
> *'I don't want to get burned again'*
> *'I want to remain neutral'*
> *'I'm only telling the truth (to others) as I see it'*
> *'I'm just following orders'*
> *'I expect it's six of one and half a dozen of the other'*
> *'My contribution won't make much difference'*
> *'I'm simply keeping my own counsel'*
> *'They brought it on themselves'*
> *'I don't want to rock the boat'*

At a management team meeting a decision needs to be made about a difficult issue for which there are no easy solutions. After some debate, and pushed by the formal leader, a decision is apparently agreed. Several participants are aware that they have not expressed in this forum views, doubts and suggestions relating to the implications of this decision which they have thought privately and have discussed with one another and with others outside the meeting. The formal leader will be held accountable for this decision at the next level above in the organisation. In holding their peace several team members have not offered assistance in a critical situation. When asked later they give a variety of explanations and rationales for their behaviour, most of which probably fall into one of the categories listed above.

This activity has been identified as bystanding. A bystander is someone who does not become actively involved in a situation in which others require assistance of some kind. Bystanding is the nemesis of organisational empowerment.

When an organisation has espoused 'empowerment' as a desired characteristic, it is tempting for all the discussion to be focused on trying to reach joint understanding of the meaning and concrete implications of this much-used term. It seems to us fruitful for people to have ways to understanding and recognising some of the dynamics of disempowerment. Our thesis is that it is not only the central players in any situation, nor only those with formal authority, nor abstractions such as management, who can significantly influence events, but that the most potent possibilities of change in many organisations lie with those who would disclaim such power — the bystanders.

Bystanding behaviour meets the following criteria:

> People are aware that something seems wrong in a situation.
> They do not actively take responsibility for their part in maintaining the problem — preventing its resolution.
> They claim they could not have acted otherwise.
> They are discounting their autonomy and power to *influence the situation.*

There are many ways of adopting the bystander role. Below we identify a dozen examples we have come to recognise. Any one organisational culture will tend to support some examples in particular. The behaviour is both a manifestation of the organisation culture and is continually recreating that culture. Each example is characterised by a typical phrase which bystanders might use to account for their behaviour.

'It's none of my business'

Here there is a conflict or difficult situation and an individual, on the basis of not being a central player, discounts any responsibility for influencing the events, when they could mediate, ask someone else to mediate, express their views, give information, etc.

'This situation is more complex than it seems'

The individual uses the complexity and variety of real life situations to justify non-involvement, rather than helping to clarify the situation or saying, in effect, *'I don't understand all that is going on here, but from what I appreciate so far ...'*

'I do not have all the information/am not qualified to deal with this'

Rarely does anyone have all the information about any situation before they are called upon to act. Indeed, the very absence of information may underline the need for action. To refuse to bystand may be to accept that *'What I do know is useful and what I don't know I can begin to find out or find out why I can't find out.'*

'I don't want to get burned again'

Someone refuses involvement because a past intervention was not effective or had negative results: *'Last time I tried to speak to X he shouted at me'*. Instead, they could reflect on and learn from the previous encounter something about effective intervention, which they experiment with now instead of withdrawing to safety.

'I want to remain neutral'

Here, someone masks their failure to decide what to do by appearing to be invested in fairness and a supposedly higher moral ground. Instead, it is possible to be interested in all the grievances people have, to be on both or all sides and to actively support everyone, or to realise that the desire to be fair to all sides may include the necessity of pointing out where one side may be being unfair.

'I'm only telling the truth (to others) as I see it'

A person jumps to conclusions and takes every opportunity to tell their version of the truth to others without checking their perceptions with, challenging, or seeking to understand the parties directly involved. Thus, they exchange a contribution to collective problem solving for the popularity of the carrier of juicy gossip.

'I'm just following orders'

A person claims they are unable to act autonomously in a situation because they are subject to higher authority or popular demand. Convenient obedience to persons or rigid bureaucratic procedures is meant to guarantee personal exoneration while allowing blaming of 'them' or the rules. The possibilities of protest or creative bending of the rules to meet the challenge of the situation are denied.

'I expect it's six of one and half a dozen of the other'

The jury concludes that the truth lies somewhere in the middle. Truth is so relative that responsibility can be abrogated.

'My contribution won't make much difference'

The politics and power of the organisation are believed to be too great for an individual to have any influence at all. A person does not deny that there is a contribution to be made, but that theirs is so insignificant as to be worthless. Instead they could join forces with others and pool resources.

'I'm simply keeping my own counsel'

Unless the person believes their own interests are threatened they do not get involved. There is a failure to acknowledge that part of taking care of yourself involves taking care of others. Everybody benefits from a more caring situation.

'They brought it on themselves'

A person justifies their non-involvement on the grounds that if something has gone wrong the key figures probably deserved it, and it behoves the audience to stay out of the way of their just retribution.

'I don't want to rock the boat'

By avoiding conflict and confrontation in the name of political wisdom, this person ignores the fact that any disturbing dynamic will eventually emerge and take effect anyway. Instead, they need to find a way of expressing their concerns even if they seem to be starting a disturbance, and then to remain committed to an effective resolution of such a disturbance, while the storm rages.

We are not advocating meddling or interfering at every single opportunity or leaping in to 'rescue' those who do not in fact need assistance. We are suggesting that it is important to realise that, in any situation about which you have knowledge or with which you are in contact, necessarily means you are already involved. As we know from modern physics all observers are part of the field; even the act of observation affects what is observed.

The question becomes 'What is the best way to be involved?' and this does not always mean doing something directly or immediately. Understanding and accepting personal responsibility for bystanding behaviour may be uncomfortable. There is a deep heritage in many organisations of covering your own back, turning a blind eye, allowing scapegoating and relishing the vicarious excitement of office politics. One important lesson is not to wait to see which way the wind is blowing, but to make choices while the story is still unfolding, to decide how to be and do before the scene is played out and while the result remains ambiguous.

In collusively bystanding cultures, which tend to have flourished in bureaucratic organisations, the advantages of such a position can seem minimal — the penalties of having 'backed the wrong horse', criticism, isolation, a black note on the file, or dwindling career prospects.

So what *are* the possible advantages? At a personal level, the satisfaction of expressing one's energy in the service of integrity and responsibility rather than turning it inwards into sleepless nights, gnawing doubts, ulcers and heart disease. Also you gain the vitality of engaging in a struggle for what you believe to be right, rather than the vicarious excitement of political gossip. There are also fertile opportunities for learning and increasing one's knowledge of how to be effective amongst the complexities of organisational life. Responsible involvement is at least one way of understanding the challenge that the call for an empowered organisational culture represents.

Petrūska Clarkson and
Patricia Shaw

Appendix III
About Protective
Behaviours*

Protective Behaviours Inc. (PBI) developed in Madison, Wisconsin, during the 1970s as a result of children approaching a school social worker, Peg Flandreau West, telling her about their problems, including violence and abuse. In her attempts to address this, Peg realised that many children were not feeling safe and as a result their schooling suffered and numerous other problems ensued. With the assistance of survivors, children, colleagues, friends and many hours, nay years, of brainstorming, visioning, laughter and tears the Protective Behaviours Inc. process was nurtured into its current form.

From the United States in 1985 Peg West went to Australia. Starting in Victoria, via police and then community networks the programme was taken up by all the Australian states. There is now a national Protective Behaviours Forum with regular meetings and conferences to share stories, information and materials.

From Australia, PBI went to the UK in 1991, again starting with police networks and then flourishing into a wider community involvement. There are many local network groups throughout the UK. Other countries using the process include Canada, Hong Kong, Norway, Papua New Guinea, the Philippines, and Vanuatu. An international journal is published twice a year.

Summary of the Programme

There are many external rules about what is safe and how to protect ourselves but these do not account for individual differences in what is perceived as safe or unsafe. All too often these rules create a sense of fear or guilt. The Protective Behaviours process believes that we cannot be scared into feeling safe and addresses this by helping us to

* This is a summary, written by Di Margetts, of the Protective Behaviours Manual, (1995) S. Gordon, (Ed.) *The Right to Feel Safe*. Adelaide: Mission SA.

recognise the difference between safe, fun-to-feel-scared and feeling unsafe. The process then teaches us how to organise and maintain systems of support and to use strategies to prevent and/or interrupt potential or actual violence.

There are two *themes* used to introduce Protective Behaviours Inc:

1.   We all have the right to feel safe all of the time.
2.   There is nothing so awful we can't talk about it with someone.

Feelings of *safety* are identified to form a baseline from which individuals can measure their own levels of 'safe' or 'unsafe'. People then identify those times when it is fun to feel scared, such as a funfair ride, scary story, making a speech, etc. Next, people identify specific body signs or *Early Warning Signs* which happen when they do not feel safe. These may include butterflies in the stomach, shaky knees, heart beating faster, etc.

In both cases, fun and not-so-fun, we feel the same body signs, but there is a fundamental difference. When it is not fun there is a lack of choice or control over what is happening and/or there is no sense of when it will finish. Many people do not listen to their Early Warning Signs, discounting their feelings and telling themselves they are being stupid. Protective Behaviours teaches us to recognise this *internal* measure on which to base our understanding of the safety or not of the *external* situation.

To understand the second theme, people explore how it feels to talk about a problem, what sort of person we would wish to confide in and how we know if someone would have these qualities. Then each person identifies their own personal *Networks* of support. A Network consists of a minimum of four people, in addition to any adults at home. Networks are personal and chosen by the network owner.

There are strategies used to help put the themes and concepts into practice. For example, *Network Review*. As we grow and change so our Network needs evolve and change. Network Review is checking our Networks on a regular basis to ensure that people are available and still suited to our needs.

Questions are always asked in a *One Step Removed* way, for example, 'How could we keep ourselves safe even if ... someone bigger than us was about to hurt us?' This generalised question may concern bullying to one person, assault to another, physical abuse to another, and to a fourth person it may not be seen as physical at all, but emotional hurts. No-one can know how another person is feeling in any given situation; the situation will vary for each person.

One Step Removed also enables a person to 'check out' someone on their Network before disclosing a problem, for example, *'What if someone told you that ... what would you do?'* According to the given reply a choice can be made whether to disclose a problem or to try someone else.

People are actively encouraged to use *persistence*. Sometimes a request for support or help is not taken seriously or the person asked will not take the necessary steps to assist us. This strategy provides a framework for us to persevere in seeking help through our prese-lected Network of trusted people, until enough happens and our Early Warning Signs subside and we feel safe again.

There are other strategies explored during training which needs a minimum of six hours and can be taken in one or more sessions. PBI's concepts and strategies are adaptable, can apply to almost any circumstance, and be used with people from any age, race or ethnic background. Abundant materials are available for all age levels to support people who wish to use the process with others.

Contacts in UK: Joc Rose or Di Margetts, Milton Keynes Health Promotions Service, Milton Keynes Hospital Campus, Standing Way, Eaglestone, Milton Keynes, MK6 5LE. Tel. 01908 661487.

References

Adams, D. (1985) *So Long and Thanks for All the Fish*. London: Pan.

Adler, G. (1979) *Dynamics of the Self*. London: Coventure (first published 1951).

Adorno, T., Frenkel-Brunswick, E., Levinson, D. and Sanford, R. N. (1950) *The Authoritarian Personality*. New York: Harper.

Aleixandre, V. (1979) *A Longing for the Light*. Port Townsend, WA: Copper Canyon Press.

Amnesty International Report on Torture (1973). London: Duckworth.

Anderson, W. T. (1990) *Reality Isn't What it Used to Be*. San Francisco: Harper & Row.

Arendt, H. (1964) *Eichmann in Jerusalem: A Report on the Banality of Evil*. New York: Viking Press.

Aristotle (1934) *Nicomachean Ethics*. (H. Rackman, Trans.), London: William Heinemann.

Ash, T. G. (1985) The life of death. *New York Review of Books* **XXXII**, 26–39.

Bailey, J. R. and Eastman, W. N. (1994) Positivism and the promise of the social sciences. *Theory and Psychology* **4** (4), 505–524.

Barnett, R. (1995) A 'gust of fresh air'. Review of *The Therapeutic Relationship* by P. Clarkson. *Counselling News* **19**, 31.

Bary, B. B. and Hufford, F. M. (1990) The six advantages to Games and their use in Treatment. *Transactional Analysis Journal* **20** (4), 214–220.

Bateson, G. (1979) *Mind and Nature: A Necessary Unity*. London: Wildwood House.

Bataille, G. (1986) *Death and Sensuality: A Study of Eroticism and the Taboo*. New York: Ballantine Books. (First published 1957.)

Bauman, Z. (1989) *In Modernity and the Holocaust*. Cambridge: Polity Press.

Bauman, Z. (1993) *Postmodern Ethics*. Oxford: Blackwell.

Becker, E. (1973) *The Denial of Death*. New York: The Free Press.

Beevor, A. and Cooper, S. A. (1994) *Daily Mail*, 23 July, pp 30–31 London: Associated Newspapers.

Berke, J. (1989) *The Tyranny of Malice: Exploring the Dark Side of Character and Culture*. London: Simon & Schuster.

Berne, E. (1968) *Games People Play*. Harmondsworth: Penguin. (First published 1964.)

Berne, E. (1972) *What Do You Say After You Say Hello?* New York: Bantam.

171

Besant, A. (1914) *The Bhagavad Gita*. Madras: Theosophical Society.

Birnbaum, L. (1964) Behaviorism: John Broadus Watson and American Social Thought, 1913–1933. PhD dissertation. Berkeley: University of California.

Black, M. (1992) *A Cause for Our Times: Oxfam, the First Fifty Years*. Oxford: Oxfam.

Blackham, H. J. (1961) *Six Existentialist Thinkers*. London: Routledge.

Bly, R. (1990) *Iron John*. Shaftesbury: Element Books.

Boadella, D. (1986) Energy and character. *The Journal of Biosynthesis* **17** (2), 1–23.

Boadella, D. (1987) *Lifestreams: An Introduction to Biosynthesis*. London: Routledge & Kegan Paul.

Bonhoeffer, D. (1955) *Ethics* (N. H. Smith, Trans.). London: Macmillan.

Bowlby, J. (1953) Some pathological processes set in motion by early mother–child separation. *Journal of Mental Science* **99**, 265.

Boyd, R. D. (1992) Book review. *Clinical Psychology Forum* **45**, 42.

Breytenbach, B. (1988) *Judas Eye and Self Portrait / Death Watch*. London: Faber & Faber.

Briggs, J. and Peat, F. D. (1989) *Turbulent Mirror*. New York, Harper & Row.

Brunner, E. (1947) *The Divine Imperative*. (O. Wyon, Trans.) London: Westminster Press.

Buber, M. (1970) *I and Thou*. (W. Kaufmann, Trans.) Edinbugh: T & T Clark.

Bywater, I. (1909) *Aristotle on the Art of Poetry*. London: Oxford University Press.

Caplan, P. J. (1985) *The Myth of Women's Masochism*. New York: Dutton.

Capra, F. (1976) *The Tao of Physics*. London: Fontana.

Capra, F. (1983) *The Turning Point: Science, Society and the Rising Culture*. London: Flamingo.

Chambers, I. (1990) *Border Dialogues*. London: Routledge.

Chilton, B. (1992) Touching Tale of the Fight to Save Whales [Letters]. *Daily Mail*, 23 July, p. 43. London: Associated Newspapers.

Christy, C. A. and Voigt, H. (1994) Bystander responses to public episodes of child abuse. *Journal of Applied Social Psychology* **24** (9), 824–847.

Chung, M. C. (1994) Learning from Viktor Frankl in disaster work. *Changes* **12** (1), 6–10.

Clarkson, P. (1975) Seven-level Model. Invitational paper delivered at the University of Pretoria, November.

Clarkson, P. (1986) Peace and the social responsibility of the integrated adult. *ITA News* **15**, 4–5.

Clarkson, P. (1987) The bystander role. *Transactional Analysis Journal* **17** (3), 82–87.

Clarkson, P. (1989) *Gestalt Counselling in Action*. London: Sage.

Clarkson, P. (1990) A multiplicity of psychotherapeutic relationships. *British Journal of Psychotherapy* **7** (2), 148–163.

Clarkson, P. (1991) Individuality and commonality in Gestalt. *British Gestalt Journal* **1**, 28–37.

Clarkson, P. (1992a) *Transactional Analysis Psychotherapy: An Integrated Approach*. London: Routledge.

Clarkson, P. (1992b) The Seven Level Model. In P. Clarkson and P. Lapworth, Systemic Integrative Psychotherapy, in W. Dryden (Ed) *Integrative and Eclectic Therapy: A Handbook*. Milton Keynes: Open University Press, pp. 41–83.

Clarkson, P. (1993a) The opening of the wall. *On Psychotherapy*. London: Whurr, pp. 233–235.

Clarkson, P. (1993b) Bystander games. *Transactional Analysis Journal* **23** (3), 158–172.

Clarkson, P. (1994a) The Nature and Range of Psychotherapy. In P. Clarkson and M. Pokorny, (Eds) *The Handbook of Psychotherapy*. London: Routledge, pp. 3–27.

Clarkson, P. (1994b) The Psychotherapist's Experience of Fame. Unpublished manuscript.

Clarkson, P. (1994c) *The Achilles Syndrome: The Secret Fear of Failure*. Shaftesbury: Element.

Clarkson, P. (1995a) *The Therapeutic Relationship*. London: Whurr.

Clarkson, P. (1995b) Vengeance of the victim. In: *The Therapeutic Relationship*. London: Whurr, pp. 53–61.

Clarkson, P. (1995c) Ethical relationships. In: *The Therapeutic Relationship*. London: Whurr, pp. 306–312.

Clarkson, P. (1995d) The Archetype of Physis: The Soul of Nature – Our Nature. Accepted for publication in *Journal for Jungian Studies*.

Clarkson, P. (1995e) *The Sublime in Psychoanalysis and Archetypal Psychotherapy*. London: PHYSIS.

Clarkson, P. (1995f) *After Schoolism*. London: PHYSIS*.

Clarkson, P. (1995g) *Researching the Therapeutic Relationship – A Qualitative Inquiry*. London: PHYSIS*.

Clarkson, P. (1995h) *Dieratao – Learning by Inquiry*. London: PHYSIS*.

Clarkson, P. (1996) *On the Sublime in Psychoanalysis, Analytical Psychology and Archetypical Psychology*. London: Whurr.

Clarkson, P. and Murdin, L. (1996) When rules are not enough: reflections on the spirit of the law in ethical codes. *Counselling* **7** (1), 31–35.

Clarkson, P. and Pokorny, M. (Eds) (1994) *The Handbook of Psychotherapy*. London: Routledge.

Cobb, N. (1992) *Archetypal Imagination: Glimpses of the Gods in Life and Art*. Hudson, NY: Lindisfarne.

Colman, A. M. (1991a) Expert Psychological Testimony in Two Murder Trials in South Africa. Division of Criminological and Legal Psychology First Annual Conference, Canterbury, England.

Colman, A. M. (1991b) Crowd Psychology in South African Murder Trials. *American Psychologist* **46** (10), 1071–1079.

Connor, S. (1989) *Postmodernist Culture*. Oxford: Basil Blackwell.

Conway, R. (1992) *The Rage for Utopia*. St Leonards, NSW: Allen & Unwin.

Cornell, W. F. (1984) Teaching people what matters. *Transactional Analysis Journal* **14** (4), 270–282.

Cottone, R. R. (1988) Epistemological and ontological issues in counselling: implications of social systems theory. *Counselling Psychology Quarterly* **1** (4), 357–365.

Davies, N. (1991) *White Lies*. London: Chatto & Windus.

Dobson, B. (1969) personal communication.

Dostoyevsky, F. (1955) *Brothers Karamazov*. (C. Garnett, Trans.) New York: Vintage.

Douzinas, C., Warrington, R. with McVeigh, S. (1991) *Postmodern Jurisprudence: The Law of Text in the Texts of Law*. London: Routledge.

* Manuscript available from 12 North Common Road, London, W5 2QB, UK.

Dryden, W. (Ed.) (1992) *Integrative and Eclectic Therapy: A Handbook.* Buckingham: Open University Press.

Dryden, W. and Trower, P. (eds) (1989) *Cognitive Psychotherapy: Status and Change.* London: Cassell.

English, F. (1979) Talk on receiving the Eric Berne memorial scientific award. *Transactional Analysis Journal* **17**, 59–71.

English. F. (1992) Personal communication.

Erdman, D.E. (Ed) (1965) *The Poetry and Prose of William Blake.* New York: Garden City.

Estés, C. P. (1992) *Women Who Run With Wolves: Contacting the Power of the Wild Woman.* London: Rider.

Farrell, B. A. (1979) Work in Small Groups: Some Philosophical Considerations. In: B. Babington Smith and B. A. Farrell (eds). *Training In Small Groups: A Study of Five Methods.* Oxford: Pergamon, pp. 103–115.

Feather, N. T. (Ed) (1982) *Expectations and Actions: Expectancy-Value Models in Psychology.* Hillsdale, NJ: Lawrence Erlbaum.

Federer, D. (1995) *The Dangers of Learned Compliance.* Madison, WI: Protective Behaviors Inc.

Festinger, L. (1957) *A Theory of Cognitive Dissonance.* Stanford: Stanford University Press.

Fiske, S. T. and Taylor, S. E. (1987) *Social Cognition* (second edition). New York: Random House.

Fletcher, J. (1966) Situation Ethics: The New Morality. London: SCM Press.

Foucault, M. (1979) Discipline and Punishment. New York: Random House.

Fox, M. (1983) *Original Blessing.* Santa Fe, NM: Bear & Co.

Frank, J. (1973) *Persuasion and Healing.* New York: Schocken.

Frankl, V. (1964) *Man's Search For Meaning: An Introduction to Logotherapy.* London: Hodder & Stoughton.

Freud, S. (1912a) The Dynamics of Transference. In: J. Strachey (Ed) *The Standard Edition of the Complete Psychological Works of Sigmund Freud,* Volume 12. London: Hogarth Press, pp. 97–108.

Freud, S. (1912b) Recommendations to Physicians Practising Psycho-analysis. In J. Strachey (Ed) *The Standard Edition of the Complete Psychological Works of Sigmund Freud,* Volume 12. London: Hogarth Press, pp. 109–120.

Fromm, E. (1960) *Psychoanalysis and Zen Buddhism.* London: Allen & Unwin.

Fromm, E. (1991) *The Fear of Freedom.* London: Routledge.

Gerard, G. and Mathewson, G. (1966) The effect of severity of initiation on liking for a group. *Journal of Abnormal and Social Psychology* **59**, 171–181.

Gergen, K. (1994) *Realities and Relationships: Soundings in Social Construction.* Cambridge, MA: Harvard University Press.

Gergen, M. (1992) From Mod Masculinity to Post-Mod Macho: A Feminist Re-Play. In: S. Kvale (Ed) *Psychology and Postmodernism.* London: Sage, pp. 183–193.

Gergen, M. (1994) Free will and psychotherapy: complaints of the draughtsmen's daughters. *Journal of Theoretical and Philosophical Psychology* **14** (1), 13–24.

Gibson, J. and Haritos-Faroutos, M. (1986) The education of a torturer. *Psychology Today* **20**, 50–58.

Gilligan, C. (1982) *In a Different Voice: Psychological Theory and Women's Development.* Cambridge, MA: Harvard University Press.

Gleick, J. (1988) *Chaos: Making a New Science.* London: Heinemann.

Goodman, P. (1991) Reflections on Racism, Spite, Guilt and Non-Violence. In T. Stoehr (Ed) *Nature Heals: The Psychological Essays of Paul Goodman.* Highland, NY: The Gestalt Journal, pp. 118–133.

Gouldner, A. W. (1970) *The Coming Crises of Western Sociology.* New York: Basic Books.

Greenberg, I. A. (Ed.) (1975) *Psychodrama: Theory and Therapy.* London: Souvenir Press.

Greenson, R. R. (1967) *The Technique and Practice of Psychoanalysis,* Volume 1. New York: International Universities Press.

Greenwald, A. G., Pratkanis, A. R., Leippe, M. R. and Baumgardner, M. H. (1986) Under what conditions does theory obstruct research progress? *American Psychologist* **93**, 216–229.

Gribbin, J. (1984) *In Search of Schrödinger's Cat.* London: Corgi.

Grinberg, L., Sor, D. and Tabak de Bianchedi, E. (1975) *Introduction to the Work of Bion.* Strath Tay: Clunie Press.

Grof, S. (1985) *Beyond the Brain: Birth, Death and Transcendence in Psychotherapy.* New York: State University of New York.

Guerrière, D. (1980) Physis, Sophia, Psyche. In: J. Sallis and K. Maly (Eds) *Heraclitean Fragments: A Companion Volume to the Heidegger / Fink Seminar on Heraclitus.* Alabama: University of Alabama Press, pp. 86–134.

Hall, J. (1993) *The Reluctant Adult.* Bridport: Prism Press.

Haney, C., Banks, C. and Zimbardo, P. (1973) Interpersonal dynamics in a simulated prison. *International Journal of Criminology and Penology* **1**, 69–97.

Hardie, W. F. R. (1968) *Aristotle's Ethical Theory.* Oxford: Oxford University Press.

Hare, R. M. (1989) *Essays in Ethical Theory.* Oxford: Clarendon Press.

Haritos-Faroutos, M. (1983) Antecedent Conditions Leading to the Behaviour of a Torturer: Fallacy or Reality. Unpublished manuscript, University of Thessaloniki, Greece.

Hauke, C. (1996) Review of *The Therapeutic Relationship* by P. Clarkson. *British Journal of Psychotherapy* **12** (3), 405–407..

Herbert, N. (1985) *The New Reality: Beyond the New Physics.* London: Rider.

Hersh, J. (1982) Model-making and the Promethean ego. *Spring,* 151–163.

Higgins, R. (1982) *The Seventh Enemy: The Human Factor in the Global Crisis.* London: Hodder & Stoughton. (First published 1978.)

Hillman, J. (1988) Jung's daimonic inheritance. *Sphinx* **1**, 9–19. London: Convivium for Archetypal Studies.

Hillman, J. (1992) The practice of beauty. *Sphinx* **4**, 13–28. London: Convivium for Archetypal Studies.

Hillman, J. and Ventura, M. (1992) *We've Had a Hundred Years of Psychotherapy and the World's Getting Worse.* San Francisco: Harper.

Hinshelwood, R. D. (1989) *A Dictionary of Kleinian Thought.* London: Free Association Books.

Hinshelwood, R. (1990) Editorial. *British Journal of Psychotherapy* **7**, 119–120.

Holland, P. (1992) *What is a Child? Popular Images of Childhood.* London: Pandora.

Holmes, J. and Lindley, R. (1989) *The Values of Psychotherapy.* Oxford: Oxford University Press.

Illich, I. (1975) *Medical Nemesis: The Expropriation of Health*. London: Calder & Boyars.

Jacobs, A. (1987) Autocratic power. *Transactional Analysis Journal* **17** (3), 59–71.

Jaspers, K. (1963) *General Psychopathology* (J. Hoenig and M. W. Hamilton, trans.). Chicago: University of Chicago Press. (First published 1913.)

Jung, C. G. (1954) *C.W.17*. London: Routlege & Kegan Paul.

Jung, C. G. (1969) *C.W.8*. (second edition). London: Routledge & Kegan Paul.

Jung, C. G. (1983) *Memories, Dreams, Reflections* (R. & C. Winston, trans.). London: Fontana.

Kagan, J. (1992) *Unstable Ideas: Temperament, Cognition, and Self*. Cambridge, MA: Harvard University Press.

Karpman, S. (1968) Fairy tales and script drama analysis. *Transactional Analysis Bulletin*, selected articles from Volumes 1–9, 51–56.

Kelly, G. (1955) *The Psychology of Personal Constructs*. New York: W. W. Norton.

Keneally, T. (1994) *Schindler's List*. London: Sceptre.

Keynes, G. (Ed) (1991) *Blake: Complete Writings*. Oxford: Oxford University Press. (First published 1957.)

Kipphardt, H. (1971) The Case of J. Robert Oppenheimer. Pact Drama. In association with Alexander Theatre, Johannesburg.

Kirschenbau, A. (1980) The bystander's duty to rescue in Jewish law. *Jewish Religious Ethics* **8**, 204–226.

Klein, M. (1984) *Envy and Gratitude and Other Works 1946–1963*. London: Hogarth Press and the Institute of Psycho-analysis.

Kohlberg, L. (1964) Development of Moral Character and Moral Ideology. In: M. L. Hoffman and L. W. Hoffman (Eds) *Review of Child Development Research*, Volume 1. New York: Russell Sage Foundation.

Kohut, H. (1959) Introspection, Empathy, and Psychoanalysis: An Examination of the Relationship Between Modes of Observation and Theory. In: P. H. Ornstein (Ed) *The Search for Self* Volume 1. New York: International Universities Press, pp. 205–232.

Kuhn, T. S. (1970) *The Structure of Scientific Revolutions*. Chicago: University of Chicago. (First published 1962.)

Kupers, T. A. (1988) *Ending Therapy*. New York: New York University Press.

Kvale, S. (Ed.) (1992) *Psychology and Postmodernism*. London: Sage.

Lao Tzu (1973) *Tao Te Ching* (G. Feng and J. English, trans.). Aldershot: Wildwood House.

Latané, B. and Darley, M. (1970) *The Unresponsive Bystander: Why Doesn't He Help?* New York: Appleton Century Crofts.

Lattimer, M. (1994) *The Campaigning Handbook: Communications, Organisation, Direct Action, Lobbying, The Law*. London: Directory of Social Change.

Leahey, T. H. (1987) *A History of Psychology*. Englewood Cliffs, NJ: Prentice-Hall.

Lefebvre, L. and Giraldeau, L-A. (1994) Cultural transmission in pigeons is affected by the number of tutors and bystanders present. *Animal Behaviour* **47** (2), 331–337.

Levin, P. (1974) *Becoming the Way We Are*. Berkeley, CA: Pamela Levin.

Lipman-Blumen, J. (1994) The Existential Bases of Power and Relationships: The Gender Role Case. In: H. L. Radtke and H. J. Stam (Eds) *Power/Gender: Social Relations in Theory and Practice*. London: Sage, pp. 108–135.

Lloyd, A. P. (1992) Dual Relationship Problems in Counselor Education. In: B. Herlihy and G. Corey (Eds) *Dual Relationships in Counseling*. Alexandria, VA: American Association for Counseling and Development, pp. 59–64.

Lowenfeld, M. (1988) *Child Psychotherapy, War and the Normal Child: Selected Papers of Margaret Lowenfeld*. C. Urwin and J. Hood-Williams (Eds) London: Free Association Books.

Lyotard, J-F. (1984) The postmodern condition: a report on knowledge. *Theory and History of Literature* **10** (G. Bennington and B. Massumi, trans). Manchester: Manchester University Press.

Macdonald, A. M. (Ed) (1972) *Chambers Twentieth Century Dictionary*. London: W. & R. Chambers.

McGuire, W. J. (1969) Suspiciousness of Experimenter's Intent. In: R. Rosenthal and R. L. Rosnow (Eds) *Artefact in Behavioral Research*. New York: Academic Press, pp. 13–57.

Macintyre, A. (1985) *After Virtue: A Study in Moral Theory*. London: Duckworth.

Macy, J. R. (1983) *Despair and Personal Power in the Nuclear Age*. Philadelphia, PA: New Society.

Mahfouz, N. (1986) *The Beggar*. (K. Walker Henry and N. K. Naili al-Warraki, trans.) Cairo: American University in Cairo Press. (First published 1965.)

The Mail on Sunday (1987) June 14, p. 32.

Mair, M. (1988) A psychology for a changing world. *Psychotherapy Section Newsletter*, No. 4. Leicester: British Psychological Society.

Malcolm, J. (1981) *Psychoanalysis: The Impossible Profession*. New York: Knopf.

Marcel, G. (1952) *The Metaphysical Journal*. (B. Wall, trans.). London: Rockliff. (First published 1927.)

Maslow, A. H. (1968) *Toward a Psychology of Being*. New York: D. Van Nostrand.

Masson, J. M. (1989) *Against Therapy*. London: Collins.

Masson, J.M. (1996) *When Elephants Cry*. New York: Vintage.

May, R. (1972) *Power and Innocence: The Search for Sources of Violence*. New York, NY: Norton.

May, R. (1991) *The Cry for Myth*. London: Norton.

Melzack, R. (1965) Effects of Early Experience on Behaviour: Experimental and Conceptual Considerations. In: P. H. Hoch and J. Zubin (Eds) *Psychopathology of Perception*. New York: Grune & Stratton, pp. 271–299.

Merleau-Ponty, M. (1962) *Phenomenology of Perception*. (C. Smith, trans.). London: Routledge & Kegan Paul.

Milgram, S. (1974) *Obedience to Authority*. New York: Harper & Row.

Mill, J.S. (1982) *On Liberty*. London: Penguin.

Miller, H. (1941) *The Colossus of Maroussi*. Harmondsworth: Penguin.

Moore, R. I. (1985) Preface. In: E. Peters. *Torture*. New York: Blackwell, pp. vii–viiii.

Moore, R. L. and Gillette, D. (1990) *King, Warrior, Magician, Lover*. New York: Harper Collins.

Moreno, J. L. (1953) *Who Shall Survive?* Beacon, NY: Beacon House.

Moreno, Z. (1975) A Survey of Psychodramatic Techniques. In: I. A. Greenberg (Ed) *Psychodrama: Theory and Therapy*. London: Souvenir Press, pp. 85–100.

Muhlhausler, P. and Harré, R. (1991) *Pronouns and the People*. Oxford: Blackwell.

Murray, G. (1915) *The Stoic Philosophy*. London: Allen & Unwin.

Newnes, C. (1991) *ECT, the DCP and ME. Clinical Psychology Forum* **36**, 20–24.

Newnes, C. (1994) Making public common knowledge. *The Psychologist* **7**, 313–314.

O'Hara, M. (1991) Horizons of reality: demystifying postmodernism. *Networker*, 71–74 (book review).

Oliner, S. P. and Oliner, P. M. (1988) *The Altruistic Personality: Rescuers of Jews in Nazi Europe*. New York: Free Press/Macmillan.

Olivier, G. (1991) Counselling, Anarchy and the Kingdom of God (1990 Frank Lake Memorial Lecture). Oxford: Clinical Theology Association.

Ostriker, A. (Ed) (1977) *William Blake: The Complete Poems*. London: Penguin.

Patchen, K. (1971) *Collected Poems*. New York: New Directions. (First published 1936.)

Perera, S. B. (1981) *Descent to the Goddess: A Way of Initiation for Women*. Toronto: Inner City Books.

Perls, F.S. (1969) *Gestalt Therapy Verbatim*. Moab, UT: Real People Press.

Perls, F. S., Hefferline, R. F. and Goodman, P. (1951) *Gestalt Therapy: Excitement and Growth in the Human Personality*. New York: Julian Press.

Peters, E. (1985) *Torture*. Oxford: Basil Blackwell.

Polkinghorne, D. E. (1992) Postmodern Epistemology of Practice. In: S. Kvale (Ed) *Psychology and Postmodernism*. London: Sage, pp. 146–165.

Polster, E. (1987) *Every Person's Life is Worth a Novel*. New York: W. W. Norton & Co.

Proulx, C. (1994) On Jung's theory of Ethics. *Journal of Analytical Psychology* **39**, 101–119.

Richardson, L. (1994) Writing – A Method of Enquiry. In: N. Denzin and Y. Lincoln (Eds) *Handbook of Qualitative Research*. London: Sage Publications.

Riesen, A. (1965) Effects of Early Deprivation of Photoc Stimulation. In: S. F. Osler and R. E. Cooke (Eds) *The Bisocial Basis of Mental Retardation*. Baltimore, MD: Johns Hopkins University Press.

Rinzler, D. (1984) Human disconnection and the murder of the earth. *Transactional Analysis Journal* **14** (4), 231–236.

Roberts, D. L. (1984) Contracting for peace – the first step in disarmament. *Transactional Analysis Journal* **14** (4), 229–230.

Rogers, C. R. (1951) *Client-Centered Therapy*. Boston: Houghton Mifflin.

Rogers Macy, J. (1983) *Despair and Personal Power in the Nuclear Age*. Philadelphia, PA: New Society.

Rosenthal, R. (1963) On the social psychology of the psychological experiment: the experimenter's hypothesis as an unintended determinant of the experimental results. *American Scientist* **51**, 268–283.

Rosenthal, R. and Jacobson, L. (1968) *Pygmalion in the Classroom: Teacher Expectation and Pupils' Intellectual Development*. New York: Holt, Rinehart & Winston.

Rowan, J. (1988) Counselling and the psychology of furniture. *Counselling* **64**, 21–24. Reprinted as Chapter 12 of Rowan, J. (1992) *Breakthroughs and Integration in Psychotherapy*. London: Whurr.

Rowe, D. (1990) A gene for depression? Who are we kidding? *Changes* **8** (1), 15–29.

Rumi, J. (1990) *Delicious Laughter: Rambunctious Teaching Stories from the Mathnawi*. C. Barks (Ed.). Athens: Maypop Books.

Russell, B. A. W. (1961) *A History of Western Philosophy and Its Connection with Political and Social Circumstances from the Earliest Times to the Present Day*. London: Allen & Unwin.

Rutter, M. (1972) *Maternal Deprivation Reassessed*. Harmondsworth: Penguin.

Ryle, G. (1960) *Dilemmas*. Cambridge: Cambridge University Press.

Sampson, E. E. (1981) Cognitive psychology as ideology. *American Psychologist* **36**, 730–743.

Samuels, A. (1989) *The Plural Psyche*. London: Routledge.

Samuels, A. (1993) *The Political Psyche*. London: Routledge.

Sartre, J-P. (1948) *Existentialism and Humanism*. Paris: Les Editions Nagel.

Sartre, J-P. (1969) *Being and Nothingness* (H. E. Barnes, trans.). London: Methuen. (First published in French, 1943.)

Satir, V. (1967) *Conjoint Family Therapy*. Palo Alto, CA: Science & Behavior Books.

Schiff, J. L., Schiff, A. W., Mellor, K., Schiff, E., Schiff, S., Richman, D., Fishman, J., Wolz, L., Fishman, C. and Momb, D. (1975) *Cathexis Reader: Transactional Analysis Treatment of Psychosis*. New York: Harper & Row.

Schimmel, A. (1993) *The Triumphal Sun*. New York: Suny.

Seligman, M. E. P. (1970) On the generality of the laws of learning. *Psychological Review* **77**, 406–418.

Severin, F. T. (1965) *Humanistic Viewpoints in Psychotherapy*. New York: McGraw-Hill.

Shakespeare, W. (1951) *The Complete Works* (P. Alexander (Ed.). London: Collins.

Shaw, G. B. (1991) *Caesar and Cleopatra* W.A. Landes (Ed) Studio City, CA: Players Press Inc.

Shotter, J. (1984) *Social Accountability and Selfhood*. Oxford: Blackwell.

Simon, S. B., Howe, L. W. and Kirschenbaum, H. (1972) *Values Clarification: A Handbook of Practical Strategies for Teachers and Students*. New York: Dodd, Mead & Co.

Simons, H. W. (1989) Distinguishing the Rhetorical from the Real: The Case of Psychotherapeutic Placebos. In: H. W. Simons (Ed) *Rhetoric in the Human Sciences*. London: Sage, pp. 109–118.

Simonton, O. C., Matthews-Simonton, S. and Creighton, J. (1978) *Getting Well Again: A Step-By-Step, Self-help Guide to Overcoming Cancer for Patients and Their Families*. Los Angeles: Tarcher.

Sivyer, J. (1996) Review of *The Therapeutic Relationship* by P. Clarkson. *Self and Society* **23**, 50–52.

Smail, D. J. (1978) *Psychotherapy: A Personal Approach*. London: J. M. Dent.

Smail, D. J. (1987) *Taking Care: An Alternative to Therapy*. London: J. M. Dent.

Smith, M. (1977) *A Practical Guide to Value Clarification*. La Jolla, CA: University Associates.

Smith, M. L., Glass, G. V. and Miller, T. I. (1980) *The Benefits of Psychotherapy*. Baltimore, MD: Johns Hopkins University Press.

Smuts, J. C. (1987) *Holism and Evolution*. Cape Town: N & S Press. (First published in 1926.)

Solzhenitsyn, A. (1974) *The Gulag Archipelago*. Glasgow: Fontana.

Sosa, E. (Ed.) (1979) *The Philosophy of Nicholas Rescher*. Dordrecht: Reidel.

Spitz, R. (1945) Hospitalism: genesis of psychiatric conditions in early childhood. *Psychoanalytic Study of the Child* **1**, 53–74.

Staub, E. (1990) The Psychology and Culture of Torture and Torturers. In: P. Suedfeld (Ed.). *Psychology and Torture*. New York: Hemisphere.

Steiner, C., Wyckoff, H., Marcus, J., Lariviere, P., Goldstine, D., Schwebel, R. and members of the Radical Psychiatry Center. (1975) *Readings in Radical Psychiatry*. New York: Grove Press.

Stern, D. N. (1985) *The Interpersonal World of the Infant*. New York: Basic Books.

Stoehr, T. (Ed.) (1991) *Nature Heals: The Psychological Essays of Paul Goodman*. Highland, NY: The Gestalt Journal.

Tacey, D. J. (1993) Jung's ambivalence toward the world soul. *Sphinx* 5, 278–287. London: Convivium for Archetypal Studies.

Tajfel, H. (1981) *Human Groups and Social Categories*. Cambridge: Cambridge University Press.

Taylor, A. E. (1902) *International Journal of Ethics*.

Taylor, H. (1954) *On Education and Freedom*. New York: Abelard-Schuman.

Thompson, A. (1990) *Guide to Ethical Practice in Psychotherapy*. Chichester: John Wiley.

Thompson, E.P. (1979) *Whigs and Hunters*. New York: Allen Lane.

Thompson, J. (1985) *Psychological Aspects of Nuclear War*. Leicester: British Psychological Society.

Ury, W. (1991) *Getting Past No: Negotiating with Difficult People*. London: Business Books.

Von Franz, M-L. (1986) *Shadow and Evil in Fairy Tales*. Dallas: Spring Publications. (First published 1974.)

Walden, B. (1994) *The Mail on Sunday*, 30 October, p. 10. London: Associated Press.

Warrington, J. (Ed and Trans) (1963) *Aristotle's Poetics, Demetrius on Style, Longinus on the Sublime*. London: Dent.

Watson, L. (1974) *Supernature*. London: Coronet.

Watzlawick, P., Weakland, J. H. and Fisch, R. (1974) *Change: Principles of Problem Formation and Resolution*. New York: Norton.

Weigert, A. (1970) The immortal rhetoric of scientific sociology. *American Sociologist* 5, 570–573.

Weiss, P. (1972) *Marat Sade*. London: John Calder & Marion Boyars.

Weldon, F. (1994) *Affliction*. London: Harper Collins.

Wertz, F. J. (1995) Yerkes' rabbit and career: from trivial to more significant matters. *Theory and Psychology* 5 (3), 451–454.

West, P. F. (1991) *Risking on Purpose*. Burnside, S. Australia: Essence Publications.

Wheeler, C. J. (1993) The lost Atlantis: myths of soul in the modern world. *Sphinx* 5, 287–302. London: Convivium for Archetypal Studies.

Whyte, C. R. (1994) Competencies. *British Journal of Psychotherapy* 10 (4), 568–569.

Wilhelm, R. (1988) *The I Ching or Book of Changes*. London: Routledge & Kegan Paul

Williams, L. (1992) Torture and the torturer. *The Psychologist* 5 (7), 305–308.

Willsher, K. and Churcher, S. (1995) Japan's secret Schindler. *The Mail on Sunday*, 19 November, pp. 48–49.

Winnicott, D. W. (1960) *The Maturational Processes and the Facilitating Environment*. London: Hogarth Press.

Winterson, J. (1994) *Art and Lies: A Piece for Three Voices and a Bawd*. London: Jonathan Cape.

Wittgenstein, L. (1967) *Zettel*. Berkeley: University of California Press.

Wolf, N. (1990) *The Beauty Myth*. London: Chatto & Windus.

Wolf, N. (1994) *Fire with Fire*. London: Vintage.

Yalom, I. (1980) *Existential Psychotherapy*. New York: Basic Books.

Zohar, D. (1990) *The Quantum Self*. London: Bloomsbury.

Index

abortion 137
  pain of foetus 143
abuse
  audience prevention of 42–3, 96–7
  desensitization to 31
  and psychotherapy 114–15
  tacit permission for 9
  see also child abuse
aggression, favoured by neutrality 59,
    61, 129
agitators, *see* 'outside agitators'
Amnesty International 67
anxiety, reduction strategies 7–8
apathy, *see* bystanding; bystanding
    apathy; inaction; passivity
archetypes 46
audience
  definition 43
  role of 8, 42–4
  see also observers
audience inhibition hypothesis 69
authoritarian personalities 86
authority
  'I'm only following orders' 79–83,
    165–6
  subject to higher 79–82
  withdrawal of consent to 82
autonomy 100
  not used 79, 80
awareness
  of problem 102–3
  to relationship, responsibility as 14

behaviour
  altruistic *v.* pro-social 28
  harmful 46–7

learned 17
  see also bystander patterns
blame
  avoiding responsibility 107
  see also patient blaming; victim blam-
    ing
bureaucratisation of sadism 113
bystander patterns 54–6
  foresight, midsight and hindsight in
    105–8
  'I don't have all the information'
    68–9, 165
  'I don't want to get burned again'
    69–72, 165
  'I don't want to rock the boat' 63–5,
    166
  'I want to remain neutral' 58–61,
    165
  identification of 54
  'I'm just keeping my own counsel'
    83–5, 166
  'I'm only following orders' 79–83,
    165–6
  'I'm only telling the truth as I see it'
    76–9, 165
  'it's more complex than it seems'
    66–7, 164–5
  'it's none of my business' 56–8, 164
  'my contribution won't make much
    difference' 72–4, 166
  overview 163–6
  'the truth lies somewhere in the
    middle' 61–3, 166
  'victim blaming' ('they brought it on
    themselves') 85–9, 166
Bystander Witness 108

181